Advance Praise for *Webs of Power*

The grave danger we are in — of enslavement,
worldwide, by the insatiably greedy — is so complex
only a witch could fully comprehend, analyze, and write
a spell to get us out of it. I am serious.
Enter Starhawk (thank goddess!) and *Webs of Power:
Notes from the Global Uprising.*
This book tells us all we need to know about the
chasm gaping at our feet. Visionary ropes are
thrown in the hope that we will have sense and soul
enough to swing ourselves across.
— A must and soonest read.

— Alice Walker, author of *The Color Purple*

Webs of Power is a must reading for all who would take
part in the essential revolution of our time:
the transition from a suicide economy to a
life-sustaining civilization. Here Starhawk provides
on-the-scene reports from the opening years of the
Global Justice Movement; then in a set of outstanding
essays, reflects on key strategic and philosophic issues.
The voice of this visionary teacher, writer, activist is
unfailingly fresh in its wisdom and relevance.
While refusing all dogmas, she inspires and guides with
wholesome, wry authority.

— Joanna Macy, author of *Widening Circles*

Starhawk is a profound example of spiritual activation —
the place where mind, heart, and spirit join in sacred,
conscious action. Her message on the importance of
diversity in the global justice movement is timely and
vitally important. This vision for a healthy world
manifests into reality when we recognize that peace
ON the Earth must happen as one with peace
WITH the Earth.

— Julia Butterfly Hill, author of
One Makes the Difference and *The Legacy of Luna*

What an important book to read right now!
Always on the cutting edge, Starhawk guides us this
time through the labyrinthine pathways of the global
justice movement. These powerful chronicles of her
experiences 'out on the streets' — beginning with
Seattle in 1999 — are an exciting read in themselves.
Her observations, and her razor-sharp analysis of the
converging elements involved in the protests provide a
framework to see this rising, world wide movement.
Starhawk's vision comes from a lifetime of service to the
Earth and all living things. Clearly she understands the
dynamics needed to make another world possible.

— Donna Read, Documentary Filmmaker,
Women & Spirituality Trilogy: Full Circle,
The Burning Times and *Goddess Remembered*

Starhawk has done it again: merging the personal, the political, and the planetary in a seamless web of words that resemble the web of life. Do yourself a favor and read every sentence of this book; then let it guide you into being an active participant in the global values revolution that is replacing money values and violence with life values and nonviolence.

— **Kevin Danaher, Co-Founder, Global Exchange**

Since the anti-WTO protests in Seattle, a dispersed and diverse global movement has better understood itself in the mirror of Starhawk's writings. Her essays consistently, and miraculously, combine how-to practicality with poetry and inspiration. She presents the best face of social justice and dares us to live up to it.

— **Naomi Klein, author of *No Logo***

webs of power

webs of power

Notes from the Global Uprising

Starhawk

new catalyst books

CATALOGING IN PUBLICATION DATA:
A catalog record for this publication is available from the National Library of Canada.

New Catalyst Books edition 2008

Cover design by Diane McIntosh.
Barbed wire image © Christoph Burki/Stone; Earth image © Photodisc.

Printed in the United States of America.

Paperback ISBN: 978-1-897408-13-1
Original ISBN: 0-86571-456-8

The following pieces were first published in *Reclaiming Quarterly*:
"Cultural Appropriation," *Reclaiming Quarterly*, Vol. 76, Autumn 1999;
"Making It Real: Initiation Instructions, Seattle '99," *Reclaiming Quarterly*, Vol. 77, Winter 1999;
"Hermana Cristina's Well,"*Reclaiming Quarterly*, Vol. 78, Spring 2000;
"Spirals: How to Conjure Justice," *Reclaiming Quarterly*, Vol. 79, Summer 2000;
"Courage and Faith in Hard Times," *Reclaiming Quarterly*, Vol. 84, Autumn 2001.

Inquiries regarding requests to reprint all or part of *Webs of Power* should be addressed to New Catalyst Books at the address below.

To order directly from the publishers, please call toll-free (North America) 1-800-567-6772.

Any other inquiries can be directed by mail to:

New Catalyst Books
P.O. Box 189, Gabriola Island, BC V0R 1X0, Canada
1-250-247-9737

NEW CATALYST BOOKS is an imprint of New Society Publishers, aimed at providing readers with access to a wider range of books dealing with sustainability issues than is usually available through the regular book trade. In keeping with our commitment to publish books with the least possible impact on the environment, all New Catalyst titles are available in paperless, electronic form, as well as in print form on an on-demand basis. New Catalyst Books' "Sustainability Classics" series is specifically designed to keep books in print that have enduring value in the field of sustainability. Please place orders directly through New Catalyst Books at the address above.

For further information, or to browse our full list of books, visit our website at: www.newcatalystbooks.com

NEW CATALYST BOOKS   www.newcatalystbooks.com

CONTENTS

ACKNOWLEDGMENTS

AS THIS BOOK CHRONICLES the growth of a movement, it is in many ways a collective story. I want to thank and acknowledge all those amazing companeras I've marched with and met with, laughed and cried and struggled with over the course of these last two years, especially those in the Living River and Pagan Cluster, the women's actions, and the pink bloc of Genoa. My two training partners in RANT, the Root Activist Network of Trainers, Hilary McQuie and Lisa Fithian, have shared many of these adventures with me, and their insights and experience as organizers have been invaluable. Penny Livingston-Stark, my permaculture teaching partner, has brought many of the concepts in this book alive for me. Charles Williams is the best scout in the world. Oak and Revel Alliance got us all to Seattle. My partner, David Miller, is an inspiration as a true nonviolent activist and a great support.

I also thank those who have taken time to read and critique parts of this book: Katrina Hopkins, Culebra, Pamela Harris, Chris Crass, Margo Adair, and Bill Aal. As well, I'm indebted to those on all sides of the nonviolence debate: George Lakey, Jaggi Singh, Bill Moyer, The black bloc, and all the rest whom I've learned from and argued with. My comrades in Argentina, Brazil, Canada, El Salvador, Europe, Mexico, and Quebec have broadened my perspective and allowed me to envision the possibility of a true global web of support and solidarity.

My housemates and partners in crime Rose May Dance, Wilow Zacubi, and Bill Simpich are true examples of a lifelong commitment to both spirit and action. Along with Jeanne, Anna, and Seretha, they create a warm and supportive home base. Madrone, Ariel, and Mary de Danan have attempted to keep me organized. And Kore Margaret Simpich is a daily reminder of why we do this work. May she grow to womanhood in a world that can celebrate every aspect of her being and offer her abundance, liberty, and peace.

Starhawk
San Francisco and Cazadero, January 2002

INTRODUCTION: THE WEB

I'M SITTING IN A COLORFUL collective flat in Montreal, on a cold January night, surrounded by women helping to plan a women's action for the protests next April against the Summit of the Americas. "I'm tired of talking," one woman complains. "Can't we do something different?"

I pull out my drum and begin a simple beat, and a soft, wordless chant above it. We all begin to sing. Over the harmonies and the rhythm, we speak of our visions for the action:

"I see webs ... webs of power ..."

"Globalization is a web that traps us ..."

"I see us weaving new webs, webs of connection ..."

"I see us weaving a movement ..."

The two years that followed the successful Seattle blockade of the World Trade Organization summit in November of 1999 saw the explosive growth of a powerful movement to contest the institutions of global corporate capitalism. The movement is often called the "anti-globalization" movement, but I prefer the more positive phrasing of the "global justice" movement.

Before Seattle, large, urban street actions involving direct action were simply not happening. Or if they were, the media were paying no attention to them. Suddenly, around the world every major meeting or summit of the global corporate capitalists was being met with countersummits, protests, blockades, and sometimes out-and-out street battles. A whole new generation was being radicalized and drawn into activism. New coalitions were being formed, and new ideologies and tactics were being forged. Alternative institutions sprang up, from collectives of street medics to IndyMedia centers that pioneered a whole new approach to journalism.

The movement has had a tremendous impact. Before Seattle, the agenda of transnational corporations was being imposed on a world largely unaware of the implications of the trade agreements and institutions that override laws passed by citizens and undermine environmental and labor standards. The virtues of free trade and a type of development that furthers corporate profits were challenged by a few dedicated organizations, but barely debated publicly. The process of globalization was considered to be both desirable and unstoppable.

After two years of protests, however, the major institutions of globalization were on the defensive. The WTO was unwelcome to meet in any democratic country in the world. The less developed countries were in revolt against its "green room" meetings where industrialized nations set the policies poorer countries were expected to follow. The International Monetary Fund (IMF) and the World Bank had cut short their annual meeting in Washington, D.C., because the city couldn't afford to police it for an entire week. Moreover, their policies were being publicly scrutinized and their track records questioned.

Throughout the summer of 2001, police violence against the movement escalated. Live ammunition was used against demonstrators in Goteburg, Sweden. Four students in Papua New Guinea were shot dead. One young protester was shot in Genoa, and hundreds were subjected to brutal beatings and torture in jail. Nevertheless, the movement was gaining momentum. The next large protest was scheduled for the end of September, when the IMF and the World Bank were due to meet in Washington, D.C.

On September 11, 2001, hijacked planes crashed into the Pentagon and destroyed the World Trade Towers in New York, killing about thirty-five hundred people. Shock, grief, horror, and panic gripped the country. The political climate changed — overnight.

The IMF and the World Bank cancelled their meeting, and major groups pulled out of the protest against them. Others decided to transform the event into a protest against the war of revenge Bush was in the process of launching. The movement suddenly faced its greatest challenge: how to continue gaining momentum in a climate of public fear and increased repression, how to focus attention on the ongoing violence and everyday terror caused by the global corporate system, how to challenge global economic policies when "capitalism" and "freedom" were being identified with each other by the media and seen by the public as the innocent victims of terrorists.

The attacks could spell the end of the global justice movement. But their shattering impact, tragic as it is, could also spur us to deepen and broaden the movement. If we respond out of fear and constrict our efforts, the movement will wither. If we respond with compassion, imagination, and vision, the movement will grow and regain its momentum.

I am writing this introduction in October 2001, when the challenge still lies ahead of us. The stakes could not be higher: at a time when every life support system on the planet is under assault, they may well include our own survival. I write in faith that we will marshal the creativity needed to move forward, and that a chronicle of the movement's first two years will be of value.

This is, of course, far from a complete chronicle. It's focused on the events I've taken part in myself and/or the global justice movement. Other major issues that I've been deeply involved in — old growth forest campaigns, justice for Palestine, Central American Solidarity, local land use issues — are not much represented here. Several major actions are missing, including those at the Democratic and Republican conventions of 2000. It is shaped by the emotional and political events in the immediate aftermath of the attacks of September 11th. And it's the chronicle of a participant, not of an objective observer, if such a thing can exist. I draw my inspiration from involvement, not from detachment. I can't just write about a movement — I need to be part of it, to sweep out the Convergence Center, wrestle with the agenda of the meeting, hand out postcards inviting people to the action, train new activists in street tactics and in how not to panic when the police attack. My writing is fed by the wisdom and the commitment of all the people I've met in this work, from the brilliant theorists and strategists who head up NGOs to the tattooed, spiky anarcho-punks eager to be in the front lines of any confrontation.

"It didn't start in Seattle ..." is one of the slogans of the global justice movement. This collection of writings, however, did start in Seattle, with a post I sent out shortly after I returned home from five days in jail following the blockade of the World Trade Organization summit in November of 1999.

Disgusted by the media misrepresentation of the action, I dashed off a quick description of how I understood the blockade had been organized. I sent it to friends, a few listserves, and some of my contacts in other countries who I thought would be interested. Much to my surprise, the post got forwarded around the world. I began receiving requests for translation into French, Spanish, and Portuguese as well as reprint requests from many, many places. At that time, I was new to the Internet, but my experience with that article showed me its potential power.

When I went to Seattle, I had been writing and working both politically and spiritually for decades. I began my involvement in activism during the Vietnam War, when I was still in high school. Through the feminist movement of the early seventies, I became interested in looking at the impact patriarchal religions had on women's development and self-esteem. From there, it was a natural step to explore alternatives, both rediscovering the ancient, pre-Christian Goddess religions and exploring new forms in ritual and collective practice.

A deepening earth-based spirituality led me into environmental and antinuclear activism, out of the sense that if the earth is sacred, we should prevent idiots from destroying her and us. Throughout the eighties and nineties I engaged in many nonviolent direct actions on the issues of nuclear power and weapons, and later on militarism, intervention in Central America, the clearcutting of redwood forests, AIDS, and other issues. I was part of a collective of nonviolence trainers and also helped to organize many of the actions. At the same time, I was writing about earth-based spirituality, teaching, creating ritual, and helping our community grow and transition from a small, local collective to an international network.

I went to Seattle reluctantly. I had more than enough commitments at home, both political and personal, to keep me busy. I went with somewhat the same attitude with which I used to go to synagogue as a child — thinking I would fulfill a somewhat unpleasant duty, feel absolved of my guilt for a little while, come home, and resume my life.

Instead, I found myself galvanized into a new level of political activity. The next big action planned was for April in Washington, D.C., at the meeting of the IMF and the World Bank. I began mobilizing people to go and volunteered to come early and help with trainings. By then, I was hooked. My partner and I devoted our vacation in Europe to doing trainings for the Prague action, although we couldn't stay for the action itself. I came home, threw over most of my paying work, and began to help mobilize for Quebec and to travel all over doing trainings for actions rather than workshops on ritual. I spent a month in South America, weeks in Canada, and in the summer made a last-minute decision to go to Genoa to the protest against the G8, the summit of the eight most powerful industrialized countries in the world.

For all of these actions, I wrote descriptions, reports, articles, and exhortations and sent them out over the Internet. Throwing a writer onto the Internet is like throwing a fish into water. I found myself in my natural element. For over two decades, I'd been writing books. While being an author is in many ways a highly satisfying occupation, it is also an exercise in delayed gratification. For years, you sit alone, writing, rewriting (before computers, children, that meant retyping!) draft after draft. When the book is done, anywhere from eight to eighteen months may elapse before it comes out. Reviews are often few and far between, and few readers bother to sit down and write a letter commenting on your ideas.

But putting a post out onto the Internet was instant gratification. Within days, sometimes hours, I might get a thank-you from someone in Thailand or a critique from a friend in Quebec. What I wrote could become part of a living dialogue, an ongoing discussion that might be reflected in the next call to action.

The articles in the first section of this book were mostly written with a sense of immediacy and urgency. They were what I felt people needed to hear in the moment. They were written on airplanes, in spare moments of time between other events, late at night or early in the morning. I have left them virtually unedited, so that they stand as a record of the events and changes of two years of powerful movement building.

Of all the posts, the most urgent was the one I sent from Genoa on the Saturday of the action. I was trapped in the IndyMedia Center while the police brutally beat sleeping people in the school across the street. I watched in anguish as they carried out stretcher after stretcher, thinking, "What can I do? What can I do?" Finally, I looked around and realized that I was surrounded by computers and phone lines. I dashed off a message describing what was happening and sent it to three people whose e-mail addresses I happened to remember: two of my closest friends, and Michael Albert of *Z Magazine*. By the next afternoon, my friends in San Francisco were hearing it read on the radio, and it had literally gone around the world, alerting the movement to the truth of what was happening.

The last posts in this section were those written in response to the attacks of 9-11. They close off this two-year phase of the movement, and I hope open directions for the next phase.

The chapters in the second section of the book are my attempts to do deeper thinking about some of the key questions confronting the global justice movement. As satisfying as the immediacy of the Internet can be, posts sent out by e-mail have their limitations. For one thing, they need to be relatively short. And the urgency with which most are written doesn't always allow for broader reflection. When I realized I was writing an actual book, I eagerly took the opportunity to expand and stretch out a bit.

In this section, I examine our relationship to nature and place, which for me is the beginning point for creating any truly alternative culture. I share some of my own experiences in directly democratic organizing and explore some of the issues in building a more diverse movement. I reexamine nonviolence and some of the pressing questions around how best to wage our struggles. Finally, I propose an economic vision based on an understanding of ecology, and some ideas about how we might get there.

All of my writing and activism comes from an alternative vision of power. Power-over, or domination, is the power we're all familiar with, the power of a small group to control the resources or to limit the choices of others. Ultimately, it stems from violence and force and is generally backed by the police and military power of the state.

But the word "power" itself comes from a root that means "ability." We each have a different kind of power: the power that comes from within; our ability to dare, to do, and to dream; our creativity.

Power from within is unlimited. If I have the power to write, it doesn't diminish your power: in fact, my writing might inspire you or illuminate your thinking.

Power-over seems invincible, but ultimately it rests upon the compliance of those it controls. No system of power can afford to use force to enforce its every decree. Instead, the fear of that force causes us to repress and police ourselves. If we refuse to comply, if we call the legitimacy of the system itself into question, ultimately the system cannot stand.

Power from within is akin to what many cultures call "spirit." The global justice movement challenges the greatest amassing of police, military, political, and economic power the world has ever seen. To do so requires great courage, and the faith that ultimately creativity must triumph over violence.

Throughout the book, I use a few terms that may seem provocative or even inflammatory and need explanation. "Pagan" as a term generally refers to earth-based traditions from Europe and the Middle East that predate Christianity. The end of the 20th century saw a great revival of interest in spirituality rooted in nature and embracing sexuality and liberatory values.

The feminist spirituality movement is especially concerned with the empowerment of women and the undermining of patriarchal values in religion as well as in other walks of life. It includes women and men who identify as Pagans, but also many who work for gender equality within mainstream religions.

"Witch," as I use the term, refers to a woman or man who honors the cycles of birth, growth, death, and regeneration as the Goddess, who makes a deep personal commitment to serve that force, and who often takes on a role of responsibility in their spiritual community, as healer, ritual maker, teacher, priestess.

"Anarchist" means someone who contests all forms of hierarchy, coercion, and control rooted in domination. Some anarchists reject the state entirely, others make some accommodation with it. Anarchism envisions a world of greater freedom, where people are governed not through fear and force but through direct democracy and voluntary agreements.

Identifying as a Pagan, feminist, Witch, and anarchist is possibly a way to alarm great segments of the general public, but at least it keeps me from sinking into a boring and respectable middle age.

From our vision of the web at the women's potluck, we dreamed up an action in which we asked women all over the world to send us weavings, which we then placed on the fence erected to keep protesters away from the Summit, transforming it into a gallery of art. It is my hope that this book will continue weaving connections that can be useful both to those who are involved in the global justice and peace movements and to those who are seeking some way to comprehend and have an impact on the political and economic forces that surround us. "Another world is possible!" is the slogan created at the World Social Forum in Brazil in 2001. Another world is also necessary, for this one is unjust, unsustainable, and unsafe. It's up to us to envision, fight for, and create that world, a world of freedom, real justice, balance, and shared abundance, a world woven in a new design.

ALPHABET SOUP: THE
INSTITUTIONS OF GLOBALIZATION

FOLLOWING, OR CONTESTING, the progress of global corporate capitalism can be like wading through a thick soup of acronyms and code words. Here's a short explanation of a few of the most important ones:

NAFTA: The North American Free Trade Agreement, linking the U.S., Mexico, and Canada. The U.S. has lost over three quarters of a million manufacturing jobs since its passage in 1994, Canada more than a quarter of a million. Its impact on the indigenous communities of Mexico has been devastating as it allows the U.S. to dump cheap products on the market that undercut the traditional agriculture of rural communities. Displaced farm workers migrate to the border, which became militarized even before 9-11. *Maquiladoras,* the factories that crowd the border, are exempted from environmental and labor regulations. NAFTA, under its Chapter 11, also allows corporations to sue governments for loss of projected profits if governments pass labor or environmental laws. Under NAFTA, a Canadian corporation has sued the State of California for banning an additive in gasoline that pollutes groundwater. A U.S. corporation has sued Canada for banning another gasoline additive that causes cancer and birth defects.

FTAA: The Free Trade Area of the Americas would extend NAFTA throughout the hemisphere, excluding only Cuba. Containing all the provisions that make NAFTA problematic, it would also remove countries' rights to control foreign investment.

G8: The G8 are the eight most powerful, industrialized nations: the U.S., Canada, Great Britain, Germany, Italy, France, Japan, and Russia. At their summits, they create policies and set agendas that affect everything from the WTO to the U.N.

WTO: The World Trade Organization (It has nothing to do with the World Trade Towers that were destroyed in New York. They were not its headquarters, nor did the WTO have any offices there. Nor does the WTO have anything to do with the United Nations.) The World Trade Organization is an international body set up in 1995 under the Uruguay Round of GATT — the General Agreement on Tariffs and Trade. Under its auspices, member countries can sue other countries for "restricting trade" if they pass laws and regulations that impose environmental or labor standards. Disputes are settled by a tribunal presided over by three judges who come from the world of business and finance and who are not elected, named, or accountable to the public. Proceedings are secret, and their judgments can override laws passed by citizens of the countries involved. For example, the WTO has disallowed laws that would have protected endangered sea turtles from being killed in shrimping nets and laws that would have banned products made with child labor.

World Bank/IMF: The World Bank and the International Monetary Fund are sister institutions. Set up after World War II, originally to loan money for Europe's reconstruction, the World Bank found its loans weren't necessary because the Marshall Plan provided interest-free money. It turned to the Third World, where it has become notorious for making loans for huge, environmentally destructive projects that primarily benefit large transnational corporations. The Narmada Dam project in India, which would displace hundreds of thousands of traditional farming families, is a current example.

The International Monetary Fund is primarily known for its imposition of Structural Adjustment Programs (SAPs) on Third World countries. By the eighties, the less developed countries were finding that World Bank loans had not, in fact, stimulated their economies and that they were unable to pay the interest on their large international loans. The IMF stepped in, offering to loan more money to service the debts on outstanding loans, but imposing policies on the countries in question that required them to orient their economies to earning foreign exchange rather than providing for the needs of their people. They were to open their resources to foreign investment and to cut programs in education, health care, or social welfare. The U.N.

estimates that six million children a year die because of policies imposed by the IMF and the World Bank.

World Economic Forum: A yearly gathering of economic and political power holders. In its educational forums and informal socializing much of the agenda of corporate globalization is set.

I

actions

*T*his section includes my writings from the last two years of activism and organizing. Most of the articles were originally written for the Internet or for small publications; they tend to be short, urgent expressions of whatever I felt the movement most needed to know at the time. I have left them relatively unedited to serve as a record both of my development and of the movement's progress.

SEATTLE

In November of 1999, the WTO met in Seattle for its high level Ministerial to attempt to launch a new Millenial Round of trade negotiations. Upwards of sixty thousand people gathered to stop the meeting in the first of the large summit demonstrations. I helped do trainings for the action and took part in the blockade on November 30, which succeeded in shutting down the conference for the first day of meetings. Demonstrators were met with an unprecedented level of police violence: tear gas, beatings, pepper spray, and rubber bullets. A small number of demonstrators, organized into a black bloc, broke the windows of targeted global corporations, setting off a great deal of controversy within the movement about violence, nonviolence, and tactics. (The "black bloc" is not an organization, but a tactic adopted in street protests where groups of demonstrators wear black and cover their faces for protection against surveillance and to demonstrate solidarity. The black bloc sometimes, but not always, engages in principled destruction of corporate property.) The Mayor of Seattle declared downtown Seattle a no-protest zone. On November 31, thousands challenged what we saw as an unconstitutional abridgment of our freedom of speech, and went downtown to protest. I was arrested and spent five days in jail.

Seattle was a once-in-a-lifetime, world-changing event. It energized a whole new movement, radicalized thousands of new activists, and opened a whole new chapter in the history of resistance to corporate globalization.

How We Really Shut down the WTO

IT'S BEEN TWO WEEKS NOW SINCE the morning when I awoke before dawn to join the blockade that shut down the opening meeting of the WTO. Since getting out of jail, I've been reading the media coverage and trying to make sense out of the divergence between what I know happened and what has been reported.

For once in a political protest, when we chanted "The whole world is watching!" we were telling the truth. I've never seen so much media attention on a political action. However, most of what has been written is so inaccurate that I can't decide if the reporters in question should be charged with conspiracy or simply incompetence. The reports have pontificated endlessly about a few broken windows and mostly ignored the Direct Action Network (DAN), the group that successfully organized the nonviolent direct action that ultimately involved thousands of people. The true story of what made the action a success is not being told.

The police, in defending their brutal and stupid mishandling of the situation, have said they were "not prepared for the violence." In reality, they were unprepared for the nonviolence and the numbers and commitment of the nonviolent activists — even though the blockade was organized in open, public meetings and there was nothing secret about our strategy. My suspicion is that our model of organization and decision-making was so foreign to their picture of what constitutes leadership that they literally could not see what was going on in front of them.

When authoritarians think about leadership, the picture in their minds is of one person, usually a guy, or a small group standing up and telling other people what to do. Power is centralized and requires obedience.

In contrast, our model of power was decentralized, and leadership was invested in the group as a whole. People were empowered to make their own decisions, and the centralized structures were for co-ordination, not control. As a result, we had great flexibility and resilience,

16

and many people were inspired to acts of courage they could never have been ordered to do.

Here are some of the key aspects of our model of organizing:

TRAINING AND PREPARATION

In the weeks and days before the blockade, thousands of people were given nonviolence training — a three-hour course that combined the history and philosophy of nonviolence with real life practice through role-plays in staying calm in tense situations, using nonviolent tactics, responding to brutality, and making decisions together. Thousand also went through a second-level training in jail preparation, solidarity strategies, and tactics and legal aspects. As well, there were trainings in first aid, blockade tactics, street theater, meeting facilitation, and other skills. While many more thousands of people took part in the blockade who had not attended any of these trainings, a nucleus of groups existed who were prepared to face police brutality and who could provide a core of resistance and strength. And in jail, I saw many situations that played out just like the role-plays. Activists were able to protect members of their group from being singled out or removed by using tactics introduced in the trainings. The solidarity tactics we had prepared became a real block to the functioning of the system.

COMMON AGREEMENTS

Each participant in the action was asked to agree to the nonviolence guidelines: to refrain from violence (physical or verbal), not to carry weapons, not to bring or use illegal drugs or alcohol, and not to destroy property. We were asked to agree only for the purpose of the 11/30 action — not to sign on to any of these as a life philosophy. The group acknowledged that there is much diversity of opinion around some of these guidelines.

AFFINITY GROUPS, CLUSTERS, AND SPOKESCOUNCILS

The participants in the action were organized into small groups called "affinity groups." Each group was empowered to make its own decisions around how it would participate in the blockade. There were groups doing street theater, others preparing to lock themselves to structures, groups with banners and giant puppets, others simply prepared to link arms and to nonviolently block delegates. Within each group, there were generally some people prepared to risk arrest and others who would be their support people in jail, as well as a first aid person.

Affinity groups were organized into clusters. The area around the Convention Center was broken down into thirteen sections, and affinity groups and clusters committed to hold particular sections. As well, some groups were "flying squads" — free to move to wherever they were most needed. All of this was co-ordinated at spokescouncil meetings, where affinity groups each sent a representative who was empowered to speak for the group.

In practice, this form of organization meant that groups could move and react with great flexibility during the blockade. If a call went out for more people at a certain location, an affinity group could assess the numbers holding the line where they were and choose whether or not to move. When faced with tear gas, pepper spray, rubber bullets, and horses, groups and individuals could assess their own ability to withstand the brutality. As a result, blockade lines held in the face of incredible police violence. When one group of people was finally swept away by gas and clubs, another would move in to take their place. Yet there was also room for those of us in the middle-aged, bad lungs/bad backs affinity group to hold lines in areas that were relatively peaceful, to interact and dialogue with the delegates we turned back, and to support the labor march that brought tens of thousands through the area at midday. No centralized leader could have co-ordinated the scene in the midst of the chaos, and none was needed — the organic, autonomous organization we had proved far more powerful and effective. No authoritarian figure could have compelled people to hold a blockade line while being tear gassed — but empowered people free to make their own decisions did choose to do that.

CONSENSUS DECISION-MAKING

The affinity groups, clusters, spokescouncils, and working groups involved with DAN made decisions by consensus — a process that allows every voice to be heard and that stresses respect for minority opinions. Consensus was part of the nonviolence and jail trainings, and we made a small attempt to also offer some special training in meeting facilitation. We did not interpret consensus to mean unanimity. The only mandatory agreement was to act within the nonviolent guidelines. Beyond that, the DAN organizers set a tone that valued autonomy and freedom over conformity and stressed co-ordination rather than pressure to conform. So, for example, our jail solidarity stategy involved staying in jail where we could use the pressure of our numbers to protect individuals from being singled out for heavier charges or more brutal treatment. But no one was pressured to stay in jail or made to feel guilty for bailing out before the others. We recognized that each person has his or her own needs and life situation, and that what was important was to have taken action at whatever level we each could. Had we pressured people to stay in jail, many would have resisted and felt resentful and misused. Because we didn't, because people felt empowered, not manipulated, the vast majority decided for themselves to remain in, and many people pushed themselves far beyond the boundaries of what they had expected to do.

VISION AND SPIRIT

The action included art, dance, celebration, song, ritual, and magic. It was more than a protest; it was an uprising of a vision of true abundance, a celebration of life and creativity and connection that remained joyful in the face of brutality and brought alive the creative forces that can truly counter those of injustice and control. Many people brought the strength of their personal spiritual practice to the action. I saw Buddhists turn away angry delegates with loving kindness. We Witches led rituals before the action and in jail and called on the elements of nature to sustain us. In jail, I was given Reiki when sick and we celebrated Hanukah with no candles, but only the blessings and the story of the struggle for religious freedom. We found the spirit to sing in our cells, to dance a spiral dance in the holding cell, to laugh at the hundred petty humiliations the jail inflicts, to comfort each other and listen to each other in tense moments, to use our time together to continue teaching and organizing and envisioning the flourishing of this movement. For me, it was one of the most profound spiritual experiences of my life.

I'm writing this for two reasons. First, I want to give credit to the DAN organizers who did a brilliant and difficult job, who learned and applied the lessons of the last twenty years of nonviolent direct action, and who created a powerful, successful, and life-changing action in the face of enormous odds, an action that has changed the global political landscape and radicalized a new generation. And secondly, because the true story of how this action was organized provides a powerful model that activists can learn from. Seattle was only a beginning. We have before us the task of building a global movement to overthrow corporate control and to create a new economy based on fairness and justice, on a sound ecology and a healthy environment, one that protects human rights and serves freedom. We have many campaigns ahead of us, and we deserve to learn the true lessons of our successes.

What's Wrong with the WTO

AT THE HEIGHT OF THE RECENT protests in Seattle, when tear gas filled the streets and many of us filled the jails, California State Senator Tom Hayden was quoted as saying, "A week ago, nobody knew what the WTO was. Now — they still don't know what it is, but they know it's bad."

Aside from its association with tear gas, police brutality, and incarceration, what is so bad about the WTO?

The World Trade Organization was set up by the Uruguay round of GATT — the General Agreement on Tariffs and Trade, the international body that is negotiating so-called "free trade" agreements worldwide. The WTO, in a sense, is the executive and judicial arm of GATT: it judges a country's compliance with the rules, enforces the rules by way of trade sanctions and monetary judgments, and expands the rules.

All of this sounds somewhat innocuous and boring. Personally, when I hear the word "tariff" I go back to half-forgotten history lessons about the War of 1812 and start to snooze. But what it means is something much more sinister. In effect, the WTO has become an agency of global corporate rule with the power to override our laws.

Huh? How? It seems inconceivable. Where does a trade organization get that kind of power? It stems from a clause in the agreement signed by our government that states: "Each member shall ensure the conformity of its laws, regulations, and administrative procedures with its obligations as provided in the annexed agreement." By joining the WTO and signing GATT, our legislators agreed for us, without a public vote or a debate, that we would make our laws conform to the rulings of the WTO tribunals.

Those rulings are made by an unelected group of bureaucrats who meet in closed-door proceedings in Geneva and who are not accountable to any citizens' organization. Their procedures are required to be secret, and their documents are confidential. Unlike at a U.S. Court proceeding, there are no public records of the arguments or evidence submitted. No citizens and no media can observe the proceedings, and there is no appeal or outside review process. Nor is there any mechanism for labor, environmental, health, or human rights considerations to have a voice in the proceedings.

All this would be frightening enough if the issues under consideration were simply arcane financial matters. But WTO rulings affect major labor, human rights, and environmental considerations. The WTO has prevented the U.S. from banning gas that contains unsafe additives and from stopping the import of shrimp caught with nets that kill endangered sea turtles. It has prevented the European Union from banning hormones in beef and stopped African governments from procuring less expensive AIDS drugs to supply to their people. Under its "intellectual property" protections, corporations can patent life forms, including seeds, plants, and even human cell lines. Corporations can prevent farmers from saving or trading seeds and can charge a "royalty" on resources that traditional cultures have used for thousands of years.

These are just some of the abuses that inspired me to go to Seattle. I don't have room or time in this forum to outline all the wrongs, but I suggest you check out the websites and books (those old-fashioned things) in the endnotes and the bibliography.[1]

Of course, if you go to the WTO website, they will tell you that all of these problems are just misunderstandings and misinformation. Their opening preamble is full of nice phrases about sustainable development and protecting and preserving the environment. One of their websites attempts to counter what they call "Ten Misunderstandings" that are actually the "Ten Reasons to Hate the WTO" taken from the Global Exchange Website.

But if you read their excuses carefully and with some background knowledge, it becomes clear that they are deliberately putting out disinformation. I only have room here for one example. The WTO tries to counter the charge that it is anti-environmental by stating: "A recent ruling on a dispute brought to the WTO (an appeals report in a case about shrimp imports and the protection of sea turtles) has reinforced these principles. WTO members can, should, and do take measures to protect endangered species and to protect the environment in other ways, the report says."

The statement doesn't make clear that the WTO essentially banned the protections that our legislators deemed to be the most effective, indeed the only way we as a nation could have an impact on this issue. In theory, we can, should, and do protect the environment — but in reality, whenever we try to actually do it, the WTO rules against the protections and for the interests of profit-making corporations.

But the WTO is only one aspect of a larger issue. Free trade is part of the process of globalization, which has freed corporations to move money and production facilities around the globe, relocating to places where labor is cheap and environmental and safety restrictions are minimal. The current economic and political dogma is that this will somehow make everybody richer and better off. The reality, however, is quite different. Globalization has meant a tremendous concentration of wealth in the hands of the rich. Lori Wallach, in her testimony opposing the WTO, cites a prominent economist at the pro-WTO, pro-free trade Institute for International Economics, who determined that 39% of the increase in income inequality in U.S. from 1973 to 1993 can be attributed to trade. And she states that according to the United Nations Conference on Trade and Development (UNCTAD), most of the gains in national income during the current U.S. recovery have been captured by profits, not wages.[2]

We all understand intuitively how this works. A textile factory in Tennessee that has sustained a community for decades closes because it can pay workers in Thailand 25 cents an hour instead of paying workers in this country even minimum wage. Perhaps in the next town over, a family-run factory with a strong commitment to the community and the well-being of its workers refuses to leave. Their products must compete in the marketplace with the cheaper goods produced abroad. Most likely, they will go bankrupt or be taken over by corporate raiders who will liquidize their assets, downsize them, or simply close them down.

We've all seen this happen again and again over the last decades. No matter how much our politicians and economists try to convince us that this process is somehow better for us all, the reality of inequality stares us in the face every time we walk out on the street and are accosted by the homeless. Already by the mid-nineties, the top 1% of U.S. households received as much combined annual income as the bottom 40%. 358 billionaires in the world owned as much as the world's poorest two and a half billion people. One man, Bill Gates, has an annual income equal to that of the entire nation of Pakistan.[3]

As someone who believes the earth is a living being and all of us are part of her life, I say this is wrong. Something is wrong with a system in which ten-year-olds in India work sixty-hour weeks making carpets and corporate executives make millions. It's not justifiable under any theory of economic growth or comparative advantage, it's just wrong. And if we truly believe that the Goddess is every human being on the planet (and a lot of other things besides), then we owe the billions of Her who are hungry and hopeless and see no future some help, fast. We owe the sea turtles and the dolphins and the redwoods a shift in our values. We need to educate ourselves on these issues, to read David Korten's *When Corporations Rule the World* or Jerry Mander and Edward Goldsmith's *The Case Against the Global Economy* as well as our e-mail. We need to think about what we buy, to consider the karma that comes with a pair of Nikes or a purchase from Wal-Mart. And we need to be willing to speak for our values and take action.

We have the power and the responsibility to be part of the reshaping of our world to reflect our values of life, love, diversity, justice, and true abundance for all.

Making It Real: Initiation Instructions, Seattle '99

Wednesday, December 1: Day 2 of the WTO Action

IT BEGINS BEFORE YOU LEAVE home in the predawn dark. Remove all jewelry, everything you truly are unwilling to lose. Leave behind your identification, forget your name. Take only what will sustain you or serve you: pockets full of apples, sandwiches, chocolate, nail clippers for the plastic handcuffs, a bandanna soaked in vinegar against tear gas.

Make your way through dark streets to the meeting place. Waving the banners that have not yet been confiscated, begin the procession. Beat the drums. They have forbidden you to gather — your challenge is to disobey.

Get as far as you can before the police stop you. Your challenge now is to walk unarmed up to the massed lines of men of known violence, to face the weapons, the clubs, the tear gas with nothing but your body and the power of your spirit.

Sit down. Hold on. Hold on to each other as the violence begins around you, protect each other as best you can. Continue to talk to the police as the clubs whip down around you, as your friends are dragged off, thrown to the ground, beaten, their faces smashed down on concrete.

Keep your focus on the meaning of what you are doing as your hands are cuffed behind you. Your challenge now and for a long time to come will be to remember, at each stage of what happens to you, that you have a choice: to acquiesce or to resist. Choose your battles mindfully — there will be many of them and you cannot fight them all. Still every instance of resistance slows the system down, prevents its functioning, lessens its power.

Take care of each other. If you have wriggled free of your handcuffs, use the clippers to free your friends. Share all the food and water you have before it is taken away from you. Greet newcomers with song, chant your resistance: "We want our lawyers now / They're just outside the door / We want our lawyers now / Or we will chant some more!" "Si, se puede!" Yes, it's possible — it can be done.

If they try to separate one of you, place your body over his. Pile on. Never mind if they pull your hair, if they threaten more violence. Each time you act, you become stronger.

Eventually the time will come to move through the next gate of this initiation. At each one, another layer of your former self is stripped away. Now they take all your outer clothing, your packs, your food, everything from your pockets, your shoelaces. No matter how they intimidate you, do not give your name.

Your challenge is to walk proudly in shackles, wrists and ankles cuffed together, a chain around your waist.

You will wait for a very long time. Always they will tell you that what you want is just at the next place they want you to go to. Do not believe them. Gather your patience — you will need great reserves. Resign yourself to hunger. Sit in a cage with your sisters — continue to tell your stories, sing your songs. Fend off exhaustion. Do what you can to heal the woman with the broken nose and loose teeth who was jumped from behind by a plainclothes cop as she stood outside of the cafe. Greet as your sisters the woman arrested for a fight with her mother, the felon turning herself in on an old charge. Inside a cage, the locked door creates the only division that counts. We are all on the same side.

Inanna descends into the underworld. Now they will strip you of your last layer of individuality. They take your clothes, issue you identical blue pants and shirts, white plastic sandals, the same size underwear for all, the same name: Jane WTO. Your challenge, locked in a small, concrete box, is to laugh, to put on a fashion show. And when they take you away and lock you up in a tiny, airless concrete cell in ones and twos, your challenge is not to despair, not to lose your connection.

Keep breathing. Remember, every molecule of oxygen that makes its way through these concrete walls is a gift of the ancestors. They are with us: close your eyes and you will see them marching in rivers that swell and grow, breaking through concrete, tearing down walls.

Morning brings a small release. In the day room, you reconnect with your sisters. You will be offered glutinous oatmeal, dry brown bread, powdered kool aid — the first food you've been offered in twenty-four hours and though it is almost inedible, eat it.

You spend the day locked up with fifty women in another airless, concrete room, waiting to be arraigned. Your challenge now is to ride the waves of energy that sweep through this airless cell. A whispered chant becomes a dance becomes a circle becomes a cone of power. A meeting becomes a circle becomes a song. A song is interrupted by a threat from the guards and becomes a meeting. You are demanding to see our lawyers in a group. The guard says it is impossible, has never been done, can never be done. Your challenge is to not believe him. Si, se puede!

Waves of elation, waves of despair. This is what you have been learning magic for: to ride these currents, to fortify the spirit, to call in our allies now. Hours go by. Tell stories. Sing again. Do not meet so long that you exhaust yourselves — play, dance. Whenever you sink, a piece of news arrives that will buoy you up again. They are marching in London, in Cuba. The Longshore Workers Union has shut down the west coast. Protestors have surrounded the jails.

You are a vessel of a larger spirit that rises up again and again. Something new is being born here, something that will not quiet down and go away when the weekend is over. Your challenge is to be a midwife. At the end of the day, locked down until the protest outside is over, dance the spiral dance. Rising, rising, the earth is rising; turning, turning, the tide is turning.

Over the next few days, your challenge will be to endure. To keep talking, to treasure the friendships you will make, the web that is woven here. To treasure the clarity that comes inside a cage: here all the workings of power are perfectly clear. There is no more disguise, no more pretense that this system is working in your interest. And when you get out of jail, you will see where the jail is thinly concealed in the shopping mall, the school, the television program. You will know that at every moment you do truly have a choice: to aquiesce, to resist, to create something new.

At night in the underworld, lying in that hot, airless cell, aching with fever, keep breathing. Use your magic, remember your power, call on the elements which exist within your body even if this place is designed to shut them off. Your cellmate massages your feet, wets towels to cool you. The air presses down but the burning within you is kindling a deeper fire. Close your eyes. A lake of burning light is rising, cracking through the concrete. Webs form, grass pushes up through cement. Structures that seemed invincible fall. Si, se puede!

Initiation. Not a culmination, but a beginning.

Hermana Cristina's Well

HERMANA CRISTINA IS A TINY WOMAN, and every day she must draw the water for her family up from a deep well. The crank is stiff and the bucket is heavy, and though she is pregnant with her sixth child she does not complain. She feels lucky, for she does not have to rise before dawn and walk the shoulders of the new highway for hours to find water, like many women do. And though her possessions and those of her husband and children would fit into two or three shopping bags, she has a home, although it is far away from the town where she was born and the family and friends she grew up with, for she and her husband fled as refugees during the war. The war was waged against those who could tolerate hopelessness and injustice no longer and so made a revolution against the rich and the powerful. But the revolution like so many things ended inconclusively, and all the blood and pain and sacrifice could win only a partial victory against the death squads and the massive military might supported by the great corporations.

Hermana Cristina never learned to read, and though she is worn and tired from bearing children she has nothing else of beauty with which to fill her home. She lives not far from the great road where women like her walk every day in the dust, searching for water. The road was financed by those same corporate interests through institutions whose name Hermana Cristina does not know. The World Bank, the International Monetary Fund, the institutions of world corporate wealth lent money to some incarnation of a government she never voted for, in private negotiations never ratified by the people, to build the great road, which is dotted with gas stations like palaces, gleaming and clean, complete with glass box fast food stops where affluent visitors from the North could find familiar brand names: Ritz crackers, Hershey bars, Oreos.

Hermana Cristina feeds her family tortillas and beans. She feels lucky because many are hungry. They are hungry, though she may not know it, because in order to pay the interest on the loans that built the great road and the beautiful gas stations and the shops full of brand name products she cannot afford, her government which she did not vote for must encourage the production of food to be sold in the countries of the rich and must allow those same corporations to build the great *maquiladoras*, the factories where her children may someday labor to produce the jeans and cell phones and computers they will not be able to afford on a wage of four dollars a day. While she is burdened with too many children, her daughters may not have children at all because the *maquiladoras* produce wastes that eat away at ovaries and wombs, and in order to service the foreign debt and attract the same corporations her government has suspended the laws she never had a chance to vote for that could have protected her daughters' health.

Her sons will dream of the rich countries to the north, of following the great road up through Guatemala, Mexico. If they reach their goal, they will stand on a street corner hungry and desperate in a foggy dawn, hoping for work. If they find great success, they may someday ride to a laborer's job down the avenue where every stoplight is the turf of another beggar poorer than even Cristina, for they have no homes. This man was broken long ago when he was sent to fight an unjust war to protect those same corporations. This woman has just come out of jail; she lost her children when she turned to drugs to ease the pain of despair. This woman has AIDS and no money for a hotel room for the night, let alone the medications. This man still has a light in his eye and a smile, but he cannot find a job because the factory that would have hired him has moved to El Salvador where the people work for four dollars a day.

The avenue is lined with the gleaming storefronts that sell jeans and computers and cell phones. An administrative assistant spoons sugar into her coffee and thinks herself lucky that she still has a job, when half her department was laid off when her company was bought out by a larger company. Her salary barely covers the costs of childcare and her credit card debt and the rent on her apartment, which is high because for twenty years the banks have encouraged speculation and so many people want to live in this city, which is headquarters for many great corporations. She does not yet know that she has cancer from the chemical residues in the food she eats, the same cancer shared by those who made the long journey north on the great road and now pick the crops and administer the chemicals which the banks require farmers to spray because the banks have made loans to the corporations that make the chemicals. Nor does she imagine that she will lose her job when she cannot work and lose her health insurance, which in the name of freedom is not provided by her government, and that she will not live to see her daughter grow up. Or that the same chemical residues which have contaminated her breasts are seeping slowly toward the groundwater that feeds Cristina's well.

These connections are the reason why we went to Seattle to shut down the WTO and why in the spring instead of planting our own gardens we will go to Washington, D.C., to shut down the World Bank and the International Monetary Fund. Because we are no longer willing to acquiesce to institutions that do not cherish Hermana Cristina and her children and the beggar on the street and the administrative assistant stirring her coffee.

But we know that it is not enough to name the connections and identify the problems. It's not enough even to put our bodies on the line to stand against injustice. We must work magic. We must hold a vision.

So let us imagine a world in which the health of Hermana Cristina, the well-being of her children, the purity of her well were the prime concern of every institution of power. We could relax in such a world for we understand that if Hermana Cristina's interests are cherished, then so will ours be.

Let us imagine that the great economic powers of the world wish to free the slight and pregnant Cristina from the task of drawing water, and to do this in the way that will most benefit her children and, later, her grandchildren. So that instead of loaning money to her government to pay a big corporation to hire engineers from the United States to build a giant hydroelectric dam that will flood the fields of small farmers, they decide to give her a solar panel and a pump. But instead of sending her equipment made in the United States, they will assure the future jobs of her sons and daughters by funding a small company in her town to make the equipment locally, a company that will pay a living wage and will hold to strict standards of safety for its workers and its environment. And they will train young men and women to install and maintain the equipment, and these young men and women will be able to afford tortilllas and beans and fruit and grain and good food for their families, and dress-up clothes to go out in and, sometimes, a meal in a restaurant. And with the water from the well Hermana Cristina can grow a garden and feed her children on papayas and bananas and fresh vegetables as well as beans, so that they grow bright and healthy and eager to learn. And the extra fruit she can sell to the young men and women for their families, and with the money she earns she can buy a new dress for each of her daughters and a new shirt for each of her sons, which are made by the woman down the street who no longer works in a *maquiladora* but has a nice little business of her own, where she can step outside in the afternoon and enjoy the sunshine. And because the purity of Hermana Cristina's well is the prime concern of the world's political and economic structures, the chemical factory down the way has been closed, the men of her district no longer travel out to cut cane on the large plantations which service foreign debt which has miraculously disappeared, but instead till their own small plots of mixed fruits and vegetables for their families, with some left over to sell, and use nothing which would contaminate the soil, for everyone knows that the health of a people depends upon the health of the soil. And the papayas, the mangos, the coconut palms sink deep roots that hold the soil and make it a spongelike reservoir, and so the springs return to the hillsides and Hermana Cristina's sisters no longer have to rise before dawn to walk the dusty roadside searching for water.

And if her sons and daughters take the long road to the North, it is for adventure, for study, for fun. And there they might sit, in a cafe on the avenue, stirring their coffee grown under shade trees that harbor thousands of birds, beside the administrative assistant who is now the administrator of a healing center where those who have been wounded and broken by life are cared for. She's lunching with the former drug addict who is now a nurse. They're eating salmon from restored streams and flourishing fisheries, and wild mushrooms from extensive forests, and are drinking organic wine, which she can afford because she lives in her own, modestly priced home built by the man with the smile and the light in his eye. And because the health of the soil and the health of the people are the prime concerns of every political and economic structure in her country, too, there are no chemical residues in her food, there is no cancer in her breast, and she will live a long and healthy life and see the daughters of her daughter grow up in a world devoted to the well-being of the land, the waters, the children.

This is a modest and possible vision. It requires no unknown technologies or new inventions. We already have the knowledge, the skills, the resources we need to make it come true.

What we need is the will and the fortitude to confront and transform the structures of political and economic power that currently govern our world. A simple "to do" list: dismantle the structures of globalization, revoke corporate power, rescue government from the influence of wealth, restore democracy — but then maybe we've never really had that in the first place.

And after lunch, the hot tub.

It's not new, the call to revolution, it's really kind of a nineteenth-century or maybe a sixties thang, and hey, we've had a few and they mostly went rotten or proved inconclusive.

But maybe those were just for practice. This time, let's get it right.

A16

Inspired by the success of Seattle, anti-globalists called another blockade against the meeting of the IMF and the World Bank in Washington, D.C., in April of 2000. I went a week early to help with trainings. Together with a small Pagan cluster, I participated in two days of actions. The plan for the blockade repeated the successful tactics of Seattle. A map of the area was divided into zones like pie slices, and affinity groups committed to blockade in certain areas. The plan was less tactically effective this time: the delegates got in. But the action was a huge political victory, sparking a larger public dialogue about the IMF and the World Bank, putting them for the first time on the defensive.

Cutting down the Pines: Why We're Taking Action against the World Bank and the IMF

FOR THE NATIVE TRIBES OF CALIFORNIA, pine nuts have always been an important delicacy. Not so long ago, their ripening was an occasion for celebration. Young men of the tribe would earn great honor and praise for their skill and daring in climbing to the top of the tall trees and shaking the branches to knock the cones down.

During the Gold Rush, it often happened that a European-American man would marry a Native woman. When pine nut season came around, she might ask her husband to gather some. Let's say that he was a kind and thoughtful husband who loved her and wanted to please her, but that he was ignorant of the ways of her people and no longer young and daring, nor patient enough to climb the trees and shake the branches. Instead, he would simply cut down a pine tree.

When pines were plentiful and settlers were few, this might seem like a rational thing to do. At first, in fact, it might create an enormous sense of abundance and prosperity. The woman might have more pine nuts than she'd ever had before — for a while.

But in time, if this practice continued, the pines would be gone and the pine nuts would be no more.

We are going to Washington, D.C., this week because we see the globalized, corporatized economy cutting down the pines all around us. In the United States, we are surrounded by an illusory abundance that creates great wealth for a few, but it is the economy of the clearcut and it destroys the resources we should be cherishing. Globally, poverty and hunger deepen as corporate profits rise. Almost two billion people worldwide live in abject poverty. The lives, the cultures, and the lands of indigenous people are being destroyed in the name of development as surely as the pine trees were cut by the settlers.

The World Bank and the International Monetary Fund are major architects of this situation. In the 70s, they loaned money to Third World countries for massive projects that enriched political elites and multinational corporations while providing little for the less privileged. In the 80s, when many countries could not repay those loans, the World Bank and the IMF pushed them deeper into the cycle of debt with "Structural Adjustment" programs that forced countries to refocus their economies on exports and debt repayment instead of on food and goods to meet their own needs. Poor countries were made to reduce spending on education and health care in order to be able to continue paying billions and billions of dollars in interest to wealthy countries. UNICEF and UN Economic Commission for Africa figures show that six million children under the age of five die each year as a result of these policies.[3]

In the developed world, we feast among the fallen pines with a growing sense of uneasiness. We have seen the health of our own communities and economies compromised as job after job is lost to lands where pay is negligible and health and environmental standards unenforced. We see family farms lost, ancient forests cut down, wild lands and open spaces paved. The interests of transnational corporations undermine our democracy and widen the chasms of wealth and power that more and more divide us.

We are going to Washington this week to say that this system is wrong. It is unjust, unbalanced, and unsustainable, and it causes untold suffering. We cannot challenge these institutions through our government because our democratic institutions are corrupted by the interests of corporate wealth. We have no recourse but the streets, no alternative but action.

The World Bank, the International Monetary Fund, the World Trade Organization, and the system they represent will not change from any one action. But they will and must transform or go down in the face of the rising social movement these actions represent. They will change when we all begin to ask dangerous questions.

Some of us will ask these questions loudly in the streets of Washington, D.C.. But all of us can begin to ask these questions in our workplaces, our offices, the places where we buy the goods we need and shop for the things we enjoy:

Are the people who produce the tools of my trade, my food, my clothing and luxuries paid a living wage? Are their health and safety protected? Are their children well educated? Can they afford to buy the products they produce? What is the true cost of this work, this product, this toy to the soil? The waters? The air? The complex and irreplaceable habitats of this earth? The health of our communities? Who pays that cost, and in what coin? Money? Cancer? Extinction? Who profits?

If we face these questions, we can begin to build an economy of true abundance. The sustainability and stability of our increasingly global economy can only come from wealth widely and fairly shared. An economy of true abundance will favor the small and diverse over the monolithic, hold corporations and individuals accountable for the true costs of what they produce, favor renewable energy, and insist on the preservation and recycling of resources. The health of that system will be measured in the health of our communities, our soil, our waters, our air, the habitats of the earth's diverse creatures. It will be seen in the pride of workers who can afford to buy what they produce, whose children are free to learn, whose lives include leisure and beauty and freedom. And it will be the source of a global creativity that may enrich all of our lives in ways we cannot foresee.

If we cherish the pines, they will produce nuts that we can enjoy now and in future generations. If we continue to cut them down, we will soon have no more.

Sunday A16

WE HAVE BEEN BLOCKADING all day in a giant spiderweb, an intersection entirely surrounded by webs of yarn that effectively prevent free movement into the street. We have been drawn here by Wilow's nose, following the energy. The intersection is held by a cluster from Asheville that includes many labor union people. In Seattle, we were cheered in jail to hear that the ILWU had shut down every port on the West Coast in solidarity with our action. Here on the streets of Washington, D.C., we are blockading arm in arm with the Ecofeminist Teamsters. In front of the police blockade, an affinity group is locked down, sitting in a line with their arms locked together. Their supporters surround them, bring them water, administer sunscreen, and hold the keys.

I am really, really happy to be part of a movement that includes a group of ecofeminist teamsters. They ask us for some help in shifting the energy, which is loud, raucous, and confrontational. I join the group of drummers in the center. I don't have my own drum today, just a bucket and sticks, which works fairly well except when it falls off the rope tied around my waist. I start to drum with the group in the center, trying to entrain as I know the only way to shift a rhythm is first to join with it. With the help of some of the singers in our group, we manage to shift into a song: "We have come too far, we won't turn around, we'll flood the streets with justice, we are freedom bound."

I'm thinking about all the energies we'd invoked at the ritual the night before, Brigid, Oya, the Norns, the Red Dragon. At that moment, a red dragon made of cloth and ribbons dances into the intersection atop of line of smiling young protesters. It circles the intersection, and the energy shifts.

This magic is played out against a background of stark though unacknowledged fear. In all our affinity group's discussions about who to invoke and how to arrange early-morning transport, I don't think we've ever simply said, "I'm afraid." I haven't said it because I've pushed the fear down so far it doesn't easily surface, and because what I'm most afraid of is that someone else, someone I persuaded to come to this action, will get hurt. And also, I suppose, because I think the group looks to me to project calm and confidence, when really what might help us all most would be to simply be able to say, "I'm scared. Are you scared, too?"

We're scared because we are out on the street risking arrest in a city that has been turned into a police state. Sixty square blocks have been barricaded off. The day before, 600 people were arrested in a pre-emptive strike at a peaceful march. They weren't warned or allowed to leave. Our Convergence Center was shut down the same morning, with thousands of people arriving that day to be trained. Our puppets and medical supplies were confiscated. Although the puppets were eventually released, the medical supplies remain under lock and key.

I spent Saturday morning wandering in the rain with a group of about eighty people for whom I was trying to do a nonviolence training. The church we headed to was flanked by police and so overcrowded we could not possibly squeeze in. We set off for a park, but a runner informed us that the police were throwing people out of it. Eventually, I just stopped on the corner and said to the group, "Look, you can come back in the afternoon and try to get into a training, or we can just do it in the road." "Let's do it!" they cried, and so we ducked into an alley, arranged a fallback point in case we had to scatter, and did the training right there, with police cruising half a block away. "I must be a Witch," I said to Wilow after she finally found us toward the end of the morning. "I just disappeared eighty people!"

We are afraid of the police: they have guns, clubs, tear gas, pepper spray, and all the power of the state at their disposal. They can beat, gas, or jail us with relative impunity. What's hard to grasp is how much they are afraid of us. Some of our group are wearing black and covering their faces and look like the folks in Seattle that broke windows and made the police look bad. Mostly, I think, the police are afraid of the unknown. Someone in the crowd could have a bomb. Those bubbling vats in the convergence kitchen could be homemade pepper spray instead of lunch. Those bottles of turpentine could have some nefarious purpose other than removal of the paint used in banner making.

Now the two groups, each perceiving themselves as righteous and the other side as potentially violent, are squaring off on the streets of our nation's capital.

Later: Wilow, Evergreen, and I are returning from a trek to the bath-
rooms blocks away. We see a barricade half-built across the street. A
dumpster has been dragged into the middle of the street, and a few
broken pieces of furniture lie atop it. Other pieces of debris strew the
roadside. A couple of cars have been lifted up and set down at forty-
five-degree angles. Our much-debated nonviolence guidlelines state
that we will not damage property. The cars are unharmed, but moving
them has certainly put them in harm's way. It is an action right on the
edge of what the guidelines allow — but then we know many people
are unhappy at having guidelines at all, and agree to them with the
greatest reluctance.

Behind the dumpster, a circle of people stands engrossed in a heated meeting. They are discussing the barricade. David, my partner, is in
the midst of them. As I listen, I soon realize what has happened. The
young man in black, the tall Rasta from the Caribbean, and some of
the others have built the barricade. David has been taking it down even
as they built it up. Now they are having a spokescouncil meeting. A
young woman from the Ecofeminist Teamsters is facilitating.[4]

The people who built the barricade see it as protective. We hear
rumors that the cops have been running over people with motorcycles.
The barricade builders view it as our defense. David sees it as endangering us, as upping the ante of confrontation and potentially provoking
violence. Most of the barricade builders are young; he is middle-aged,
he looks and sounds like somebody's Dad, which in fact he is. He's
somebody's granddad, for that matter. He's also a man who burned his
draft card in the Vietnam War and spent two years of his youth in Federal
Prison. His lifelong pacifism is staunch and unshakable, and I've never
known him to back down on a matter of principle. Next to him is a
young, black-clad, masked protester who looks like the classic image of
the anarchist/terrorist. He is listening thoughtfully to the discussion.

I look at that circle and see all the tensions, fears, and hopes that
have surrounded this action. I've been here for close to a week, doing
trainings, going to meetings, sitting in on every spokescouncil. I know
that we have deep divisions among us on the question of how this
action should be conducted. In the spokescouncils, the strongest voice
generally seems to belong to those who want a more confrontational
action, who chafe against the nonviolence guidelines and are ready to

do battle in the streets. But in the nonviolence trainings I've done, and on the street itself, I hear the voices of those for whom the guidelines are vitally important and who want a stronger commitment to nonviolence, to communication as well as confrontation.

This is the kind of issue that has torn movements apart. Those of us who are old enough to remember the sixties have seen it happen again and again. We know how easy it is for this energy to turn sour and dissipate. We've seen strong organizations splinter apart around questions of tactics. Much stronger than any fear I might have of the police is my fear that this blessed wild unlooked-for movement, this rising tide of rage and passion for justice, will founder in the same way I've seen movements founder before, that we'll end up denouncing each other instead of the IMF, or that small splinter groups will take us too quickly into forms of action so extreme they leave our base of support far behind.

This energy is rare and precious. It's the one thing that can't be organized or created. When it's present, it's unstoppable, but when it goes, it's gone. And in thirty years of political activism, I've learned how quickly it can go.

"What's amazing," I say to the group, "is that we're having this dialogue. Under all this tension and in the middle of the action, we're willing to discuss this and listen to each other. That may be as important as anything else we do on the street today."

The black-masked anarchist, the Rasta, the Ecofeminist Teamster facilitator, the other affinity group representatives, and even David are all nodding in agreement. Eventually, a compromise is reached: David will not take down any more of the barricade, and no one else will add to it or build it up. I don't know which amazes me more: that the barricade builders agree or that David does. By the end of the day, the dumpster has become a giant drum, a symbol both of our differences and of the process we use to resolve them, a living testimony to the true democracy we have brought to confront the systems of political and economic control.

We are in the Ellipse. The blockade is over. The march and rally are done. We are lying in the shade, napping after an exhausting day, when someone comes running.

"The cops are trying to sweep the park! There's Riot Cops massing over there in the corner!"

We can't really believe the police would do something so unprovoked and stupid, but a few of us go to see what is happening. A line of Park Police on horseback are threading their way through clumps of people seated on the grass and alarming a small contingent of the Daughters of the American Revolution in pink suits and pearls, who scatter toward their building across the way. We follow the horses, and they move out into Constitution Avenue, form a line, and begin, or so it seems, to try to push the crowd off the street. Half the crowd is panicking and the other half are shouting at the cops and challenging the horses and in a moment, many people are going to get badly hurt. It's a situation so dangerous and unprovoked that I'm ready to get arrested just in protest of its stupidity, or so I tell Dan Fireheart, who is right behind me. But suddenly I know that I have to get to the front of the crowd. I catch hold of some lightning bolt of energy and streak through, checking myself as I go, "Is this really for me to do?" I know it is because suddenly I'm there, doing it, yelling, "Sit down! Sit down!" And doing it myself with enough conviction that others follow suit. In a moment, the crowd is sitting down or lying in front of the horses, who stop.

I am sitting with my legs out toward a horse whose feet stand between my ankles. One of my arms is outstretched as if to say, "Stop!" I can't seem to move it or put it down. Dan Fireheart reaches forward from behind me and takes my other hand. The horse is very big. The policeman on his back will not look me in the eye. Down the line, a cop tells a young woman protester, "I don't want to trample you but if my boss orders me to move forward, I'll have to." I've been teaching people for twenty years in nonviolence trainings that horses do not like to walk into uneven ground and won't trample people if you sit down or lie down in a group in front of them, but I've never tested it before. The horse shifts its weight. I remember that we called on the spirits of the land itself to support us. I can feel all the rings of magical energy and protection being sent to this action. They surround me like ripples in a pond, converging toward me instead of dispersing out. I still cannot seem to put my hand down.

Half the people around me look like they're part of the black bloc. In this moment, we have total solidarity. There are no more questions of tactics or style or guidelines; we are simply there together, facing the same threat, making the same stand, facing the same fear.

There's a line of riot cops behind the horses, so they can't move back. We all sit, frozen in time. I reach up, let the horse sniff my hand. The horse and I, we're in complete agreement. He doesn't want to step on me, and I don't want him to. Behind us, someone from the Committee for Full Enjoyment begins a chant: "It's not about the cops, it's about the IMF!" The crowd takes it up, and the energy unifies.

Then I realize there is a second line of horses behind our horses, facing the other way. It seems as if they've just come in from somewhere. They form a kind of open V with the riot cops in the middle. The crowd facing those horses begins to shout and panic. They're yelling at the horses and trying to push them back and throwing horse manure at the cops. The riot cops get out of the way. The horses are dancing and stumbling and being pushed into our horses who will have nowhere to move and stumble except on top of us. We begin chanting at the other crowd to sit down. They don't listen. "Sit down! Sit down! Sit down!" we chant. Finally they get it. They sit down. The horses stop. We breathe again. At some point in the melee, one young man does get stepped on and is left with a broken leg.

Now the horses are trapped. They have nowhere to go. I look up at the policeman who still won't meet my eye. "Officer, you have created an incredibly dangerous situation here, for us, for yourselves, for the horses! What were you thinking of? And how can we get you out of this?" I am fully prepared to try to negotiate with the crowd to let the horses out, but he still won't look at me. Off to the side, the riot cops move in. They begin literally throwing people around, until they clear a passage where the horses can file out. We scoot forward and then stand up and follow them, taking over the street, chanting, "Whose streets? Our streets!" At the other end of Constitution Avenue, a line of riot cops stands, batons ready. We are willing to be arrested, but they don't move, simply hold their own blockade as the drums thunder and the victory dance begins.

Spirals: How to Conjure Justice

"Wake Up Muggles! Conjure Justice!"
(The Revel Alliance sticker for the A16
action against the World Bank/IMF)

THIS IS HOW IT WORKS: Someone has a vision. Donald goes to the Bear Mounds and is told, "Make spirals. Make them of impermanent materials, on the steps of institutions, governments, banks."

We are in Washington, D.C., on the second day of actions against the World Bank and the International Monetary Fund. We join a march that takes over the downtown streets. We are drumming, chanting, singing. Giant puppets march with us, and above our heads float beautiful banners emblazoned with ears of corn and slogans of justice. I am with Culebra, Evergreen, and Lea, who is eighty-three years old. A cold, drenching rain falls and our voices echo off the walls of stores and corporations.

I am warily keeping my eye on the police who line each intersection as we pass. I don't want Lea to get trapped and arrested. But she does not want to leave. With every step, she seems to shine with a brighter inner glow. The march swells and grows. A fierce joy rises from our chanting, and I see it reflected in Lea's eyes.

And then we are trapped, in a massive intersection where many streets come together. The police who guard the streets have on their riot gear. They have covered their badges. "Go with Evergreen," we say to Lea. "Tell them you're eighty-three years old, they'll probably let you out."

"But I don't want to leave," Lea says.

I don't blame her. I don't want to leave either. I want to stay in the midst of these thousands of brave and crazy people willing to face tear gas or arrest in order to stand up for justice. So we wait. We bring reporters over to talk to Lea. We borrow a cell phone and call the rest of our cluster. We wait some more. The rain pours down.

At last Lea begins to get cold. Reluctantly, she decides to go, and Evergreen goes with her. We have heard that there is a way out further down the street. Culebra and I move deeper into the crowd. "Sit down! Sit down!" someone is calling, and we do, although the street is wet. We sing, as the rain pours down. "Hold on, hold on, hold the vision that's being born." We hear voices chanting in Spanish behind us, and shift to "Si, se puede!" Someone brings a small sound system over and Culebra stands up and teaches the Spanish chant to the crowd. "It means, 'Yes, it's possible. It can be done!'" she tells them. "Cesar Chavez used it in the farmworkers' struggle, and many, many people have used it." The Latino affinity group behind us joins in with vigor. The Spanish language media come over and interview all of us.

The police put on their gas masks. We put on ours. Dan, from our cluster, has joined us. The rain falls in cold sheets. We sit down, waiting for some form of violence to begin. I find chalk in my pocket and draw a spiral on the street. I write, "Justice." Next to me is a young man in black, masked and hooded. I hand him the chalk. He studies it for a long moment, then draws a Circle A and writes, "Resist!" I find another piece of chalk and begin passing it around. The rest of our cluster joins us, with boxes of chalk. It circulates through the crowd. We draw spirals, and the rain dissolves our marks almost as soon as we make them.

We do not know this at the time, but up at the front of the line, the police chief is negotiating with what the media later describe as "a woman dressed as a tree." Mary Bull, wearing a foam redwood, works out a deal. The police uncover their badges. They take off their gas masks. They call for anyone who wants to get arrested to move forward. Someone hands the Chief of Police a bouquet of roses.

The tension eases. Jugglers appear, and fire eaters dancing with flames, and radical cheerleaders, and drum circles. We stand up, hovering together as the cold rain falls. Under our feet is a labyrinth someone has drawn, which the rain does not wash away.

This is how it works: The Police Chief, who two days before illegally arrested 600 people, goes on T.V. holding his roses and talks about democracy. Meanwhile those who volunteered to get arrested in order to make a statement about justice are kept in handcuffs for many, many hours. They are hit in the face for smiling or for asking to see a lawyer. They are kept in wet clothes shivering with hypothermia. They are not given food, or water, for so long that some end up drinking from the jail toilets. They are brutalized, intimidated, lied to. In one holding cell deep in the underworld, Cullet leaves a spiral torn from scraps of a dollar bill.

This is how it works: There are twelve of us, and the rattlesnake makes thirteen. We are in the redwoods, next to the river we have been fighting to defend, among the trees that will be cut if the Timber Harvest Plan goes through. The snake is in a bucket — she appeared on the driveway as one of our friends was leaving to come to the ritual. We have with us a pile of letters that have been written, a petition that all the neighbors have signed. We know that the man who will take possession of this land, if the Timber Harvest Plan goes through, has lied and cheated, has destroyed ancient trees, and has desecrated graves with bulldozers. The California Department of Forestry has no mechanism for integrating this information. There is nothing in its process that truly allows the voice of our concerns for the river, the land, the community to be heard, as there is nothing in the deliberations of the World Bank or the International Monetary Fund or the World Trade Organization or the political processes that support them that truly opens an ear to concerns of justice. Within these institutions are good people who sincerely desire to protect the forests, to help the poor. Yet whatever efforts they make, and regardless of what is stated in press conferences or political campaigns, injustice is embedded in the very structure of these bodies, in the procedures that must be followed, in the questions that can and cannot be asked, in the way the debate is framed.

If we want justice, we have to conjure it up from another framework. We have to step outside the institutions, walk out into the streets and forests, drawing impermanent spirals in the face of fear.

So we gather in the woods to claim this forest as sacred space, to charge our letters, our petition, our phone calls with magic, that extra something that may shift the structures just a bit, create an opening for something new. We sing, we chant, we make offerings, we claim this land as sacred space. We dare to call upon the ancestors although we recognize ourselves as the inheritors of stolen lands. Out of these contradictions, out of our willingness to listen, to guard the soil and the trees and the rivers, to cherish each other and the love that arises from our history of everyday work and our quarrels and our common song, we intend to conjure back the salmon, the ancient groves, the community of those indigenous to this place.

We draw spirals in the dirt. We leave feathers, yarn, a shell — our altar. We release the snake from her bucket. She is beautiful, the scales on her back glistening in diamond shape, her tale crowned with many rattles. She leans her chin on the shell filled with waters of the world and listens as we sing to her. When we go, she will coil her body into a spiral and remain, a fitting guardian for this land.

This is how it works: Someone has a vision that arises from a fierce and passionate love. To make it real, we must love every moment of what we do. Impermanent spirals embed themselves in asphalt, concrete, dust. Slowly, slowly, they eat into the foundations of the structures of power. Deep transformations take time. Regeneration arises from decay. Si, se puede! It can be done.

PRAGUE

In September of 2000, the IMF and the World Bank held its larger annual meeting in Prague. Again a demonstration was organized. I was in Europe for the summer and answered a call put out by the organizers for help with trainings. Through the international listserves, we organized two trainings: one weekend in London and a three-day action/training camp in Prague before one of the general meetings.

The European movement is different in many ways from that in the U.S. In the U.S., the traditional Socialist/Communist left was pushed underground during the McCarthy era and remains a movement on the margins. In Europe, Socialists and Communists have seats on national parliaments. In the Czech Republic, the Communists are the overthrown establishment; the former dissident rebels are now in power. In the U.S., although militant factions may argue for the necessity of high confrontation or the effectiveness of property damage as a tactic, they do so against a background of assumed nonviolence. In Europe, the assumption is that an action involves conflict with the police, that "direct action" often does mean property damage, and while many groups practice a dedicated and disciplined nonviolence, it's not the assumed mode of protest.

On the West Coast, where I live, the linking of the spiritual and the political is part of the culture; in Europe, it is almost unheard of. But Europeans are often much more politically sophisticated; they spend long hours happily discussing theory and ideology, so long that at one point I asked one of the Italians from the Ya Basta! group how long meetings lasted at home. "Oh, we often go on all night," he said. "In the U.S.," I told him, "people hate meetings. The first thing people say when you begin a meeting is, 'When is this going to be over?'"

"Really? How can that be?" He truly couldn't believe that political people could hate meetings, but I assured him it was so.

The action was organized by a handful of young Czech anarchists, aided by a few international volunteers who were equally young. The average age was probably around twenty-two, and many of the Czechs were still in their teens. Whereas the direct action groups in Seattle and A16 had had funding, the support of NGOs and unions, and some highly experienced organizers, in Prague they had virtually no resources to draw on. Only in the last decade, since the Velvet Revolution overthrew the Soviets, had protest been allowed. The dissidents who had mounted a successful campaign in earlier years were now the government that was hosting the meeting.

The training camp included myself and my partner David, a lifelong pacifist who spent two years in Federal Prison in the sixties for burning his draft card, some of the Czechs, some of the organizers of Reclaim the Streets from Britain, and a whole contingent of the Ya Basta! groups from Italy who mount the White Overalls actions where they pad themselves, build shields and defensive structures, and walk through police lines. There were other groups from many parts of Europe, and more who came for the International Meeting. We stayed at an ecological farm on the outskirts of Prague, sleeping on what David called the "post-Soviet mattresses": thin pads covered with a rough and noxious plastic. Groups took turns cooking — the Italians definitely produced the most edible pasta.

The International Meeting stands out for me as the single most difficult meeting I've ever tried to facilitate in a long career of difficult meetings. The large room was crammed with sixty or eighty people from dozens of nationalities and a broad spectrum of political cultures. There were representatives from unions, from the Socialist Workers' Party, from obscure dissident Communist groups in Eastern Europe, there were German anarchists and cheerful Catalans and a sprinkling of feminists and every other group imaginable, all wanting their turn to expound, denounce, and speechify, but not necessarily being familiar with the consensus process. And every speech had to be translated into Italian and Czech. We spent nine hours on the question of whether to have one big march or several separate marches that would converge or split apart. The

Socialists wanted One Big March, for unity: the anarchists wanted many autonomous marches and creative affinity group actions. The Italians felt we hadn't discussed the underlying political ideology enough.

In truth each side had a point. With thousands of people coming in buses from all over Europe just for the day, there did need to be some common meeting point and some simple, unified action for them to do. But with thousands of others forming affinity groups and wanting to actually disrupt the meeting in creative ways, a big march alone was not sufficient. Eventually, the group came up with a creative synthesis: one big march that would split into different groups with different destinations and different styles.

I wasn't able to stay in Europe for the action, but the plan worked effectively. The groups became color-coded: The blue group was the hard-core militants who got into a clash with the police that included rocks, bottles, and Molotov cocktails. The yellow group followed the White Overalls to the bridge in front of the Congress Center and got into a standoff with the police for hours. The pink group, including the pink-and-silver samba band, was the nonviolent group, and they somehow snakedanced their way up to the Congress Center itself. The resulting chaos was so strong that the meeting was disrupted.

From accounts of my friends, the police were relatively restrained on the street although they did use tear gas, pepper spray, percussion bombs, and the like. But those who were arrested, many of whom were peaceful protesters arrested at random, found a very different situation in jail. The Velvet Revolution was a transfer of power, but it didn't dismantle the previous system. Many of the police and prison guards were the same as under the Communists, and they harassed, beat, and tortured some of the prisoners. Many of us who had long admired Vaclav Havel were deeply disappointed and disillusioned by his failure to intervene.

Letter to the Third Element

(IN THE LEAD UP TO THE ACTION, as the media and police were predicting violent riots, the situation in Prague became more heated. Havel had earlier called for a dialogue between the protesters and the IMF/World Bank, and the anarchists had hotly debated whether or not to participate until it became clear that they were not the "respectable" protesters who would be invited. As tension increased, a few of the former dissidents became concerned. They formed a group called the Third Element, to try to serve as a mediating force between the protesters and the state. Jan Urban sent a letter to INPEG, the Czech organizing group, proposing "terms of engagement" — essentially, an orchestrated nonviolent action of ceremonial arrests. His proposal was out of synch with the political aims of the groups involved, who hoped to effectively disrupt the Congress, not simply to make a symbolic statement. Originally his letter was sent privately to a few organizers and key people; later it was put out directly on the listserve created for international organizing.

The Third Element did prove helpful and supportive when the action was over, in pressuring for better treatment and release of protesters being held in jail.

Here is my response to their letter.)

Dear Third Element,

I'm glad to see that you have brought your concerns and proposals directly to these listserves. I know that you've previously written some of us privately but I think this discussion is much more appropriate and effective when it is open and includes as many voices as possible.

When we're organizing or participating in an international action, it's easy to focus on the global implications and lose sight of the local impact. I thank you for bringing to our awareness the question of how this will impact the Czech Republic.

It was my great privilege to be in Prague in August to help with preparations and the international meeting, and my great sadness that I can't return on the 26th. I hope to participate in our support actions here in

San Francisco. I was in Seattle last November, and in Washington, D.C., in April, and I have been helping to organize and participate in actions for thirty years or more, so my remarks stem from that experience.

INPEG, the group that is organizing the direct action, has had a lot of discussion online about whether or not to participate in Havel's offer to set up a dialogue with representatives of the World Bank/IMF. But, as I understand it, soon it became clear that INPEG was not actually invited to be part of the dialogue. INPEG was identified as the "irresponsible" demonstrators who "only want to make trouble," in spite of their very clear statement that they will not initiate violence nor destroy property. The direct action component of these actions has throughout been demonized and misrepresented by the press and by some Czech officials to create a climate of fear. So the following is my attempt to express why direct action is important.

The anti-globalization movement IS a democracy movement. Democracy means that people have a voice in the decisions that affect their lives. The IMF and the World Bank along with the WTO are three of the major institutions used by corporations to protect their profits at the expense of the quality of life of billions of ordinary people, and at the expense of the environment that supports life.

These institutions are not accountable to ordinary people through any existing democratic process. The power of wealthy corporations continually subverts our democratic institutions. Perhaps this is especially clear in the United States where elections have become blatant fundraising competitions, but it applies worldwide.

These institutions, through their policies, impose a deadly, daily violence against the bulk of the people in the world. If we allow them to continue unhampered, we participate in a violence far greater than anything that might occur in street action.

Direct action is a way of making these institutions accountable. Direct action means interfering with the operations of injustice. We attempt to stop or disrupt their meetings from the same impulse you might feel to stop a man beating a child or kicking a dog. We're saying, "Hey, these institutions are illegitimate. They should not be allowed to continue functioning because they are causing immediate harm." If a man is kicking his dog, you have to stop him before you can discuss his behavior with him.

Dialogue is meaningless without accountability. It becomes simply an exercise in public relations, making the institutions in question look sensitive while the violence of their policies continues unabated.

Direct action is the only way we've found so far to hold these institutions accountable. Only the actions against them over the last year have created any real public debate about their policies. Personally, I think it's great that respectable members of NGOs will debate the IMF and the World Bank and that the dialogue will be broadcast on public television. But that dialogue will be very different because of the presence of thousands of people in the streets.

Within our movement, there are many different ideas of how best to disrupt these institutions. To use our analogy, there are some who believe the only moral way to stop the beating of the dog is by putting our own bodies between the dog and the stick. There are others who say, "To hell with that, grab the stick, or knock it out of his hand." And still others who might say, "Distract him, come up from behind, and do something totally unexpected."

But there is no one in our movement saying, "Shoot the guy." There is no one at this time calling for violence or armed struggle. In our actions in the United States, we have repeatedly seen police use alleged "bomb threats" as a way of closing down our meeting places and illegally arresting people. At the Democratic Convention, they used a bomb scare to prevent the broadcast of the dialogue taking place at the counter convention. NONE of these allegations have proved true. NONE have been founded on any true evidence. The media have consistently reported the rumors and ignored the reality, to create a climate of fear around these actions.

The more open and respectful the discussions we have within the movement around our tactical and ideological differences are, the more creative and effective our actions get. There is no one, not in INPEG or any other organization, who can negotiate "terms of engagement" for everyone who will come to these demonstrations. INPEG has already put out a clear statement: they will not initiate violence nor destroy property. The fact that they are the main on-the-ground organizers, and the people who know the local situation, gives their voices a certain weight, but it does not mean they can control what others do. However, just because someone believes property damage is a viable or even vital tactic and argues for that position on these lists does not mean they will be necessarily smashing the windows of small shopkeepers in Prague.

In reality, the violence at these actions has come from the police. I'm speaking of my experience in the United States, and the Czech Republic may be quite different. However, the FBI has been in Prague for months, presumably advising the local police, so I think our experience is relevant. In Seattle, the police began using tear gas and pepper spray long before a single window was broken. In Washington, D.C., where no property damage occurred, demonstrators were beaten and brutalized in jail after just such a negotiated, totally nonviolent arrest as you propose in your letter. Illegal, preemptive arrests have become the police strategy of choice. I could go on with examples, but this post is already far too long.

What we've seen so far in Prague is an immense buildup of police power and a concerted media campaign to paint the demonstrators as violent terrorists. The elements are already in place to justify police violence, regardless of what actually occurs in the demonstrations.

I would ask you, what can you do to restrain police violence, to prevent preemptive arrests, to assure that if people take creative action and make costumes, puppets, and other elements of street theater, they will actually be able to use them? Or that those who want to come for a legal march and demonstration will be able to do so? Can you use your influence with the media to allow the true voices of the demonstrators to be heard, to assure that they check out the truth of rumors, to prevent the continued fearmongering?

In return, we need to ask ourselves if we can do more to educate our own movement about the Czech Republic. The more people know about Czech history, culture, and political realities, the more intelligent their choices of tactics will be.

And can we do more outreach to the Czech people? INPEG is a small group with very limited resources, but that's certainly a question that can be discussed. At the very least, a flyer in Czech could be distributed before the 26th.

In the end, we have to trust in the good sense of those of you who will be in Prague on the 26th. The rest of us around the world will be supporting you, and looking ahead to carrying this movement on.

Starhawk

Reply to Molly Mayhem

(AFTER PRAGUE, MUCH debate arose and much criticism was aimed at those who took part in major conflicts with the police. This is an excerpt from my reply to a post by a very angry woman objecting to the criticism of the violence and attacking the style, motives, and impact of the non-violent contingent.)

… I think the debate going on on this list is the crucial one we need to be having as a movement right now.

One part of that debate is the question about the role of experience in our movement. Personally, I think we'd be criminally stupid NOT to share our experience. The police are certainly sharing theirs. One of those American women Molly complains about was one of the major organizers of Seattle, A16 in Washington, and the protests at the Democratic Convention. Are you telling me you DON'T want to hear what she's learned from all that?

I volunteered to do some trainings in both London and, a month early, in Prague because I've been an activist for more than thirty years. I've been training people in direct action for twenty, and I've been arrested more times than I'll admit on a list undoubtedly being monitored by the cops. I've learned that when people are going into extremely tense and dangerous situations, it's really helpful to have played them out ahead of time, to have thought through some of the possibilities and options, and to have in the back of their minds some possible responses they might not think of otherwise. That's why police and armies train people. I don't tell people what to do or what to think; if I did, they wouldn't accept it anyway. I know my experience is not necessarily going to translate across different cultural contexts, but I have enough respect for those who might be in the trainings to know they'll take what I offer and figure out what might work in their situation. And I learn from the experience of the other activists who come. In Prague, the "trainings" I and my partner did were more in the nature of mutual sharings: "This is how we did it

Seattle, this is how Reclaim the Streets does it, this is how Ya Basta! does it." It was an incredibly rich experience to share political cultures.

I've also read some posts that seem to object to the very existence of organizers who come early and help plan an action. But what happens on the day of an action is just the tip of an iceberg in terms of the immense amount of work required to set the stage for it to happen. A lot of that work is dull and unglamorous and not nearly as exciting as battling it out with the cops — it's about making a thousand phone calls and going to endless meetings and setting up the websites and the listserves and printing the flyers and raising the money to print the flyers, and it's about being there after the action is over to support the people in jail and to mobilize the political pressure to get them out and to raise the money for their court cases, and a whole lot more. I say when people are willing to do that work, we should be supporting and appreciating them. That doesn't mean we shouldn't criticize their mistakes, but there are ways to do that constructively.

We bring different things to actions from our different cultures and histories. From the United States, especially from the West Coast, we bring tools and insights from allied spiritual and psychological movements. That comes out of our culture where those ideas do seem to mix more freely than they do in Europe, where people in spiritual movements and political activists seem much more divided. We have a strong history here of social movements rooted in spirituality — from the Quaker abolitionists to the Church-supported black Civil Rights movement in the South. A lot of us have done support work for indigenous groups, for whom spirit and culture are a matter of survival. And many of us have found that we can only sustain our activism over the long haul when we have some regular connection to nature, to the larger cycles of birth and death and rebirth around us, and some way of collectively supporting each other and sharing that connection.

The spiritual/political/psychological edge is one I've been walking for twenty five years — and ecology teaches us that edges where different systems meet are often the most fertile places. I came to that edge thirty years ago for the same reason I think it's an important one now: because when you open your eyes to the incredible destructiveness and injustice of this system, you experience profound rage, along with grief, hopelessness, terror, and despair. That rage is enough to drive us all mad, to turn any one of us into a maniacal, head-holding, frothing-at-the-mouth flaming madwoman. There's not a day of my life when I don't feel the urge to simply pick up a brick and smash the hell out of something or someone.

But we have to find ways to transmute that rage. Otherwise it will simply kill us, saving the cops and the authorities the trouble of doing it themselves. And worse, we tend to turn it on each other because it's a hell of a lot easier and safer to attack our allies than our enemies. Or maybe because the small failures of our allies hurt us more than the attacks by our enemies. Action helps, but each action puts us in situations where the injustices become so clear and personal that the end result is more rage.

This is a violent system. Unlike Molly, however, I don't believe it can be defeated by violence. They have assault rifles; we have rocks. This is sane self-defense? But I believe the system can be dismantled if we mobilize our radical imagination, if we create an alternative so inspiring and compelling that the masses of people who yearn for both freedom and abundance will join us.

In fact, I believe that the more we turn toward violence, the more we throw away the advantages we do have. Whether you sit down and lock arms, or pick up a rock or a Molotov cocktail, you're operating in a space allowed us by police restraint. Because the reality is that they have the firepower and the state backing to shoot all of us if they chose to do so. Maybe that's more evident here in the U.S., where our police regularly do shoot people, especially people of color, for actions much less threatening than throwing a rock at a cop.

That restraint is created by a web of subtle forces that may not be visible on the street in the moment of confrontation. In part, it may come from the inner reluctance of some of the police to hurt or kill people. Yeah, some of them are heartless fascists, but not all. However, the larger restraints come from a broader web of forces: public opinion, potential political repercussions, orders from above, potential legal repercussions, and direct resistance.

If you haven't built a political base to support you, then as soon as you pick up a rock, you rip that web to shreds. And not just for yourselves, but for what is usually a much larger group of people who want to practice powerful, effective nonviolence. But what's worse, you've limited your own imagination. You've accepted the terms dictated by a system that is always telling us that force is the only solution. You've let them alienate you from those people working in McDonald's and eating at McDonald's. You can no longer imagine that they might come to be on our side, and you can no longer think clearly about how we might win them over.

We're at a crucial point right now. We can evolve further into an unpaid militant mercenary army, travelling to actions that get more violent, smaller, more isolated, and less effective, or we can look at what it takes to build a movement — which involves reaching out to people who don't look like us or think like us already, figuring out how to communicate our vision, and orchestrating a whole range of actions people in widely varying life circumstances might be inspired to take.

Nonviolence is about not waiting for the revolution, but living it now, in this moment. What kind of world do we want? Maybe we can't always articulate it, but we can embody it in how we organize, and in how we treat each other. We can treat each other with respect, regardless of how we treat the authorities. I respect Molly's courage, and her rage, even if I don't agree with her way of expressing it.

Political action, nonviolent or violent, always involves self-sacrifice. What makes it worthwhile is the community we create in the face of all their violence.

November 2000

Organizing in the Face of
Increased Repression

SINCE THE VERY FIRST MORNING of the Seattle blockade a year ago, the police forces of the world have greeted the anti-globalization movement with a high level of violence and repression. As the international movement has continued on, the repression has fallen into a pattern discernible from D.C. to Prague and beyond. This pattern involves the following:

- A concerted media campaign by the police and government forces that begins long before the demonstration, painting the activists as violent terrorists. All previous demos are equally characterized as violent, regardless of the actual facts.
- Surveillance of meetings, e-mail lists, phones, listserves, etc.
- Attempts at preemptive control, which range from mass illegal arrests in D.C. the night before the action, shutdowns of convergence centers and IndyMedia centers, and border closures to declaring a 5-kilometer no-protest zone five months before the planned action in Quebec.
- Less obvious violence on the street. Seattle taught them that tear gassing whole sections of the city was a bad idea. However, tear gas, pepper spray, beatings, projectile weapons, water cannons, concussion grenades, etc. are routinely used now from Prague to Cincinnati.
- Random arrests and targeting of peaceful protesters while those throwing rocks are often let go. Maybe nonviolent protesters are easier to catch? Or maybe this is a concerted effort to discourage wider participation in these actions?
- Use of provocateurs. I am not saying that all who throw rocks are provocateurs. However, there is a growing body of eyewitnesses and stories of "protesters" seen one moment throwing a

rock at a window and the next being sheltered behind a police line, indicating that provocateurs are being used. Along with them, we can suspect the whole range of fun Cointelpro tactics (Cointelpro was the CIA Counterintelligence Program of the seventies that involved surveillance, infiltration, entrapment, and disinformation.).

- Intimidation and brutality in jail, which reached levels of out-right torture in Prague.
- Some sporadic attempts to identify and neutralize "leaders," i.e., holding John Sellers of Ruckus on a million dollars bail for charges that were later all dropped.

What fun! It's enough to make you think we're being effective, especially when, as in Prague, the protesters still managed to disrupt the meeting and send the banksters home a day early.

What can we do about it? Are we doomed to have our actions become more and more dangerous, and smaller and smaller? Or can we succeed in building a mass movement in spite of repression?

1. The greatest restraint to police violence during an action is the organizing and alliance building we're doing before the action ever happens. We need to counter their disinformation campaigns with our own community outreach, to leaflet, to talk to people, to go door to door, to explain to the community what we're doing and why long before we do it.

2. We need to build alliances with labor (like the meeting of the local or the folks down at the union hall), churches, NGOs, all the groups who are fighting the same vested interests. We don't have to do the same work they do, we don't have to change our hair-styles or analysis to accommodate them, but we do need to build bridges so that we can call on them to defend our — and their — civil rights, at the border, on the streets, or in jail.

3. We need to train and prepare as many people as possible. The more people have had a chance to play out a dangerous situation, to think out possible responses, and to try out different tactics, the calmer and more resilient they'll be on the streets. Even a few centered people in a crowd can be enough to prevent panic and spark an effective moment of resistance. Trainings need to stress flexibility

and developing a range of possible responses to widely varied situations so activists are prepared in the moment to make choices about what to do.

4. We also need ever more flexible and creative tactics. The more we can plan for orchestrated spontaneity, the harder we'll be to stop. For example, in Prague part of the plan was for smaller marches led by flags of different colors to break away from the main march and go in different directions. While this tactic had been discussed at open meetings for at least a month before the action, it still seemed to confuse the authorities.

5. We may need to focus more on preparation for surviving jail, for resisting intimidation, and for being prepared for interrogation than on the classic jail solidarity tactics we've used in the U.S. Those tactics focus on attempting to stay in jail where our strength of numbers allows us to pressure the system to drop or lower charges and helps us to protect individuals at risk. These tactics were developed, however, in a very different time, when the authorities often were interested in releasing most protesters and when jail experiences were hard and uncomfortable but relatively decent. At times those conditions still prevail and that kind of jail solidarity has been effective in Seattle and D.C. and in many other places. However, if people are being chained to the wall and beaten, the focus needs to shift to getting them out of jail. Solidarity then becomes what people outside jail do to put political pressure on the system, from calling on allies, phoning, faxing, and e-mailing the authorities to blockading the jail itself.

6. Organizing an action needs to include planning post-action and post-jail support, debriefing, trauma counseling, etc.

7. We need to continue building a broader, larger movement, to find ways to encourage participation at varied levels of risk, to support a wide variety of forms of protest that can mobilize different groups of people, to confront the racism, sexism, classism, etc. in our own groups, and to reach out to more diversity. Most of all, we need to clarify our vision of the world we want to create so we can mobilize people's hopes and desires as well as their outrage. And we need to be creative, visionary, wild, sexy, colorful, humorous, and fun in the face of the violence directed against us.

BRAZIL

When I returned from Europe in the fall of 2000, I underwent a midlife crisis. The actions and trainings had been, up to that point, something I fit into an already full and creative life of writing, teaching, lecturing, and other activities such as wandering in the woods, gardening, making apple butter, and baking pies. But now some inner voice said, "This is it. This is the time you've been preparing for, and you can't afford to waste a moment of it. Your first priority now needs to be the work of political change."

Accordingly, I threw aside most of my paying work. The inner voice was followed immediately by an e-mail from Brazil. Groups that had formed to do actions in solidarity with Prague were looking for trainings and help from those with experience in direct action.

My friend Hilary McQuie, who was one of the major organizers in Seattle, had spent time in Brazil working on public health and AIDS issues. We formed a collective to offer trainings and organizing support to actions, and invited one other member, Lisa Fithian, a labor organizer and also one of the organizers in Seattle, A16, and the Democratic Convention. In Europe all summer, I'd missed the actions in the U.S., but major protests took place both at the Republican Convention in Philadelphia and at the Democratic Convention in L.A.

Hilary and I found funding and went to Brazil, together with her new baby Ruby (the world's best travelling baby!) and the baby's father Mike Dolan, another Seattle organizer, who came from the world of the NGOs rather than from direct action. We began at the World Social Forum, a mammoth gathering of 17,000 people held in Porto Alegre as a counter to the World Economic Forum being held at the same time in Davos, Switzerland.

We attended the forum and gave a rather wild training to the Brazilians and a good contingent of Argentinians who were planning their own actions for April, when the working meeting for the FTAA was planned in Buenos Aires. We went on to offer trainings in Sao Paolo, while Mike did childcare. I then did a training workshop in Belo Horizonte and went on to spend a week in Buenos Aires.

The Brazilian anti-globalists, like the Czechs, were mostly very young. Pablo, our contact, was in his late twenties — the old man of the group. We were impressed with their dedication, courage, and a kind of Brazilian irrepressibility. Brazil, too, is not long removed from a military dictatorship, and the police can be brutal. The activists were a wonderful mix of punks and university students, bright, cheerful, often pierced, tattooed, studded, and spiked in amazing and creative ways, and seemingly unfazed by a series of actions in which the police met them with clubs and dogs.

We were, perhaps, not what the South Americans expected. The Argentinians told our friend Culebra, who had come with us to the Social Forum, that when they heard two women had come to train them in direct action they had pictured two jack-booted hard-core militants in army fatigues. Instead, they got one gray-haired grandmotherly type (me) and the Madonna-like Hilary nursing her angelic baby. However, they coped.

Hilary and I spent a lot of time thinking about how to transfer what we knew of direct action to a completely different political culture. In training, we use the Empowered Learning model, derived from the Brazilian educator Paolo Freire's work. In that model, education is not so much about the transfer of information as about providing a framework for reflection on experience. Teachers or trainers are not trying to push their agenda or philosophy, but to create a process in which learners develop their own.

Our trainings were active, focusing on role-plays and experiential exercises which we would then debrief. When we shared our experiences, it was always with the warning that the Brazilians would need to adapt this to their own circumstances.

I was also fortunate enough to visit two encampments of the MST, the Movimiento Sim Terre, which occupies unused land to create new settlements for landless rural people. (My experience is described later in the book, in the chapter entitled "Our Place in Nature.")

As well, I was warmly welcomed by the Brazilian Witches. I hadn't realized that a thriving Wiccan movement existed there. Even though two of my books had been published in Brazil, I was gratified to learn that people were actually reading and using them.

The difference between Brazil and Argentina is the difference between the exuberant samba and the melancholy tango. I went on to spend a week in Buenos Aires, to attend a marathon of political meetings, and to do trainings for a group there. The Argentinians were a much more mixed group in terms of age and experience. Argentinians my age are those who survived one of the most brutal dictatorships in history, in which more than 30,000 people were tortured, murdered, or "disappeared." I was able to spend an afternoon walking in the Plaza de Mayo with the Mothers of the Disappeared, who still circumambulate the plaza calling for justice for their lost children as they did when during the days of the dictatorship they were almost the only group who could protest publicly and survive.

The Argentinians were struggling, too, with many of the issues addressed in this book: how to make an impact on systems that are not set up for public input, how to find a method of protest that is neither just a safe, legal march nor a riot, how to decide whether nonviolence could actually be effective in a country with a history of such brutal repression. Argentina was at the time also being put through major financial crises — it still is — and my friends were concerned with how to respond. Their crisis has since escalated into a full-fledged insurrection, which saw the President removed from office and left dozens of people dead. Argentina, the country upon which neoliberalism was most fully imposed, has become a dramatic warning of that model's failure. I wish now that I had written more specifically about my time there, but I was not thinking about keeping a journal then; I was concerned about keeping up with my schedule and trying to understand what people were saying in their high-speed Argentinian Spanish.

What became clear to me on the trip is that the global justice movement truly is global. All over the world, people are struggling with the same issues out of their different histories and circumstances. The same questions were being addressed in Prague, Sao Paolo, and Quebec City, and the same institutions were being fought. Rather than being simply against globalization, the movement stands for a different sort of global connection, one of support, exchange, and solidarity rather than exploitation. Although we went to South America presumably to train, what we really did was learn.

What I Learned from the
World Social Forum

ALTHOUGH I'VE SPENT A LOT of the last year and a half at anti-globalization actions and meetings, many of which included forums of various sorts, and although in at least some of my incarnations I am a Respectable Adult with a college education and books to my credit who even gets asked to speak at conferences and universities, and even though some of my best friends work for NGOs, this is the first time I've actually made it up out of the direct action trenches and into the conference rooms. I found it highly educational (although, like most university education, it had its moments of airless, deadly boredom). The amazing number of participants, thousands more than expected, coupled with limited translation facilities and a high degree of confusion meant that I often didn't get to workshops I would have liked to attend or didn't know about events until after they happened. What follows, therefore, is an extremely limited picture of all the immensity of discussion and debate and strategizing and organizing that went on around hundreds of issues. In order to get this out, I've limited my focus to issues that affect groups I'm currently working with.

WATER

Water is a key issue worldwide, as there is a strong push from corporate interests to privatize water resources and water delivery services. The FTAA, the WTO, and a whole list of smaller bilateral and regional trade agreements open the door to the privatization of water. For me, this issue had eerie echoes of the negative society I imagined in my novel *The Fifth Sacred Thing*, where the poor could not afford to drink and people were imprisoned for stealing water. The Global Justice movement now must assert that water is a human right, linked to the right to life. There is no substitute for water; therefore there must be a limit to private ownership and control of water resources.

WOMEN'S ISSUES

They are key in the global justice struggle. There was a powerful work-shop on feminist perspectives on globalization, and many other workshops on women's issues. The main morning panels, however, tended to be quite male-dominated, and there was much talk of the need for an even stronger focus on women. I was able to connect indi-vidually with some of the women working on anti-globalization, and I hope that our women's action in Quebec City in April will bring our issues more to the forefront. There was great interest in it among women I met and as soon as the call is finalized, I will be able to get it out to some of the women's networks I've connected with here.

INDIGENOUS PEOPLES' STRUGGLES

For me, the most moving and clear talks I heard in the entire five days were two indigenous speakers who spoke so heartfully and poetically (and in such clear, blessedly slow Spanish!) that I felt like I was drink-ing cool spring water after days of stale coffee. There was an encampment of youth, the MST (Movimiento Sim Terre, a landless rural workers' movement), and indigenous groups, but unfortunately it was separate from the main campus; also, there was no clear announcement of the fact that there were ongoing meetings, speech-es, and presentations of the indigenous peoples' networks. Had I known, I probably would have spent most of the conference there. As it was, I got there only almost at the end, in time to learn that the sit-uation in Chiapas is not happily resolved under Vicente Fox, that he is trying to outlaw abortion, and that the growing struggle in Chiapas will also focus on water rights. High on the corporate agenda is con-trol of the hydroelectric potential represented by Chiapas' rivers — Bay Area folks, take note in light of our current energy "crisis!"

THE FTAA

I knew about the FTAA, I knew it was bad enough that I'm devoting most of my time currently to organizing against it, but I didn't know in detail just how bad it is:

- **Privatization of services.** Education, medical care, libraries, water delivery — the FTAA would open those areas to regulation by international trade agreements. It's one of the things the WTO hadn't quite gotten around to yet. Presumably, that could mean a corporation that runs prisons could sue a government for providing its own and thereby limiting the company's potential profits. Ditto with water, schools, health care, etc. Of course, for most countries in Latin America the World Bank and the IMF have already dealt with their health care and educational systems. But the FTAA would make it difficult or impossible for local or national governments to take control of their own schools, health care programs, or utilities and to run them for the benefit of their own citizens instead of for corporate profit.

- **Agriculture.** This is probably the most important aspect for the South — for farmers and indigenous people. The FTAA would make it impossible to support small farmers, to ensure biosafety standards around genetically engineered foods and seeds, and to prevent market manipulations and crop dumping that destroy traditional cultures.

- **Natural resources and the environment.** The FTAA would undermine every legislative and regulatory tool for conservation of resources and environmental protection, from the Endangered Species Act on down, and override local and federal laws.

- **Investment.** Remember the Multilateral Agreement on Investments that was defeated back in '97 by the opposition of civil society? This agreement brings it back, opening the door to "investors' rights" and to the control of government regulations and financial systems.

- **End run around the WTO.** The FTAA, along with a whole lot of other bilateral and smaller multilateral agreements, is part of the new strategy of the corporate globalists. Since the body blow that was dealt to the WTO in Seattle, what they're trying to do is put in place piecemeal the provisions they haven't yet been able to put into the WTO.

The WTO

It may or may not hold its next meeting in Quatar in November — although the media are reporting it as a sure thing, it will actually be a couple of weeks before they confirm the decision. It is less of a priority for corporate interests, however, because their strategy has shifted to bilateral and regional trade agreements that essentially put the WTO's noxious provisions into place.

DIRECT ACTION

We did do one forum on direct action in FTAA organizing, with groups from Brazil and Argentina. But in general, direct action is sort of the stepchild of the NGO world. It happens around the edges: the MST (The Landless Rural Workers Movement) did a great action pulling up bioengineered crops on the first day of the conference. Unfortunately we were still en route and couldn't take part. The Respectable Adults know about direct action; they often support it, and some of them actually take part in it. The introduction to the Forum Schedule credits the movement sparked by Seattle and D.C. and Prague. But many of the groups seem to have a bit of difficulty actually focusing on the direct action component of that movement or thinking about it as part of their strategy. Of course, they have funding to protect, so maybe they're better off not linking to us too directly. Maybe we don't need joint strategies, and these parallel worlds can just continue to exist semi-separately. But I can't help but think that we're their best friends — we're the reason why the World Bank is going to read a letter of protest with alarm and concern, or look at a petition, or pretend to have a dialogue. And that it might be nice occasionally, or smart strategically, for that to be a little more clearly acknowledged. Our direct action movement gains a lot when we do work together with the groups which have a level of sophistication and expertise that paid staff can develop — for example, in our San Francisco organizing around the FTAA there are a number of NGOs and also some union people who bring an incredible amount of knowledge and sophistication to the issues. But I'd also like to see more of the high-level strategists come down to the convergence center and actually listen to the anarchists and the dreadlocked youth and the black bloc who have a level of radical clarity that can get lost after years of reading reports and pressing for minor policy changes. Anyway, I amused myself by tossing out radical proposals: "Great — you guys send out a joint letter of protest and meanwhile we'll shut down every major stock exchange on the planet." And some people seemed genuinely interested.

There are, however, awesome groups down here that are organizing around direct action. There are groups in Sao Paolo, Belo Horizonte, and Buenos Aires that did solidarity actions around the S26 protests in Prague and are now gearing up for actions around the preliminary FTAA (ALCA in Spanish) meeting April 7 in Buenos Aires. They're serious, determined, and radical — the Argentinians want to make the Quebec City protests unnecessary by shafting the FTAA before it ever gets to Quebec. It's a joy and a privilege to be down here sharing some of our experiences and helping in that endeavor.

Brazil: The First Training

OUR FIRST TRAINING IN BRAZIL brought to mind the expression "herding cats," except that it was more like herding wildcats distracted by new hunting opportunities and pursued by mad dogs. But it certainly wasn't boring!

We began at the encampment for youth, indigenous people, and the MST that was set up for the World Social Forum at Porto Alegre. We had originally planned two days of trainings, but the encamped students felt that the facilities were so poor they wanted to go home and do the second day in Sao Paolo the following weekend. We gathered near the showers around nine — people slowly began arriving. First the Argentines, who are culturally more time-conscious than the Brazilians, and then gradually we woke up the students and gathered a crowd. However, immediately there was an issue: as the forum was ending, Jose Bove and an activist from the Columbian revolutionary group FARC had been arrested for leading a direct action against genetically engineered crops the day before. They were going to be deported — and for the FARC activist this would be a death sentence. Many of our potential trainees wanted to go off and do a support action. (I would have myself except that we had a commitment to the training.) About fifty of them did, leaving us still with fifty or sixty.

We started with a role-play: a march through the camp, also to gather whatever late sleepers were left. We told them they were marching to the Trade Ministry but planted a shill who at one point shouted out, "There's McDonald's — let's get it! The group immediately ran off, began battling our poor "police" with great spirit and exuberance, and completely lost focus on their original objective. We had someone else yell out, "The Trade Ministry!" and got them back on track, staged what turned out to be another "battle," and eventually got them to the area under the trees we had picked for the training site.

Everyone enjoyed the role-play immensely — they were all laughing and engaged by the time we started, and it taught us a lot about their expectations and political culture. We started in on our agenda, which was to debrief the role-play, introduce ourselves, and then have them do an active listening in pairs about what victory looks like. Brazil being one of those cultures where people talk a lot, often simultaneously, we thought active listening might be important to introduce. I spoke in Spanish, with occasional help, and the Brazilians seemed quite able to understand it. I'm not as eloquent as I can be in English, but I apparently can manage to do a training in Spanish although there were moments toward the end where I bogged down and switched to English with translation. Hilary spoke in English, with translation into Portuguese, and our fellow organizers translated for us.

During the dyads, Pablo, our key organizer, confessed to me that there was still a problem: there were still people who wanted to go to the action. Hilary and I said okay, we'll bring it to the group as a consensus role-play, just jump ahead in the agenda. Their groups have a strong tradition of open assemblies and democratic decision-making, but not all that much experience, in a formal, structured way with the consensus process itself. We introduced some of the concepts and facilitated a group decision: those who wanted to stay would and we would have enough to do a training, but those who wanted to go would go with our message of solidarity. It was a bit rocky and hard to contain the group's energy and keep focused, but we did it and in the end about five people left and fifty or so stayed on.

At that point, we went back to our agenda, having people introduce their partner's ideas of what victory would look like, doing some talk about strategy, about how direct action works, how your ultimate intention sets your strategy and your strategy determines your tactics (in that ideal world we all long for!). We divided into two groups: the Brazilians and the Argentines, to plan potential actions for April — the particular division came about because the Argentines have an actual meeting to potentially shut down, while the Brazilians will be doing more of a solidarity/movement-building action.

Just as we were going to report back, the group noticed a man standing up on a nearby table taping with a big video camera. He was wearing an MST headband and had two completely different-colored eyes, a rictus smile, greasy hair, and something of the look of a madman, although most people thought he was a cop. Someone went over to confront him, but he refused to stop taping. Others went over and jumped into the fray. One young man, from some kind of Eastern spiritual tradition, was using classic nonviolence techniques (calm voice, eye contact, active listening) quite effectively, except that the rest of the group was yelling, joining in a circle and screaming, taunting, chanting, and threatening to physically take his tape away. I tried to support the nonviolence but our intruder would absolutely not focus on me; I couldn't make myself heard over the noise of the group, and he probably couldn't understand me. I went back and Hilary and I made various attempts to regain the group's attention, but it was hard because our main organizer/translator was completely invested in not going on until the guy was stopped. Hilary did suggest that physically taking his tape was possibly violent and that she could not support it but most of the group was still off engaged in the conflict and in the end they did take the tape away. Finally camp security came, the guy calmed down, we started drumming, and eventually security led him away and we got the group back together again. Neither one of us felt very good about the incident but neither could we think of any way we could have, at that moment, kept control of the group given the language barriers and the early point in the training. We debated simply debriefing the whole thing as a lesson in violence/nonviolence but decided to wait and use it as an illustration later in the training, as debriefing at that moment would have necessitated a long discussion.

We carried on with the next item on our agenda: spectograms. In retrospect, I highly recommend writing out the poles of your spectrum. Violence/nonviolence was our first pole, would do it/wouldn't do it was our second. With a spectogram, one side of the room represents violence, one nonviolence — you throw out a situation and people arrange themselves according to whether they feel it's violent or nonviolent. You can add the second pole to give a cross-graph — so people can move toward violent/would do it or violent/wouldn't do it, nonviolent/would do it or nonviolent/wouldn't do it or anywhere in between. We then debriefed one person from each corner and one from the middle, as an example of how we all have varying perspectives on what violence is and how we need to respect each other's perspectives. The situations we used were eating meat (Hilary's suggestion, to bring home the fact that violence/nonviolence is not just an issue in protests but in everyday life as well, and one that always opens up a lively dialogue), throwing a pie in someone's face, and trashing the mock clocks set up in honor of 500 years of Brazil's "discovery". They went well and people seemed to appreciate the discussion and be deeply engaged with the question in a thoughtful and sophisticated way. We had planned a hassle line and a beginning section on nonviolence but because of the distractions and interruptions, it was lunchtime and we took a break.

We came back and went into the "practical protest" section — lots of active instruction on what your options are in blockading, in withstanding a police charge, in absorbing a person into a sitting or standing crowd, in protecting yourself while being hit on the head, etc. Hilary suggested we focus on a march scenario in which a mass of people were not officially organized into affinity groups or trained, to better simulate the situation in most protests, and she came up with a great sequence of challenges for them. We did it as a kind of fishbowl — half the group enacting the technique and the other half witnessing, then trading off. Lots of discussion about how in Brazil you wouldn't sit down because the police would just beat you up, but others said no, you might — if the media were there, if you had public support, if the police perceive you as nonviolent, they would be more restrained. Again, we were stressing all of these techniques as options to have in mind, as choices, as political decisions that the group could make. We taught a very brief grounding exercise, did a hassle line and some talk about classic de-escalation techniques like staying calm and keeping eye contact, went through going limp, tear gas and pepper spray, etc. etc. This part went well although it was at one point interrupted by one of the punks who had been in the training earlier, who was very angry about something that had happened to his girlfriend in the restaurant at lunch that he felt was discrimination and he apparently wanted us all to do something about — what, was not clear. But the group actually wanted to do the training, so he stormed out and didn't return.

The practical stuff took a long time and even then there was a lot we didn't get to, like dogs, horses, and a second hassle line. Nor did we get to O-shaped or U-shaped containment circles for out-of-control people — an oversight that cost us later! But time was getting short, so we moved on to a brief review of the consensus process and a discussion of affinity groups, roles, support, etc. We formed mock affinity groups and had them go through a quick consensus, taking our real situation of the morning: an activist has been arrested, is going to be deported, is potentially facing a death sentence — what are you going to do? The groups then reported back to a spokescouncil. There was a lot of commonality in the plans: set up a media center, write cards and letters, do phone calls, blockade the prison. We would have loved to give them time to truly go through a consensus process, but time was short so we jumped ahead into a final role-play. We identified a nearby picnic table as the jail, I was the prisoner, we set up a line of police, and they blockaded us. Hilary, my guard, tried to take me out through the blockade. The nonviolent yogi somehow got past the police line and distracted them so thoroughly that their prisoner actually escaped! Not totally realistic, but it went quickly and it was striking how much more they were able to act together as a group and keep their focus than in the morning.

We went on to a short section on jail, which, due to time constraints, had to be mostly discussion. Several of them had been arrested in actions, and we would have liked to hear more of their experience. We stressed setting up outside support, both before the action and when people are in jail, marshaling political pressure, etc. rather than our in-jail solidarity because of both time constraints and our real doubts about whether that kind of solidarity is workable or appropriate here. Then, just as we were wrapping up and closing, back came our mad cameraman, shouting and frothing. A few of us tried to contain him and move him out, but I couldn't explain U-shaped containment loud enough or fast enough or comprehensibly in Spanish — to be honest, I couldn't have done it even in English, so Hilary started to move the group away from him. He ran over to follow the group, the group moved back and then linked arms in a circle, effectively blocking him out, and began to Om loudly. He was at first infuriated but began to lose energy when he couldn't get through and then Security came over and he calmed down a bit again. The group was able to act as a whole and I think felt much better about how they handled the intrusion this time. We had earlier made the point that the cops can win as much by distracting us from our work as by actually taping us, and this time we were able to hold our center. We ended by singing, "Si, se puede!" It's a pleasure to work with people who can sing and clap with spirit and who naturally raise energy. Then everyone had to run for the busses, and we were ready for dinner and general collapse.

So, there it is. You'll note it's short on theory and history; generally we bring those out through the debriefing process but in this case, in the general chaos and madness, we had no chance even to touch on the history of nonviolent direct action. On the one hand, we hope we taught them something valuable. On the other hand, a one-day training for fifty people — even the series of trainings we hope to do here — seems such a small effort toward helping them build the political culture they want. It left us both with a lot of questions about how particular models of organizing can transfer from culture to culture, and stimulated a lot of thought. It was one of the most challenging days I've ever spent — but also one of the most exciting.

QUEBEC CITY

The Summit of the Americas, the gathering of all heads of state from all the Americas except for Castro, was planned for Quebec City in April of 2001 to ratify progress toward extending NAFTA throughout the hemisphere in the form of a Free Trade Area of the Americas. Organizing for a countersummit and protest began in the autumn. In January, Lisa Fithian and I joined with trainers in Montreal for a preliminary weekend of trainings and preparations. I spent much of the spring in one way or another organizing or mobilizing people for the action.

Already the police were planning a new level of defence, in the form of a nine-foot-high fence anchored in concrete around four kilometers of Quebec City, which would keep protesters away from the meetings and prevent a repetition of Prague or Seattle. They emptied an old prison in preparation for the event.

Quebec has its own history and political culture. In many ways it is more European than North American. The history of resistance to English rule creates a strong sympathy for those who resist authority. Yet the Quebecois police are known for their harshness, and politics there can also be extremely factionalized and divided.

A group called the Table de Convergence formed to organize the countersummit and other protest activities. But a division developed between the groups that were mobilizing for direct action.

SalAMI is a direct action group with a strong commitment to non-violence. They had organized several other powerful actions, and they had very strict nonviolence guidelines for Quebec.

CLAC, the Anti-Capitalist Convergence in Montreal, and its sister group CASA in Quebec City were organized around respect for diversity of tactics. While not advocating violence, they were opposed to setting strict guidelines and uninterested in an orchestrated, ceremonial arrest. The divisions between the groups were exacerbated by personal conflicts, as divisions always are. CLAC and CASA were more attuned to the Internet, one of the prime ways of mobilizing, and had more connections with the broader direct action wing of the movement. SalAMI had more experience in the actual organizing of an action, and more connection to the NGOs and unions who were either unaware of CLAC or deliberately choosing to ignore them. Many people worked to try to bring the groups together. But in the end, SalAMI decided to focus on an action of their own in Ottawa at the Parliament, on an Avenue of the Alternatives safely away from the wall, and on the Women's action. CLAC and CASA were left to organize the main direct action, on the principle of diversity of tactics.

I struggled with my conscience about organizing Pagans to go to Quebec. It was clear to me that it would not be a safe and peaceful event. Finally, I decided to just lay out the situation as I saw it and let people make their own decisions.

Many people in the larger Pagan community shared my sense that this was an important turning point. We participated in the Women's Action and put out a call for an action of our own that we called "The Living River," to draw attention to issues of water in the FTAA. In the end, we had a group of ninety to a hundred that swelled to twice that many during parts of the action itself. We were able to hold a calm and visionary energy in the midst of chaos, to pioneer new, fluid tactics, and to allow people to participate at varying levels of risk and come away empowered and ready for further actions. Quebec did indeed prove to be both a political and personal turning point.

Quebec: Letter to the Pagan Listserve

January 15, 2001

I AM TREMENDOUSLY EXCITED by the possibilities I'm sensing around April. AND I can see the many, many ways that this could go wrong. It will not be safe. Even if everyone involved were impeccably nonviolent and utterly nonconfrontational, it would not be safe. The authorities are becoming more repressive around these globalization actions. And there is a strong possibility that at least some of the protesters will be more confrontational, even more destructive, than many people in our community will feel comfortable with.

I feel personally called to be part of this action in every way I can. For me, that comes out of not just my magic but the political assessment that has been growing in me all this year — that we need nothing less than a global economic, social, political, and spiritual revolution and that this is the next big step in making it.

And now I find myself in somewhat of a dilemma. I know that I have a lot of influence in our community, yet I don't want to use that influence unduly to persuade anyone to do anything that doesn't feel utterly right to you. But I have to be honest and say that I also feel that we as a community are called to help shape this action. That we have exactly the skills that are needed and that people are hungry for and that have the potential to shift the balance to make this action a world-changing moment in a creative and visionary way.

But I ask each of you to really do some deep magic and soul searching and divination about what you are called to do. Because world-changing moments that confront the massed police powers of the state can be costly on many levels. If you do this, you could get hurt. You could get arrested in a situation that will likely not be easy or pleasant. You could end up in jail in a foreign country.

There will be ways to support this action on every level of risk, from the complete personal safety (but vital necessity) of being home support, to participating in the many, many solidarity actions that will be organized all over, to going to Quebec and participating in the legal and educational parts of the action, to risking arrest. My own intention is not to get arrested in Quebec. But I am realistic enough to know that there are no guarantees ...

Weaving a Web of Solidarity: A Feminist Action against Globalization

Summit of the Americas on the FTAA
Quebec City, April 2001

On the weekend of April 20-22, leaders of thirty-four countries will come to Quebec to tie a new strand in the web of corporate globalization: the Free Trade Agreement of the Americas (FTAA), the regional accord that will expand NAFTA (North American Free Trade Agreement) throughout the hemisphere. In response, thousands of us will come to Quebec City to resist them. From Canada to Argentina, women and men will take action to express our opposition to the extension of the corporate web.

Women bear the brunt of the violence of globalization, yet despite all the oppression, repression, and exploitation, women continue to rise up. This is a call to rise up as we join together in a Women's Action, to take place alongside the many actions and events of the weekend.

We are taking action because we will no longer tolerate the web of corporate control that binds us down and constricts our lives. We will not allow this system to continue. We have taken its measure — its time is done. Instead, we will become spiders, spinning a new web of connection, of solidarity out of our rage, out of our love.

We will, as women, weave together our hopes and dreams, our aspirations, our indictments, our testimony, our witnessing, our demands, our visions. We will write on ribbons, on strips of cloth, on rags. We will draw, paint, knot cords, braid yarn, whisper into pieces of string. And from these materials we will weave our web.

If they ignore our voices and continue their deliberations, the cries of women will haunt them and undo all their plans. Though they erect a fence to stop us, we will twine our web through its mesh to be the visible symbol of the power of women, of the revolution we weave. When they try to wall us out of their meetings, they will only wall themselves in. We claim all of the world beyond their wall.

We ask our brothers to support us, to honor our women's space so that we who have so often been invisible can stand forth and be seen. We ask you to support us by looking honestly at the ways that, even within our own movements, women are ignored, suppressed, or discounted. And when you support us in this action, where we stand together as women, it will spark actions where we fight side by side. For we know that you, too, are weavers of this web.

We ask the ancestors to stand with us. For the web of life links the living and the dead. We ask the generations of the future to stand with us, for we fight for the world you will inherit. We ask the spirits of the earth to support us and be our ground, for we fight for the continuance of life.

We are invincible, for life itself weaves with us.

— This call was written by the collective of
women organizing the action.

81

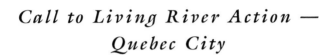

Call to Living River Action —
Quebec City

In respect for the diversity of means and tactics in our movement, we wish to clearly state our vision for this action and invite others to join who can support our intentions.

The heads of state and their ministers who will attend the Summit of the Americas believe they have come to endorse the process that will lead to ratifying the FTAA. We say this process is illegitimate and must be stopped. This secret treaty, which will override the laws of our countries, has not been subjected to public comment or democratic vote. Every effort has been made to insulate the negotiators from hearing the voice of the people. Quebec City has been turned into a militarized zone.

In the world proposed by the FTAA, every basic element of life and community is up for sale, including the health of the environment, the safety of workers, and the whole spectrum of efforts we citizens have made to provide education for our children, care for the sick, hope for the poor, and all basic services of government.

We say that our lives, our communities, the health of the earth's ecosystems, the cultures of indigenous peoples, the dreams of children are too important to be subsumed to profit. Another world is possible: a world of justice, freedom, ecological balance, and true abundance, and we will make it real.

Led by voices from the global South, we begin with water. After the people of Cochabamba, Bolivia, succeeded in retaking their water from privatization, they issued the following declaration:

THE COCHABAMBA DECLARATION

"For the right to life, for the respect of nature and the uses and traditions of our ancestors and our peoples, for all time the following shall
be declared as inviolable rights with regard to the uses of water given
us by the earth:

1. Water belongs to the earth and all species and is sacred to life; therefore, the world's water must be conserved, reclaimed, and protected
   for all future generations and its natural patterns respected.
2. Water is a fundamental human right and a public trust to be guard-
   ed by all levels of government; therefore, it should not be
   commodified, privatized, or traded for commercial purposes. These
   rights must be enshrined at all levels of government. In particular,
   an international treaty must ensure these principles are noncontro-
   vertible.
3. Water is best protected by local communities and citizens who must
   be respected as equal partners with governments in the protection
   and regulation of water. Peoples of the earth are the only vehicle to
   promote earth democracy and save water."

Here on the banks of the St. Lawrence/Magtogoek, with the river as
our ally and the ancestors marching with us, we will become a living
river, to bring this declaration as a challenge to the world's governments and an inspiration to her peoples.

Although the negotiators of the FTAA believe they have fenced out
dissent, we believe they have walled themselves in. We intend to liberate them so they can hear the voices of the people, the land, and the
waters. No army can stop the spring flood, no fence can hold back a
river. In our organization of this action, we will embody the principles
of openness, participation, empowerment, and real democracy that are
the foundation of the world we strive to create.

We intend to carry out this action with vision, imagination, creativity, humor, and joy, with respect for the lives, enterprises, culture, and
heritage of the people of Quebec City, and in a manner that encourages
all to join us.

The Bridge at Midnight Trembles:
My Story of Quebec City

UNDER THE FREEWAY, they are drumming. Clad in black, hooded in sweatshirts, they pick up sticks and beat on the iron railings, on the metal sculptures that grace this homeless park, on the underpinnings of the overpass that links the lower town to the upper levels of Quebec City. They are mostly young and they are angry and jubilant, dancing in the night after two days on the barricades. From above, the cops fire volleys of tear gas. It billows up in clouds and drifts down like an eerily beautiful phantom fog, but the dancers keep on dancing. The sound and the rhythm grow and grow, a roar that fills the city, louder than you can imagine, loud enough, it seems, to crack the freeways, bring the old order down. The rumbling of the rapids as you approach the unseen waterfall. A pulsing, throbbing heartbeat of something being born. A rough beast, not slouching but striding toward Bethlehem, in solidarity and pride.

A carnival, a dance, a battle. Images of war: the tear gas clouds, the spray of the water cannons, the starbursts of exploding gas, and yes, the rocks and bricks and bottles. No one has come here expecting a safe or peaceful struggle. Everyone who is here has overcome fear, and must continue to do so moment by moment.

In the chaos, the confusion, the moments of panic, there is also a sweetness, an exuberance. Spring after winter. Freedom. Release. The rough tenderness of a hand holding open an eye to be washed out from tear gas. The kindness of strangers offering their homes to the protesters: come up, use our toilets, eat these muffins we have baked, fill your bottles with water.

We are the Living River: a cluster within the action that sometimes swells to a couple of hundred people, sometimes shrinks to fifty. Our core is made up of Pagans, who are here because we believe that the earth is sacred and that all human beings are part of that living earth.

Many of us have known each other and worked together for years; others are new, drawn together from outlying places by the Internet and the organizing. One woman has brought her teenage children; our oldest member, Lea, is eighty-four. Our goal is to bring attention to issues of water, we say, although our true goal is to embody the element of water under fire.

We carry the Cochabamba Declaration (see p. 83), which was written by a group of people in Bolivia who staged an uprising to retake their water supply after it had been privatized by Bechtel Corporation.

This Declaration is the alternative. It's what we are fighting *for*, not against. Our goal is to bring it into the Congress Center, declare the FTAA meeting illegitimate because it is not supported by the people, and suggest they begin negotiating to protect the waters. Failing that, we will get as close as we can and declare the Declaration wherever we are stopped.

As we are mobilizing, our friends in Bolivia stage a march for Life and Sovereignty, which is violently repressed. Oscar Olivera, one of the framers of the Declaration, is arrested, charged with treason, but then released. As we are tear gassed, so the March is tear gassed, again and again. In Bolivia, two people die, one asphyxiated by the gas. In Quebec, there are near deaths, a man shot in the trachea by a rubber bullet, asthma attacks from the tear gas, a finger torn off in the assault on the fence. In Sao Paolo the youth blockading the Avenida Paulista are brutally attacked and beaten. Broken arms, broken wrists. Toya, one of our closest friends, is beaten on the head so hard her helmet is split in half, but she doesn't leave because she is a medic. At the private hospital, they refuse to treat the protesters. The police chase them away with live ammunition. Those arrested are tortured, held on their knees for over three hours in tight handcuffs while every fifteen minutes the police come by and beat them on the back. Most are under eighteen.

Our River has banners and flags and blue cloth suspended on poles and blue costumes and water songs. In theory, the action is divided into zones: a green zone for nonarrest, safe actions; a yellow zone for nonviolent, "defensive" actions; a red zone for confrontational actions. In practice, aside from two designated green areas, no one knows exactly where these zones are or what they are supposed to mean. Anyway, we're the blue group, something outside of the plan. We are prepared to be nonviolent and confrontational. However, many of us are ten to twenty years older than the average protester, most of us are women, and for many of the group, this is their first action ever. Some of us are prepared to go over the perimeter, if the chance arises, to risk arrest and physical confrontation. Others are not. So the river has four streams within it. Each will follow a flag of one of the elements. The green Earth flag will always make the safest choice in any situation. The blue Water flag will rally those willing to take the greatest risks. The red Fire and yellow Air flags will support the blue but not directly risk arrest. Affinity groups may stay together to follow one flag, or decide ahead of time how they will split when a moment of danger comes. Each person in the river has a buddy, someone they always keep track of, so that no one can get lost. Our scouts — Charles, Raven, Laura, and Lisa — run ahead and check routes, come back and report, or phone in. At times, the river is able to stop and make a choice collectively about what to do. At other times, it is impossible to meet or even hear each other, and the flag bearers decide.

Friday afternoon. The River has spiraled at the gate at Rene Levesque, where the night before the Women's Action hung our weavings. As we wind up the circle, beginning to raise the power, Evergreen comes up to me with a man in tow who is decked in the Cuban flag. He is part of a small group of indigenous people who have been holding a vigil at the gate, and our group is so metaphoric (and we never quite got the signs made that said clearly what we were doing) that somehow he has gotten the impression that we are for the FTAA. We are singing, "The river is flowing," and he is from Honduras and his land is flooded from ecological breakdown and hurricane Mitch, and the only way we can demonstrate our solidarity, he says, is to join him in his chant. "Why not?" I shrug and we begin to chant in Spanish and English, "El pueblo, unido, jamas sera vencido!" "The people, united, will never be defeated!" The shout has a rhythm of its own, an angry and hopeful power.

We dance on down to St. Jean Street, singing, "Fleuve, porte-moi, ma mère tu restera; Fleuve, porte-moi, vers l'océan." The news comes from our scouts — the CLAC march has reached the gate we've just left, and the fence is already down. I literally jump for joy. Quickly we regroup, and the blue, red, and yellow flags decide to head back up for the gates.

We move up the street, stop in an intersection. Our scouts are ahead of us, checking out the side streets. We make a circle, begin to sing, "Hold on, hold on, hold the vision until it's born."

We begin a spiral, start to wind the power up, and suddenly I know clearly that we need to move up the hill, into the battle. I look at Wilow, our Blue flag bearer, who smiles because she knows what I'm thinking. We nod, and she waves the flag. We advance forward. Up to René Levesque, into the avenue, and out in front of the theater, singing and drumming. We receive cheers — "Hey, it's the River." Closer to the gate, the cops are firing tear gas at the crowd. Young men run out of the crowd, shadows in the fog, and throw the canisters back. The gas billows up and is blown back onto the police lines. We are still able to breathe and sing, so we start a spiral. The circle grows: other people join hands and dance with us, moving ever closer to the gate, not running away, not giving ground. All along it has been hard to decide what the *action* of this direct action should be. Now we all see that the fence is the action. Challenging it, pulling it down, keeping up the pressure on the perimeter, refusing to go away, demanding to stay and be seen and heard.

We spiral and dance, the drums pounding against the thunder of the projectiles as they shoot tear gas canisters overhead, laughing with the sheer liberation and surrealism of it all. Until at last one shot lands close to us, the gas pours out and engulfs us in a stinging, blinding cloud, and we are forced away.

Down the hill we stop, wash out our eyes, rejoin the red and yellow flags. We help other people who also need their eyes washed. I am grateful for the training Laura gave us — grateful to remember that I can breathe through the tear gas, though it hurts, to know how to wash eyes properly, how to rinse my throat, spit, rinse, spit before drinking.

We decide to flow on, to the blockade on the Cote d'Abraham a few blocks away. A couple of young people beg us to stay, to go back up the hill, and I'm tempted. They want the energy we bring, and they feel safer when we're there. But we hear that the Cote d'Abraham gate could also use some energy, and the mission of the River is to flow, so we go on. We could use ten, a hundred Rivers.

The gate at the Cote d'Abraham is a stage — elevated above the lower city, it closes off one of the main thoroughfares where three highways converge. A crossroads. We can look out over the lower city and the faraway hills where a red sun is about to set. When we arrive, the energy feels fragmented. Some people are drumming and dancing, others milling around, some tossing things at the police lines behind the fence, others just not quite knowing what to do. We synch to the beat of the drummers and begin a circle that grows and grows. Three or four hundred people are holding hands when we begin to spiral. The drummers move into the center and we wind and wind the spiral until the chant gets lost in the drum jam beat. Behind us, Donna has moved over to the fence and is scolding the police, especially the one woman among them: "How can you do this? You — a woman! A Canadian! What are you thinking of!"

The area has been so heavily gassed that many of us can't stay long. The energy peaks, not into a cone of power but into a wild dance. Our scouts report that riot cops are massing down the street, heading toward us to clear the area. I ask the drummers to stop for a moment so we can inform people but they just shrug, "So what?" They won't let a little thing like a police attack interrupt their music. The Living River flows on. Behind us, we can look back and see the spray of the water cannons, arching high in the air, filled with light like a holy and terrible rain that plays upon the black figures who hold their ground below.

Saturday morning: About twenty of us gather in the house where we're staying. Everyone is braver than before. I am awed. Some of us have been activists for decades and carry into the actions a slow courage that has grown over many, many years. But some of our people have made that internal journey in one night.

All along I've been carrying a feeling of responsibility for these new people. I know they are all adults; they have made their own choices with their eyes wide open. But still, I know that many of them would not be here in this place of danger if I hadn't urged people to come.

And it's one thing to decide, in the safety of your home, to go to a demonstration. It's another thing to face the reality of the chaos, the tear gas, the potential for violence.

I am here, I have done my best to inspire and encourage other people to be here with me, because as scared as I might be of the riot cops and the rubber bullets, I'm a thousand times more scared of what will happen if we aren't here, if we don't challenge that meeting going on behind these walls. In the beauty of the woods, in the quiet of the morning when I sit outside and listen for the birdsong, in every place that should feel like safety, I know by the feel of the current that we are headed for an irrevocable edge, an ecological/economic/social crash of epic dimensions, for our system is not sustainable and we are running out of room to maneuver. The mostly men running the governments and the corporations and the economic institutions of the world seem incapable of grasping reality: that nature is real, and has limits and needs of her own that must be respected; that neither human beings nor forests nor oil reserves can be endlessly exploited without causing great damage to the world; that the basic life support systems of the planet are under assault. In the meeting we are protesting, the Congress Center protected by the fence and the wall and the riot cops and the army, they are planning to unleash the plundering forces and remove all controls. Water, land, forests, energy, health, education, all of the human services communities perform for each other will be confirmed as arenas for corporate profit making, with all of our efforts to regulate the damage undermined.

And I am here because I am inspired by the incredible courage, the energy, the commitment of the mostly young people in this struggle. And because I have felt, all along, a vortex of forces converging on this time and this place — and a cadre of Witches is just what is needed to work those energies.

And what I hear from my friends now confirms my feelings. "I know, now, why you do this." "This is what we have been training for, all these years." "This action itself is a training ground. We're just beginning."

We circle, sing, raise power, and make our decision. We will go to the labor march, whose leaders have planned to walk safely away from the wall. But we will join the groups that plan to break off and return to challenge the perimeter.

Saturday afternoon: I am standing in the alley with Juniper who has never been in an action before and with Lisa who has been in many. There is an opening in the wall, but the riot cops stand behind, defending it, their shields down, impermeably masked, padded and gloved and holding their long sticks ready to strike.

Wilow moves forward, begins to read the Cochabamba Declaration. The cops interrupt, shouting something, and move out from behind the fence. Their clubs are ready to strike; one holds the gun that fires tear gas projectiles and points it at us. Lisa and I look at each other, one eye on the cops, the other on the crowd behind us. "What do we want to do here?" she asks me. The cops begin to advance. "Sit down," someone calls behind us, maybe someone we ourselves trained to sit in this very situation.

We sit down. The cops tense. Juniper begins to cry. I am going to tell her she doesn't have to be in the front line, but she smiles through the tears and says, "It only gets good when you start to cry," and I know that nothing could make her leave. We are holding hands. I consider whether we should link up, make a stronger line.

We pass the Cochabamba Declaration back to someone who speaks French and begins to read it out loud. I pass my drum back, hoping one of my friends will pick it up.

I see one of the cops slightly lower his baton. Another wavers — their perfect line now shows some variation. They are beginning to relax.

A rock sails out of the crowd behind us, flies over our heads, and lands at the cops' feet. In a second they are on alert, moving toward us. "NOOOOO!" the whole crowd behind us cries in one outraged voice to the thrower of the rock. "Peace!" they call out to the cops, raising their arms and flashing peace signs. In the front line, we are still, holding hands, waiting. Breathe and ground. The cops slowly relax again.

From behind, someone passes up flowers. Heather brought them in the morning, saying she wanted to do something nonviolent, give them to the police. I remember thinking that hers was an idea so sweet that it belonged in some other universe than the one I anticipated being in that day. She had not looked too happy when I explained that we intended to follow CLAC and the black bloc up to the perimeter.

"People might think we're supporting them," she said. "Well, we are supporting them," I explained. At least, for some of us that's what we felt called to do — to be right up there with them in the front lines, holding the magic, grounding the energy, not preaching about non-violence but just trying to embody it. Now Heather and her flowers are here.

Lisa gets up, holding out her hands to the cops in a gesture of peace, and attempts to give them the Declaration. I watch, holding my breath, ready to back her up if they attack. "We can't take it," one of them whispers to her through clenched teeth. She lays it at his feet. A young man comes forward, lays down a flower. A woman follows with another. Somehow, in that moment, it becomes the perfect gesture.

Everyone relaxes. After a time, we decide to make our exit. The River must flow on. Others move forward to take our place. We snake back to the intersection. Behind us, the young men of our cluster are helping to take down the fence along the cemetery. We begin a spiral in the intersection — masses of people join in with us. From a rooftop above, two of the local people shower us with confetti. We dance in a jubilant snow. The power rises, and as it does, an absolute scream of rage tears out of my throat. I'm drumming and wailing and sending waves and waves of this energy back at the Congress Center, and at the same time we are dancing and confetti is swirling down while behind us the tear gas flies and the fence comes down.

When we stop, a woman comes up with news. The only way to be heard in the din and thunder is for the cluster to repeat each sentence. The news becomes a chant:

"I've just heard" — "I'VE JUST HEARD!"

"That so much tear gas" — "THAT SO MUCH TEAR GAS!"

"Has been blown back into the Congress Center" — "HAS BEEN BLOWN BACK INTO THE CONGRESS CENTER!"

"They've had to close down the meetings for two hours." — "THEY'VE HAD TO CLOSE DOWN THE MEETINGS FOR TWO HOURS!"

We erupt in cheers.

In front of the gate on St. Jean Street, five young men and one woman stand, their backs to the massed groups of riot cops behind the barrier, their feet apart, one arm up in a peace sign, absolutely still in the midst of chaos, unmasked, unprotected, in a cloud of tear gas so strong we are choking behind our bandannas.

We file behind them, read the Cochabamba statement, and then flow on. They remain, holding the space as their eyes tear, steadfast in their silence, their courage, and their power.

When the Bay Bridge fell in the last San Francisco earthquake, we learned that structures resonate to a frequency. A vibration that matches their internal rhythm can bring them down.

Beneath the overpass, they are drumming on the rails. The city is a drum. Massive structures tremble.

And a fence is only as strong as its point of attachment to its base.

("The bridge at midnight trembles" is a line from a Bob Dylan song,
"Love Minus Zero/No Limits".)

Quebec City: Beyond Violence and Nonviolence

I HAD A HARD TIME COMING back from Quebec City. I know because, almost two months later, I still have the map in my backpack. In part it was exhaustion, tear gas residue, and the sense of having been through a battle in a war most of my neighbors are totally unaware of. But deeper than that is my sense that something was unleashed in that battle that can't be put back, that underlying the chaos, the confusion, the real differences among us, and the danger we were in was something so tender, exuberant, and wild that I don't want to let it go, something that smells and tastes and feels like the world I'm fighting for.

How we achieved this sense of sweet unity on the street is a mystery to me. In the lead-up to the action it often seemed that every single group involved was either actively disagreeing with some other group or ignoring their existence. The conflicts were mostly around issues of tactics, in particular the question of nonviolence. Quebec City was the first time since Seattle that a major anti-globalization direct action in North America was organized by groups that were committed to a "diversity of tactics" rather than to an explicit set of nonviolence guidelines.

I admit that I came into the preparations for the action uneasy about the concept of a "diversity of tactics." I'm fifty years old; I've been an anarchist and an activist since I was in high school back in the streetfighting days of the sixties. I've also been an advocate for nonviolence for many, many years, in part because of what I experienced in the sixties and seventies, when mostly male-dominated militant groups moved to clandestine actions, sectarianism, and armed struggle that left their base of support far behind. I experienced the nonviolent direct action groups of the eighties, with their commitment to feminist process and nonhierarchical structure, as far more empowering, effective, and liberating.

My fear about a "diversity of tactics" was that it would open a space for people to do things that I thought were stupid and wrong. That, it fact, proved to be partly true — at least, people did do things I would never have agreed to. But what surprised me was that it didn't seem to matter in the way I thought it would.

I thought people would only come to a mass action if it had clear nonviolence guidelines, but people came to Quebec City anyway. I thought high levels of confrontation would lose us popular support, but we had the strongest support ever from the local people, many of whom joined us or opened their homes to give us water, food, and access to toilets. I thought people new to direct action would be terrified by the level of conflict we experienced. But our cluster included many people who had never been to an action before. The first day, yes, some were terrified. By the second day, more were ready to go to the wall. By the third day, they were demanding better gas masks for the next one.

There's an ethic and a strategy about nonviolence that's clear and easy to understand: that violence begets violence; that if we resort to violence we become what we're fighting against; and that a nonviolent movement will win us more popular support, gain us legitimacy, heighten the contrasts between our movement and what we oppose, and perhaps even win over our opponents.

That's a powerful and persuasive set of values that I've held to for many years. But they're not the only values I sympathize with. Some advocates of nonviolence assume the high moral ground in any argument and tend to see those who disagree with them as unethical. In Quebec City, "diversity of tactics" meant respecting that those who employ other tactics do so not out of a lack of principles, but out of their own politics and values.

High-confrontational struggle has its own principles: that a high level of confrontation is appropriate in the situations we now face; that people have the right and responsibility to defend themselves against police violence; that many people are already angry and mostly not saintly and a political movement needs room to express that rage; that active self-defense can be empowering and may also win people to our cause; and that in order to bring down an economic and political system that worships property, property must be attacked.

And there is also an ethic behind a "diversity of tactics" that the phrase itself does not convey: that people should be free to make their own choices; that a nonauthoritarian movement doesn't tell people what to do; and that we should stand in solidarity even with people whose choices we disagree with.

I can't do justice to any of the positions in a few sentences, and they by no means represent all of the debates in the movement, especially when it moves beyond North America with our particular political cultures and histories. But I think it's worth the trouble to try and articulate what they are. The debates have continued since Quebec. Some people are now hailing "diversity of tactics" as the new watchword while others call us to get back to Gandhian nonviolence.

My sense is that many people coming to Quebec wanted something that is not fully described either by "nonviolence" as it has come to be practiced or by "diversity of tactics." I'm talking about people who know there is no set-in-stone definition of what constitutes violence, or right and wrong. Who want an action that's real, not just symbolic, but don't equate that with throwing rocks at fully armed riot cops. Who understand that an effective action means that we're going to face a higher level of confrontation and repression, but who, given a choice, would rather de-escalate police violence than heighten it. Who wanted to see the fence go down and cheered when tear gas canisters were thrown back toward the police lines, but who also know that we're in danger whenever we dehumanize another group of people, even cops. Who don't necessarily want to sing "We are a gentle angry people" and hand out flowers to the dear policemen, but who do want to remember that under the Darth Vader outfits the cops are human beings who are capable of changing and whose class interests are actually with us rather than with our opposition. And who believe that however the cops might be behaving in the moment, setting them or any human being on fire is wrong. People who are willing to risk arrest or injury when necessary, but who would rather succeed in an action and get away with it than go to jail or be martyred. Who don't see suffering as transformative, but are willing to suffer if that's what it takes to change this system. Who will act in solidarity with others they may not agree with rather than leave them to suffer alone. Who want to take actions that are powerful, visionary, creative, and empowering. And there were many moments, interludes, clusters of such actions in Quebec City, from the breaching of the wall to our River Cluster spiral dancing in the midst of the tear gas.

I'm not suggesting some middle ground between the Gandhians and the black bloc. I'm saying that we're moving onto unmapped territory, creating a politics that has not yet been defined. And to do so, we may find that it's time to leave Martin and Malcolm arguing around the dinner table with each other and Emma, Karl, Leon, and all the rest, and to step out into the clean night air.

The debate around "violence" and "nonviolence" may itself be constricting our thinking. From a magical point of view, the term "nonviolence" doesn't work well. Every beginning Witch learns that you can't cast a spell for what you don't want — that the deep aspects of our minds are unclear on the concept of "no." If you tell your dog, "Rover, I can't take you for a walk," Rover hears "Walk!" and runs for the door. If we say "nonviolence," we are still thinking in terms of violence.

I'm old enough to have seen a lot of revolutions fail or go wrong. In fact, for someone of my generation to even dare use the word "revolution" is like someone who has been really badly hurt in an affair daring to risk love again. I'm willing to take that risk — the risk of being let down, disillusioned, betrayed, and maligned as well as the ongoing risk of being jailed, gassed, beaten, thrown around, and generally stomped on in the street — but not merely to change who holds power in this system. I want a revolution that changes the very nature of how power is structured and perceived, that challenges *all* systems of domination and control, that nurtures the empowerment of individuals and the collective power we can wield when we act together in solidarity. As an anonymous writer on the Crimethink website put it, "The revolution isn't some far-off single moment … it's a process going on all the time, everywhere, wherever there is a struggle between hierarchical power and human freedom."

I don't yet have a catchy name for this approach to political struggle. For lack of anything better, I've been calling it "empowered direct action." And it's already evolving in our movement.

The goal of an empowered direct action is to make people believe that a better world is possible, that they can do something to bring it about, and that we are worthy companions in that struggle. And then to bring to life that world in the struggle itself, to be the revolution, to embody and prefigure what we want to create. Empowered direct action doesn't simply reject or restrict certain tactics; it actively and creatively searches for actions that prefigure and embody the world we want to create. It uses symbols skillfully but is more than symbolic: it gets in the way of the operations of oppression and poses confrontational alternatives. Empowered direct action means embracing our radical imagination and claiming the space we need to enact our visions; it's magic defined as "the art of changing consciousness at will." It challenges the structure of power itself and resists all forms of domination and all systems of control. It undermines the legitimacy of the institutions of control by embodying freedom, direct democracy, solidarity, and respect for diversity in our organizations and our actions. And it starts with clarity of intention before we get around to diversity of tactics. That is, before we decide what tactics to adopt we need to know what we're trying to do.

WHAT WE'RE TRYING TO DO

- Make people believe that a better world is possible, that they can do something to bring it about, and that we're the fun sort of folks they want to do it with. Build the movement.
- Undermine the legitimacy of the institutions of global corporate capitalism. Expose their hypocrisies and lies. Make visible the violence inherent in their structures and policies. Interfere with their ability to function. Link the global issues to local issues and strengthen and support local organizing. Pose alternatives that are creative, attractive, and sane. Heighten the contrast between our vision and theirs.
- Claim space outside the logo-ized, corporatized, media-colonized realm — whether that's Reclaim the Streets taking back public space, Witches creating ritual space in the midst of a battle, the Zapatistas establishing enclaves in Chiapas, forest defenders staking a claim to an old-growth forest, Ya Basta! pushing through police lines without attacking, the MST in Brazil resettling families on unused land, protesters pushing down the wall in Quebec City, adbusters, billboard alterations,

banner drops, or the thousands of other creative ways we find to do it.

• Encourage defections from the ranks, both from within the corporate institutions and from the ranks of those who are drafted to do their dirty work, like the police and the military, who are acting against their own class interests when they repress us.

• Create the alternative society. Live the revolution. Build the support networks we need as a movement, and in local communities, both to wage this struggle and to begin exploring just and sustainable ways to feed, house, clothe, shelter, care for, and employ ourselves.

WHAT EMPOWERED DIRECT ACTION MIGHT LOOK LIKE

• We'd start not with debates about tactics but with clarifying our intention. What would victory look like? Is it the political gains we make, the delegitimizing of the institutions? Or is it actually shutting the meeting down, or disrupting it? How important is a tactical victory to the political victory? Is there a possibility of inspiring dissension in the ranks of our opposition? (Dissent within the military was a huge factor in ending the Vietnam War, for example.) Are there ways in which we can embody an alternative in the moment of protest itself? How do we make the action have real, not just symbolic, impact?

• In those initial discussions, we'd look for dialogue among as wide a spectrum of groups as possible, with no single organization or group preempting the turf. We'd actively seek a diversity of race, class, and gender as well as diversity of political philosophies. We'd understand that no one group or tactic gets to own or define the movement; that there are times when we want to organize together and need to compromise and negotiate, and other times we might want to organize in parallel but separate structures.

• We'd encourage the formation of clusters or blocs as well as affinity groups. (I prefer the term "cluster," as "bloc" sounds more fixed and static.) Clusters — groups of affinity groups — might develop their own unique goals and tactics within the framework of the action, focusing on a specific issue, target, or style of action. For example, in Quebec City the Medieval Bloc brought the catapult. Our cluster became a Living River to focus attention on water issues, to practice fluid and mobile street tactics, and to bring the Cochabamba Declaration to the action.

- We'd encourage the development of a spectrum of targets, tactics, and strategies that encompass many levels of risk. Mobile street tactics as well as blockades. Art, music, dance, puppets, ritual, street theater, processions, parades, all the things we already do as well as things we haven't thought of yet. Diversions and surprises. Humor. Doing the unexpected. Never being boring, tedious, or stereotypical. We'd do our best to orchestrate our different approaches, to negotiate time, space, and targets, to make them most effective.

- We'd also understand that the more confrontational the tactics, the more lucid the message needs to be and the more we need to be sure we have a base of support for the tactics we employ.

- We'd accept that we can't necessarily make our actions safe. We don't control the police, and their response has escalated even for clearly nonviolent actions when they are more than symbolic. But people can face danger if they have preparation and support, and choices we make in an action can increase or decrease the risks in the moment. We'd provide trainings and preparations that teach a spectrum of responses to crisis situations, prepare groups and clusters to act together, spread effective street tactics, prepare people for jail and for solidarity actions, and teach de-escalation as a tool and an option, not a moral imperative. We'd encourage the formation of affinity groups, but would also develop many other forms of support.

- We'd set up ongoing networks of support for those who end up in jail, fight legal battles, or get hurt, physically or emotionally, in actions.

- Instead of decreeing a set of guidelines telling people what not to do, clusters and groups would state their intentions for what they *do* want. For example:

> "We will carry out this action in a manner that prefigures the world we want to create, and act in the service of what we love.

"We will use means consistent with our ends.

"We will act with respect for this community, for its homes and enterprises, and in a way that encourages all to join us.

"We hold open the possibility that those who are currently our opponents may change their allegiance and join us.

"We will protect and care for each other in this action, and act in solidarity even with those whose choices differ from ours."

Or, as Scott Weinstein, one of the medics in Quebec, suggests:

"We will creatively target the agents of repression and capitalism — and ensure our tactics do not endanger our sister and brother activists. We will attempt to defend our spaces such as the convergence center and the neighborhood from any police take-over or trashing. We are warriors for global justice — and our greatest weapon is our solidarity with each other and the planet. Therefore this action is not over until each of us is safely out of jail (and the planet is liberated)."

In many ways, Quebec City embodied these ideas. But what didn't quite happen in Quebec City is what many of us dreamed of: masses of people swarming the fence, taking it down in so many places at once it couldn't be effectively defended, flooding the area around the Congress Center, and utterly stopping the meeting. What is so tantalizing about the action, in retrospect, is the sense that it could have happened — that with only a little more coordination, a little more trust, a little less fear on everyone's part, we could have done it.

And we will.

GENOA

When we got home from Quebec City, we already felt like we'd been through a short war. The level of violence against protesters continued to escalate throughout the summer. Four students were killed in Papua New Guinea. Live ammunition was used against protesters in Goteburg, Sweden. Genoa seemed to be shaping up to be another standoff, and I wasn't intending to go. But a week before the action, as I describe in one of the following pieces, I suddenly knew I had to be there. Lisa was going, and I hoped to support her in the trainings she'd been asked to do, and to work with the group of women who were organizing a women's action. Hilary had been to a conference they'd organized in June, bringing Ruby, the now well-traveled baby, and the Italian press had covered "The Sweet Protest of Mama Hilary."

You may be wondering at this point, 'How do they fund all this travel? Don't they have jobs?" We've funded our work through private donations and occasional grants. As a writer, I can work anywhere. Mostly our funding has covered expenses; on occasion we take a stipend for longer trips. On many of my trips, I can combine paying lectures or talks at universities. The trainings we offer are generally free, but sometimes organizations pay for them or we collect donations to cover costs.

I've written so much about Genoa that I will keep this introduction short. The action was organized by the Genoa Social Forum, a coalition of over seven hundred groups, NGOs, unions, and political parties. They also had a counterforum, and tremendous resources compared to the Quebec or Prague actions. But they were expecting to organize a political protest, not a battle.

In Genoa I also reconnected with some of the people I'd met in Prague. We joined with them in the "pink bloc", the group that wanted to bring creativity, joy, and frivolity to the action. Frivolity in the midst of a war zone may seem an odd concept, but joy itself can be a liberating force.

Genoa was a painful, shattering, but also illuminating experience. As you will see, I wrote a lot about it. I couldn't stop writing. At one point, a thirteen-year-old boy on the Pagan listserve advised that I sounded angry, that I should let it all out, scream. "Writing is my way of screaming," I told him.

Genova — Friday, 7/20

AT THIS POINT IT'S STILL not clear to me how many are actually dead. I've heard one young man, I've heard two, four. I've heard that the police shot into the crowd, that someone was clubbed to the ground and, unconscious, run over by a car, I've heard it was the White Overalls, the black bloc, I don't know. I know what I saw.

The day started as a spirited, peaceful demonstration. I was on the Piazza Manini with the Women's Action and Rette Lilliput, a religious ecological network. Both groups were completely committed to non-violence. My friend and training partner Lisa Fithian was down at the convergence center with the pink bloc, the group that wanted to do creative, fun street theater, dancing, and music as part of their action. Lisa is a great person to be with in an action: she's experienced, never panics, moves fast and knows what to look for, has a voice that can carry over a huge crowd, and a great ability to move people. I wish she were going to be with us, but I feel like we've divided our talents well. I'll help move the smaller Women's contingent, help them with ritual, and work some magic. Lisa will help the much larger and boisterous pink bloc become mobile and coherent. We hope to meet up some-time during the day.

Around 1 pm, the women march from the piazza down to the wall with probably three or four thousand people. The women gather in a circle for a spiral dance, singing, "Siamo la luna che move la marea," "We are the moon that moves the tides, we will change the world with our ideas." We brew up a lovely magical cauldron — a big pot full of water from sacred places and whatever else women want to add: rose petals, a hair or two, tobacco from a cigarette, anything that symbol-izes the visions we hold of a different world. It's a sweet, symbolic action — not quite as satisfying, perhaps, as tearing the wall down, but empowering to the women who take part. The police are relaxed; these groups are clearly no threat to anyone. Monica negotiates with the police, and we are allowed to go up to the wall in small groups to pin up underwear (residents of the Red Zone were threatened with fines if they hung out their laundry during the G8 — apparently the site of washing might unnerve the delegates), banners, and messages, and to spill our water under the fence.

(Helicopters buzz the house as I write, the news is discussing violence and nonviolence in Italian, and I stretch my memory of high school French to ask one of the women staying here in a phrase we never covered, "How many people died today?" One," she tells me, "and one is in the hospital in critical condition.")

Then the pink march arrives, trapped in a cross street by our march. We open a lane and let them through. They are delightful, mostly young, some all punked out in wildly colored hair or dreadlocks or bright pink wigs, drumming, dancing, cavorting through the crowd. They turn the corner and filter into the next square down the wall, only a short half-block from the street we've occupied.

On our street, everyone is sitting peacefully and having lunch. I walk over to the pink bloc to see what's going on. I drum for a while with the accordion player. People are milling about — there's nothing clear that's happening, when suddenly a line of police has blocked one of the exits. Dancing youth are wildly leaping and stomping in front of them, but that's all they are doing. Much of the pink bloc has moved on, they appear a block or two above the square, with the police now trapped between groups of pink. I am just thinking that this is not a good situation when a tear gas cannister lands in front of me. I start to move away, back down to the street where the women are. Just a mild hit, I wash out my eyes, help a few others whose eyes are streaming and red. Lisa appears, and we go back for another look. This time the gas catches us in a bad situation, with the way back to the street blocked, and another exit up a staircase too full of bodies. I am getting hit heavily, my lungs and eyes burning, but I remember that helpful hint from all the trainings we have done. I can breathe, I really can breathe, and fear is the most powerful weapon. Lisa has better eye protection, she takes my hand and leads me out. I wash them out again. This seems like a good moment to leave. I gather up what's left of the women, Lisa and others get the pink bloc together, I begin a drumbeat and we start up the street, which is also up a hill. The march feels powerful and joyful. We are retreating, but in a strong way, moving on to the next action, still together.

The good feeling lasts until we reach the top of the hill. Somehow the black bloc has become trapped between the pacifist affinity groups and the police. Monica is on the cell phone, upset and tearful, when she learns that the black bloc has trashed an old part of the city. "It's over," she says, "after all our months of work! Let's go home."

I am trying to find out what the women want to do while Lisa is trying to find out what the pink bloc wants to do, when suddenly massive amounts of tear gas fill the square. I am moving away from it, down a side street, trying to convince myself that I can breathe, when I notice that I'm somehow in the midst of the black bloc. They run past me, younger, faster, much better equipped, and the police are behind them. I do not want to be here. I'm fifty years old, and I was never very fast even when I was young. For the first time, I come close to panicking.

But below is a side street, and the wind blows the gas away. I can breathe. I duck down the alley. Like most of the streets on this hillside, it winds around the side of a ridge, with a sheer drop below, and snakes back to the main street. A small clump of pink is sheltering there. I join them, we wait as the black bloc thunders by one street away. Lisa appears to tell us that the riot cops are coming up from below. They're beating people brutally. We check the exits, fearing we're trapped, but suddenly the street we came in on is clear. I and a few others make a break for it, get across and head up a stairway on the other side. Lisa goes back to see if she can help move the others. Before she can, the police have found the alley. They beat people hard, going for the head. They beat pacifists who approach them with their hands up; they beat women. A battered crowd gathers on the stairs, moves up a level or two. I comfort a young man with a head wound, a woman who is crying, her thigh covered with the blood of her boyfriend who has been taken to the hospital. We are all shaken.

Slowly, a pink contingent gathers on the stairs. We move up and up; in this part of town, half the streets are stairways that rise in endless zigzag flights. Below us, we see contingents of riot cops sweep the streets. The helicopter above moves on, following the black bloc. Lisa is moving back and forth across the street and back to the square, checking out rumors, trying to figure out what's going on and where we might go. We eventually make our way back to the square. One of the women has been gassed so badly she's been vomiting, but she wants to stay. Another woman from our contingent was hit in the head by a cop and taken to the hospital. A whole lot of people have been badly hurt, people who clearly and unmistakably are not rock-throwing, streetfighting youth, people who believed they were going to be in a peaceful and reasonably safe place. Lisa and I had done a training for the women, trying to give them some sense of what they might face on the streets from our experience in other actions. But there's no real way to prepare for a cop beating a peaceful, nonaggressive middle-aged woman on the head.

The pink bloc begins a long journey back to the other side of town. We're joined by some of the others from the square and by some of the Italian pacifist affinity groups who have been trying to hold space on this side. As we're trying to make our decision, with translation into English, Italian, Spanish, and French, some of the black bloc drift up from below and ask if they can join us to make our common way to the bottom of the town. Some of the group are angry at the bloc and unwilling to take the risk of joining them or being associated with them. Others feel that we should hold solidarity with everyone, and not leave anyone vulnerable to the police. Eventually, the group offers to accept them if they'll unmask and leave their sticks behind. They won't do that; they say we should each respect each other's way of doing things, so they'll go down alone, letting us go first.

There's more, mostly a series of moments of being trapped in an intersection here or a stairway there, but after around two or three hours we made it back to the convergence center. I'm far too tired to make sense of this day right now, it's all I can do to describe it, and it's after midnight and people have to go to bed. Someone is dead, and the night is not over.

From the IMC — Saturday, 7/21

I THINK THAT I'M CALM, that I'm not in shock, but my fingers are trembling as I write this. We were up at the school that serves as a center for media, medical, and trainings. We had just finished our meeting and were talking, making phone calls, when we heard shouts and sirens and the roar of people yelling, objects breaking. The cops had come and they were raiding the center. We couldn't get out of the building because there were too many people at the entrance. Lisa grabbed my hand and we went up, running up the five flights of stairs, up to the very top. Jeffrey joined us; people were scattering and looking for places to hide. We weren't panicking but my heart was pounding and I could hardly catch my breath. We found an empty room, a couple of tables, grabbed some sleeping bags to cover our heads if we got beaten. And waited. Helicopters were buzzing over the building, we could hear doors being slammed and voices shouting below, then quiet. Someone came in, walked around, left. I couldn't seem to breathe deep and had an almost uncontrollable cough, but I controlled it.

I lay there remembering we had lots and lots of people sending us love and protection, and finally I was able to breathe. The light went on. Through a crack between the tables, I could see a helmet, a face. A big Italian cop with a huge paunch loomed over us. He told us to come out. He didn't seem in beating mode, but we stayed where we were, tried to talk to him in English and Spanish and the few Italian words I know: "paura", "fear," and "pacifisti."

He took us down to the third floor, where a whole lot of people were sitting, lined up against the walls. We waited. Someone came in, demanding to know whether there was someone there from Irish IndyMedia. We waited. Lawyers arrived. The police left. For some arcane reason of Italian law, because it was a media place we had some right to be there, although the school across the street was also a media center and they went in there and beat people up. We watched for a long time out the windows. They began carrying people out on stretchers. One, two, a dozen or more.

A crowd had gathered and were shouting, "Assassini! Assassini!" The police brought out the walking wounded, arrested them, and took them away. We believed they brought someone out in a body bag.

The crowd below was challenging the cops and the cops were challenging the crowd and suddenly a huge circle of media gathered, bright camera lights. Monica, who is hosting us and is with the Genoa Social Forum, came up and found us. She'd been calling embassies and media and may have saved us from getting hurt once the cops finished with the first building. All the time there were helicopters thrumming and shining bright lights into the building. A few brave men were holding back the angry crowd, who seemed ready to charge the line of riot cops that was formed up in front of the school, shields up and gas masks on. "Tranquilo, tranquilo," the men were saying, holding up their hands and restraining the crowd from a suicidal charge. I was on the phone home, then back to the window, back to the phone. Finally, the cops went away. We went down to the first floor, outside, heard the story.

They had come in to the rooms where people were sleeping. Everyone had raised up their hands, calling out, "Pacifisti! Pacifist!" And they beat the shit out of every person there. There's no pretty way to say it.

We went into the other building: there was blood at every sleeping spot, pools of it in some places, stuff thrown around, computers and equipment trashed. We all wandered around in shock, not wanting to think about what is happening to those they arrested, to those they took to the hospital. We know that they have arrested everyone they took to the hospital, that they have taken people to jail and tortured them.

One of the young Frenchmen from our training, Vincent, had his head badly beaten on Friday in the street. In jail, they took him into a room, twisted his arms behind his back and banged his head on the table. Another man was taken into a room covered with pictures of Mussolini and pornography, and alternately slapped around and then stroked with affection in a weird psychological torture. Others were forced to shout, "Viva il Duce!!"

Just in case it isn't clear that this is Fascism. Italian variety, but it is coming your way. It is the lengths they will go to defend their power.

It's the lie that globalization means democracy. I can tell you, right now, tonight, this is not what democracy looks like.

I've got to stop now. We should be safe if we can make our way back to where we're staying. Call the Italian Embassy. Go there, shame them! We may not be able to mount another demonstration tomorrow here if the situation stays this dangerous. Please, do something!

Fascism in Genoa

I WAS THERE WHEN THE carabinieri raided the IndyMedia Center and the Diaz school, in Genoa, at the end of the protest against the G8 meeting. We heard the shouts and screams, couldn't get out the door, ran upstairs, and hid, fearing for our lives. Eventually the cops found us, but we were the lucky ones. A Member of Parliament was in our building; lawyers and media arrived. There was some obscure Italian legal reason why the police could be deterred. They withdrew.

But nothing could save our friends across the street, at the school where people were sleeping and where another section of the Independent Media was located. The police entered; the media and the politicians were kept out. And they beat people. They beat people who had been sleeping, who held up their hands in a gesture of innocence and cried out, "Pacifisti! Pacifisti!" They beat the men and the women. They broke bones, smashed teeth, shattered skulls. They left blood on the walls, on the windows, a pool of it in every spot where people had been sleeping. When they had finished their work, they brought in the ambulances. All night long we watched from across the street as the stretchers were carried out, as people were taken to the jail ward of the hospital, or simply to jail. And in the jail, many of them were tortured again, in rooms with pictures of Mussolini on the wall.

This really happened. Not back in the nineteen-thirties, but on the night of July 21 and the morning of July 22, 2001. Not in some Third-World country, but in Italy — prosperous, civilized, sunny Italy. And most of the victims are still in the hospital or in jail, as I write this four days later.

I can't adequately describe the shock and the horror of that night. But as terrifying as it was to live through it, what is more frightening still are its implications:

- That the police could carry out such a brutal act openly, in the face of lawyers, politicians, and the media, means that they do not expect to be held accountable for their actions. Which means that they had support from higher up, from more powerful politicians. A report published in *La Republica* quoted a police-man who took part in the raid as saying that when the more democratic factions within the police complained that the Constitution was being violated, they were told, "We don't have anything to be worried about, we're covered."

- That those politicians also do not expect to be condemned or driven from office means that they too have support from higher up — ultimately, from Berlusconi, Italy's Prime Minister, himself.

- That they could beat, torture, and falsely arrest Italians means that they do not expect to be held accountable by their own people.

- That they could beat, torture, and imprison internationals shows that they do not expect to be held accountable by the international community. And indeed, who is going to hold them accountable? George Bush, the unelected, unmandated heir of a coup? Sweden, which just used live ammunition on protesters? Canada, builders of the Wall of Shame?

- That Berlusconi could support such acts means that he must be certain of support from other international powers and that these overtly fascist actions are linked to the growing international escalation of repression against protesters.

- That the Italian government used tactics learned from Quebec — the wall, the massive use of tear gas — and that the RCMP had observers in Genoa in preparation for next year's meeting in Calgary means that police repression is also a global network. As we learn from each action, so do they.

- That the Italian government is now targeting the organizers of the Genoa Social Forum shows where their agenda was heading all along: towards the discrediting of the anti-globalization network, the discouraging of peaceful and legal protest as well as of direct action. The leader of the Forum has lost his job. Others are fearing for their freedom and safety.

It's hard to make sense of all that happened in Genoa. So much happened so fast, and in the middle of it, it was hard to know what was going on. The black bloc suddenly appears in the midst of a square that is supposed to be a safe space for peaceful gatherings; the police gas and beat the women and the pacifists and let the bloc escape. We are having a quiet lunch in the convergence center by the sea, when suddenly tear gas cannisters are flying into the eating area and a pitched battle begins directly outside, not a hundred yards away from the main march. Prisoners report being tortured until they agree to shout, "Viva il Duce!" The police rationale for the attack on the school was the supposed presence of members of the black bloc — but they never attacked the actual black bloc encampment, and by the night of the attack most of the black bloc had left the city.

I'm not an investigative reporter — I'm an activist, and once upon a time when life was not so overwhelming I was a novelist. I don't like conspiracy theories but I make sense of the world through stories. Genoa makes sense to me if this is the plot:

Memo: Italian Security to Italian Government/U.S. and International Advisors
Subject: Covert Security Plan for Genova

Top Secret!

The overt Security Plan for the Genova G8 meeting has been covered in a separate memo. The subject of this memo is the covert plan.

Phase One — Lead up to the action: This phase is characterized by two major aspects. One, the creation of a climate of fear and anticipated violence by the stockpiling of body bags, deployment of missiles, etc. And second, a concerted effort to undermine the popularity of the stronger, radical groups such as the Tute Bianca or White Overalls through smear campaigns, accusations that they cooperate with the police, etc. If necessary, we will plant actual bombs to increase the climate of fear.

Phase Two — Recruitment and infiltration: We will concentrate on infiltrating the black bloc and strategically placing provocateurs who will be in positions to instigate attacks, violence, and the destruction of private property, which will turn the population against the protesters. In addition, we will encourage Fascist groups to run as segments of the bloc, which will then give us an excuse to attack the main body of protesters.

Phase Three — Friday, 20 July. We arm the police and carabinieri with live ammunition rather than rubber or plastic bullets. With luck, deaths will result. Our 'Bloc' can appear strategically near any group we wish to attack, giving us the excuse to gas and beat the 'nonviolent' demonstrators. Protesters should be severely beaten and arrested protesters tortured to deter them from further demonstrations. In addition, our 'Bloc' will instigate the destruction of property, particularly small shops and private cars, and will attack and beat other demonstrators, perhaps even a nun or two, further discrediting the anarchists. A high level of violence and destruction should lessen the numbers expected for Saturday's march.

Phase Four — Saturday, 21 July. Our strategy here is directed to undermine, divide, and disperse the march. We instigate more property damage and police battles in the morning near the assembly point of the march. One of our factions will attack the Tute Bianca during the march itself. Shortly after noon, we begin a battle just outside the convergence center, near the corner where the march turns north, giving us the excuse to gas the convergence center. We attempt to drive the battle into the march, splitting or disrupting it and providing the rationale for attacking the march with tear gas and other dispersal agents.

Phase Five — Post-march. We continue the climate of fear with a midnight raid on the main communications center and sleeping quarters of the protesters. Severe force is justified by rumors of black bloc presence. We uncover 'evidence' of connections between the Genova Social Forum and the bloc, thereby discrediting them. Beatings, arrests, and torture will discourage future involvement with protests.

Phase Six — Sunday, 22 July, and beyond: We continue harassment and random arrests of foreigners and suspected protesters. We begin a campaign of accusations against the Genova Social Forum, connecting them with the black bloc, moving against their employment, their credibility, and possibly taking legal action against them. This will also force them to disavow the black bloc, further splitting the movement.

This memo is fiction, but I believe it's essentially true. Like a mathematical proof, it has a simple internal consistency that makes sense of the known facts. And there is more and more evidence that the "black bloc" in Genoa was significantly composed of organized fascist groups working in collaboration with the police.

If it is true, even partly true, what does it mean for us?

It means that the response to the events in Genoa will determine what level of force can be used against future demonstrations, whether we will see smashed skulls and more deaths in Calgary, and blow-torches in the armpits in the Third World.

There are signs, however, that their strategy may backfire. On Monday all over Italy 250,000 people took to the streets. The pressure is on for the Minister of the Interior to resign; Berlusconi's government is threatened. There were demonstrations at Italian embassies all over the world.

We need to keep the pressure on, to make sure the issue doesn't fade away. Keep calling and writing the embassies. Get your political organization, union, workplace, or group of best friends to write and call. Ask your local news media why they are not telling this story. Now is not the moment to be ideological and purist; now is the moment to call in all our allies, set aside our differences, and act in solidarity. For if this level of repression goes unchallenged, no one is safe, not the most legal NGO, not the most reformist organization with the mildest demands. If we don't act now, when a political space remains open to us, we may lose the space to act at all.

Continue to organize and mobilize for the next one. Fear is their most powerful weapon. The fact that they must resort to fascist violence shows that we are a serious threat.

If we want to continue to be a threat, we also need to look critically at our own movement, to identify what we do that leaves us wide open to infiltration and manipulation.

And we need both better preparation and better networks of support for these actions.

A Woman Is Dead in Padua

A WOMAN IS DEAD IN PADUA, her naked body found strangled in a canal. One of our sisters, someone who marched with us on the streets in Genoa, who marched again in her home town in support of those beaten, arrested, and tortured — Maria Jose Olivastri, a union organizer and postal worker, mother of a daughter, forty-two years old.

The post that gives us this news begins with the words: "This appears not to be a political killing, after all."

I say that it was.

Yes, it is important to know if she was targeted for her political activities or not. If so, the implications are far-reaching and grave. But whether she was specifically targeted or not, her death was political.

If someone killed her because she was an organizer and an activist, the killing was political. If someone murdered her in revenge for Genoa, because she took part in demonstrations and marched in protests, the killing was political.

And if someone killed her because she was a woman, the killing was also political.

Violence against women is political violence. When a woman cannot safely walk the streets of her city, when a woman is afraid to go out alone at night, it's political. When a woman goes with eagerness and hope to meet a new lover, and ends up dead in a gutter, that's political.

If we doubt the connection, consider how many of our comrades in Genoa reported being tortured in rooms with pictures of Mussolini and pornography on the walls.

Fascism is fueled by the fear and hatred of women's bodies. Capitalism is sustained by women's low-paid and unpaid labor. All forms of hierarchy are supported by the power men wield over women.

We need to understand these connections if we are going to overthrow the underlying structures of power and not just exchange one set of masters for another. Our brothers in this movement are courageous and beautiful, but we need you to name these connections, too.

Then we can trust that we are truly building another world, in which women's courage and beauty and intelligence are honored, as well as men's.

I didn't know Maria, but I cry for her. I mourn her as a sister, as a comrade in this struggle, and as a victim of political violence.

I would like to think that the streets of Italy, and every city, would be filled with marchers protesting her death, as she marched to protest Guiliani's.

It shouldn't need to be said, in 2001, but it does need to be said, and I say it again: Her death was political.

Why We Need to Stay in the Streets

SINCE GENOA, THERE HAS BEEN lots of healthy debate about where the movement needs to go. The large-scale protests are becoming more dangerous and difficult. The summits are moving to inaccessible locations. The IMF and the World Bank and the G8 and the WTO continue to do their business. Are we being effective enough to justify the risks we're taking? Should we be focusing more on local work, building our day-to-day networking and organizing?

I was in Genoa. Because of what I experienced there, including the moments of real terror and horror, I am more convinced than ever that we need to stay in the streets. We need to continue mounting large actions, contesting summits, working on the global scale.

Our large-scale actions have been extraordinarily effective. I've heard despairing counsels that the protests have not affected the debates in the G8 or the WTO or the IMF/World Bank. In fact they have, they have significantly changed the agendas and the propaganda issuing forth. In any case, the actual policies of these institutions will be the last thing to change. But for most of us on the streets, changing the debate within these institutions is not our purpose. Our purpose is to undercut their legitimacy, to point a spotlight at their programs and policies, and to raise the social costs of their existence until they become insupportable. Contesting the summits has delegitimized these institutions in a way no local organizing possibly can. The big summit meetings are elaborate rituals, ostentatious shows of power that reinforce the entitlement and authority of the bodies they represent. When those bodies are forced to meet behind walls, to fight a pitched battle over every conference, to retreat to isolated locations, the ritual is interrupted and their legitimacy is undercut. The agreements that were being negotiated in secret are brought out into the spotlight of public scrutiny. The lie that globalization means democracy is exposed, and the mask of benevolence is ripped off.

Local organizing simply can't do this as effectively as the big demonstrations. Local organizing is vital, and there are other things it does do: outreach, education, movement building, the creation of viable alternatives, the amelioration of some of the immediate effects of global policy. We can't and won't abandon the local, and in fact never have: many of us work on both scales. No one can go to every summit: we all need to root ourselves in work in our own communities. But many of us have come to the larger, global actions because we understand that the trade agreements and institutions we contest are designed to undo all of our local work and override the decisions and aspirations of local communities.

We can make it a conscious goal of every large-scale action to strengthen local networks and support local organizing. Aside from Washington, D.C., Brussels, or Geneva, which have no choice, no city is ever going to host one of these international meetings twice. Even now, we hear rumors that Washington is considering relocating or limiting the upcoming IMF/World Bank meeting. But if we find ways to organize mass actions that leave resources and functioning coalitions behind, then each grand action can strengthen and support the local work that continues on a daily basis.

Summits won't remain the nice, juicy targets that they are for long. Over the last two years, we've reaped an agenda of meetings that were set and contracted for before Seattle. Now that they are locating the meetings in ever more obscure and isolated venues, we need a strategy that can allow us to continue building momentum.

As an example, some of us have been talking about linked, large-scale regional actions targeting stock exchanges and financial institutions when the WTO meets in Qatar in November. The message we'll be sending is this: "If you move the summits beyond our reach and continue the policies of power consolidation and wealth concentration, then social unrest will spread beyond these specific institutions to challenge the whole structure of global corporate capitalism itself." Marches, teach-ins, countersummits, programs of positive alternatives alone can't pose this level of threat to the power structure, but combined with direct action on the scale we've now reached, they can.

Of course, the more successful we are, the meaner they get. But when they use force against us, we still win, even though the victory comes at a high cost. Systems of power maintain themselves through our fear of the force they can command, but force is costly. They cannot sustain themselves if they have to actually use force in order to accomplish every normal function.

Genoa was a victory won at a terrible price. I hope never to undergo another night like I spent when they raided the IMC and the Diaz school, knowing that atrocities were being done just across the way and not being able to stop them. I ache and grieve and rage over the price. I would do almost anything to assure that no one, especially no young person, ever suffers such brutality again.

Almost anything. Anything except backing away from the struggle. Because that level of violence and brutality is being enacted, daily, all over the world. It's the shooting of four students in Papua New Guinea, the closing of a school in Senegal, the work quota in a *maquiladora* on the Mexican border, the clearcutting of a forest in Oregon, the price of privatized water in Cochabamba. It's the violence being perpetrated on the bodies of youth, especially youth of color, in prisons all over the United States, and the brutality and murder going on in Colombia, Palestine, Venezuela ... And it's the utter disregard for the integrity of the ecosystems that sustain us all.

I don't see the choice as being between the danger of a large action and safety. I no longer see any place of safety. Or rather, I see that in the long run our safest course is to act strongly now. The choice is about when and how we contest the powers that are attempting to close all political space for true dissent.

Genoa made clear that they will fight ruthlessly to defend the consolidation of their power, but we still have a broad space in which to organize and mount large actions. We need to defend that space by using, filling, and broadening it. Either we continue to fight them together now when we can mount large-scale, effective actions, or we fight them later in small, isolated groups, or alone when they break down the doors of our homes in the middle of the night. Either we wage this struggle when there are still living forests, running rivers, and resilience left in the life support systems of the planet, or we fight when the damage is even deeper and the hope of healing slim.

We have many choices about how to wage the struggle. We can be more strategic, more creative, more skillful in what we do. We can learn to better prepare people for what they might face, and to better support people afterwards. We have deep questions to consider about violence and nonviolence, about our tactics and our long-range vision, which I hope to address in a later posting.

But those choices remain only so long as we keep open the space in which to make them. We need to grow, not shrink. We need to explore and claim new political territory. We need the actions of this autumn to be bigger, wilder, more creatively outrageous, and inspiring than ever, from the IMF/World Bank actions in Washington, D.C., at the end of September to the many local and regional actions in November when the WTO meets in Quatar. We need to stay in the streets.

After Genoa: Asking the Right Questions

GENOA WAS A WATERSHED FOR the anti-globalization movement. It's clear now that this is a life-or-death struggle in the First World as it has always been in the Third World. How we respond will determine whether repression destroys us or strengthens us. To come back stronger, we have to understand what actually happened there.

The media are telling one story about Genoa: a small group of violent protesters got out of hand and the police overreacted. I've heard variations on this from within the movement: the black bloc was allowed to get out of hand to justify police violence. But that's not what happened in Genoa, and framing the problem that way will keep us focused on the wrong questions.

Let's be clear: in Genoa we encountered a carefully orchestrated political campaign of state terrorism. The campaign included disinformation, the use of infiltrators and provocateurs, collusion with avowed Fascist groups (and I don't mean "fascist" in the loose way the left sometimes uses the term, I mean "Fascist" as in "direct inheritors of the traditions of Mussolini and Hitler"), the deliberate targeting of nonviolent groups for tear gas and beating, endemic police brutality, the torture of prisoners, the political persecution of the organizers, and a terrorist night raid on sleeping people by special forces wearing "Polizia" T-shirts under black sweatshirts, who broke bones, smashed teeth, and bashed in the skulls of nonresisting protesters. They did all this openly, in a way that indicates they had no fear of repercussions and expected political protection from the highest sources. That expectation implicates not only the proto-Fascist Berlusconi regime of Italy, but by association the rest of the G8, especially the U.S. since it now appears that L.A. County Sheriffs helped train the most brutal of the special forces.

Italy has a history of employing such tactics, going back to the "strategy of tension" used against the left in the nineteen-seventies, in fact, even further back to the twenties and thirties which don't seem all that far away any more once you've heard prisoners describe being tortured in rooms with pictures of Mussolini on the walls. Maybe even back to the Renaissance, if not the ancient Romans. The same tactics have, of course, been used extensively by U.S. agencies and other countries. Italy also has a political culture of highly confrontational actions and street-fighting with the police, as well as strong pacifist groups and groups like the White Overalls who are exploring new political territory that goes beyond the traditional definitions of violence and nonviolence. All of this set the stage upon which the events of the G8 protest were played.

The police used the black bloc, or more accurately, the myth and image of the black bloc, very effectively in Genoa — for their ends, not ours. Some aspects of black bloc tactics made that easy: the anonymity, the masks and easily identifiable dress code, the willingness to engage in more confrontational tactics and in property damage, and, perhaps most significantly, the lack of connection with the rest of the action and the organizers.

But the black bloc was not the source of the problem in Genoa. The problem was state, police, and Fascist violence. Acts were done in Genoa, attributed to protesters, that were irresponsible and wrong by anyone's standards — but it seems likely now that most of them were done by police. Or if not, police provocateurs were so endemic that it's impossible to tell what might have been done by people in our movement or to hold anyone accountable. So the question Genoa presents us with is not "How do we control the violent elements among us?", although that conceivably might be an issue someday. It's "How do we forestall another campaign of lies, police-instigated violence, and retaliation?"

There's no easy answer to that question. The simplest strategy would be to go back to a strict form of nonviolence, which many people are proposing. I don't know why I find myself in resistance to that answer. I'm a longtime advocate of nonviolence, I have no intention of ever throwing a brick through a window or lobbing a rock at a cop myself, and in general I think breaking windows and fighting cops in a mass action is counterproductive at best and suicidal at worst.

One reason might be that I can no longer use the same word to describe what I've seen even the most unruly elements of our movement do in actions and what the cops did in Genoa. If breaking windows and fighting back when the cops attack is "violence," then give me a new word, a word a thousand times stronger, to use when the cops are beating nonresisting people into comas.

Another might be just that I like the black bloc. I've been in many actions now where the black bloc was a strong presence. In Seattle I was royally pissed off at them for what I saw as their unilateral decision to violate agreements everyone else accepted. In Washington in 2000, I saw that they abided by guidelines they disagreed with and had no part in making, and I respected them for it. I've sat under the hooves of the police horses with some of them when we stopped a sweep of a crowded street using tactics Gandhi himself could not have criticized. I've choked with them in the tear gas in Quebec City and seen them refrain from damaging property there when confronted by local people. I'm bonded. Yes, there have been times I've been furious with some of them, but they're my comrades and allies in this struggle and I don't want to see them excluded or demonized. We need them, or something like them. We need room in the movement for rage, for impatience, for militant fervor, for an attitude that says, "We are badass, kickass folks and we will tear this system down." If we cut that off, we devitalize ourselves.

We also need the Gandhian pacifists. We need room for compassion, for faith, for an attitude that says, "My hands will do the works of mercy and not the works of war." We need those who refuse to engage in violence because they do not want to live in a violent world.

And we need space for those of us who are trying to explore forms of struggle that fall outside the categories. We need radical creativity, space to experiment, to carve out new territory, to invent new tactics, to make mistakes.

There are campaigns being waged now that are defined as clearly and strictly nonviolent: the School of the Americas, Vandenberg, and Vieques, among others. Those guidelines have been respected, and no black-clad brick-throwing figures have attempted to impose other tactics.

But the actions directed against the big summits have drawn their strength from a much broader political spectrum, from unions and NGOs to anarchist revolutionaries. All these groups feel a certain ownership of the issue and the fat, juicy targets that the summits represent.

How do we create a political space that can hold these contradictions, and still survive the intense repression directed against us? How do we go where no social movement has ever gone before?

Maybe these are the questions we really need to ask. In a life-or-death situation, there's a great temptation to attempt to exert more control, to set rules, to police each other, to retreat to what seems like safe ground. But all my instincts tell me that going back to what seems safe and tried and true is a mistake. As an anarchist, I'm not interested in doing any kind of police work. I want to call each other to greater, not lesser freedom, knowing that that also means greater responsibility and greater risk.

Using provocateurs to instigate violence which can be blamed on dissenters and used to justify repression is a time-tested, generally successful way of destroying radical movements. But it's a strategy that thrives on the familiar, the expected. Identifying provocateurs in the midst of an action is like trying to spray for a pest in the garden: the toxicity of the spray, of the suspicion, the secrecy, and the lack of trust may be as great as that of the pest.

But plants can resist pests if they are grown in healthy soil. To forestall infiltration and provocateurs, we need to examine the soil of our movement. I'd like to suggest three nutrients that can make us more pest resistant: *communication, solidarity,* and *creativity.*

We have to be in *communication.* We can no longer afford to wage parallel but disconnected struggles at the same demonstration. We need to clearly state our intentions and goals for each action, and ask others to support them. We may need to argue and struggle with each other, to negotiate, to compromise. Articulating a clear set of agreements about tactics may at times be the best way to forestall provocateurs. But agreements are only agreements when everyone participates in making them. If one wing of the movement attempts to impose them, they are not agreements but decrees, and, moreover, decrees that will not be respected and that we have no power to enforce.

That kind of communication involves risk on both sides, but those risks have to be taken, intelligently and thoughtfully, of course. We need to put a higher priority on our communication than on our standing with our funding sources or our security culture. If my tactic of choice makes it impossible for me to talk to you, I need to question whether it's an appropriate tactic for a mass action.

In that dialogue, we actually have to struggle to respect each other. No one gets to claim the moral high ground. None of us get to exclusively set the agenda, determine the form of what we do, or decree the politics. Those who advocate nonviolence, a chief tenet of which is to respect your opponent, need to practice it within the movement. You can't just dismiss the black bloc and other militant groups as "negative rebels" or immature adolescents acting out. They have a political perspective that is serious and thoughtful and deserves to be taken seriously.

But it also means that more militant groups need to stop dismissing those who advocate nonviolence as middle-class, passive, and cowardly. The black bloc is widely respected for its courage, but it takes another kind of courage to sit down in front of the riot cops without sticks or rocks or Molotovs. It takes courage to have your identity known, to organize in your own city where you can't disappear but must stand and face the consequences. "Nonviolent" does not equate with "nonconfrontational," or with wanting to be safe on the sidelines. The essence of nonviolent political struggle is to create intense confrontations that highlight the violence in the system, and then to stand and openly take the consequences. In today's repressive climate, where 88-year-old nuns are being given yearlong prison sentences for completely pacific actions, the risks of nonviolence may be much higher than the risks of anonymous streetfighting.

We need to communicate clearly with the larger community as well — proactively, not reactively. We have to let people know what our intentions are and what the parameters of the action might be. Imagine the black bloc putting out a Crimestopper Leaflet: "If you see a group of masked figures looting small shops, burning private cars, and endangering your children, get their badge numbers! They are the Cops! Because we're the black bloc, and that's not what we do ..." We need to talk to the not-already-converted, door to door, face to face, not to lecture them but to ask about their lives and the effects these issues have on them, and to ask them to show support for us.

We need to be in real *solidarity* with each other. Solidarity is not just about refraining from denouncing each other to the media, or about holding vigils for those in jail. It means putting the good of the whole above our immediate individual desires or even safety. It means supporting each other's intentions and goals, even when we only partially agree with them. Not just by saying, "You do your thing and I'll do mine," but by actually taking responsibility for our actions and for the impact they have on others beyond ourselves or our immediate group. Greater freedom demands greater responsibility.

In a mass action individual decisions have a collective impact. Some tactics are like the loud-voiced guy in the meeting: they take up all the available space and make it impossible for anyone else to be heard. Cops are not creatures of fine distinctions. If one group is throwing Molotov cocktails and smashing shop windows, it may well affect how the police react to the pacifist group a block over. The community, too, may miss the subtle difference between burning the neighborhood bank and burning the neighborhood store. So, just as the loud guy has to learn to step back occasionally and shut up to give others a chance to be heard, high confrontation tactics sometimes need to be restrained just to allow other possibilities to exist.

Solidarity is about what we do on the street. It means protecting each other as best we can, and certainly not deliberately endangering each other. Of course, one group's idea of protection may be another group's idea of endangerment. A barricade may seem protective, but if your strategy is to de-escalate tension, a barricade may actually make your situation more dangerous. We need to respect each other's choices. Solidarity means that if I'm sitting down in front of a line of riot cops and you're behind me, I can trust that you're restraining the crowd behind from trampling me, that you're not throwing a rock over my head. And it also means that if you push through a line of cops and I'm behind you, I'm there to support you, not to restrain you. We have a right to ask for solidarity from everyone who wants to be out on the street together.

Solidarity is also about holding each other accountable, critiquing what we do together with the purpose of learning from our mistakes and becoming more effective. Critiquing is not attacking: a good critique is a mark of respect, it's saying, "I know that you and I share a common interest in making this work better."

Perhaps most of all, we need *creativity*. Maybe, just to stimulate our thinking, we need to mount one action with one simple guideline: No tired, overused tactics allowed. No cross-the-line symbolic arrests, no bricks through the windows of Starbucks. And please, please, no boring chants that have been recycled since the Vietnam War, if not before ("Hey hey, ho ho, King George the Third has got to go!"). At least this would be a useful thought experiment.

We need to think outside the fences and the boxes. We need to do the unexpected, change clothes, change tactics, be where they don't expect us to be, doing what they don't expect us to do. If they expect us to trash McDonald's, we're there disrupting its operations by giving out free food and asking the workers how globalization affects them. If they expect militants to dress in black, then the militants go lavender and the pacifists stage a Funeral for Democracy, surrounding the White House dressed in black mourning and veils. If they expect us to walk up quietly in groups of five to get arrested, we disappear and reappear somewhere else entirely. If the hardcore streetfighters pull down a fence, the 88-year-old nuns are the first through into the red zone. If they block off the meeting and concentrate their defenses on a wall, we claim the rest of the city. If they hide the summits in inaccessible locations, we choose our own turf.

These are hard challenges, but these are hard times, too — and they're not getting easier. I've already seen too many movements splinter and fail or grandstand themselves to death in ever more extreme and suicidal acts, or suffocate from self-righteous moralism. I want to win this revolution. I don't think we have the ecological and social leeway to mount another one if this fails. And the odds of winning are so slim that we can't afford to be anything but smart, strategic, and tight with one another. We need to stand shoulder to shoulder, even when we disagree. And if we can do that, if we can hold these differences within our movement, we'll have taken a step toward meeting the much greater challenges we'll face when we do win, and come to remake a deeply diverse world.

(Thanks to Lisa Fithian, Hilary McQuie, and David Miller
for discussions that contributed to this piece.)

Courage and Faith in Hard Times

SINCE GENOA, A LOT PEOPLE have been telling me how brave I am. I've always thought it was a mistake to get a reputation for courage, on the grounds that if you acted bravely once, people would expect you to act courageously again, and you might be having an off day. Be that as it may, I've been thinking about courage. It's not such a rare or unusual trait. It's just that combination of denial and fatalism that gets us out onto the freeway every day, or up in an airplane, or into any of the thousand ordinary situations in which we have a higher chance of dying or being hurt than in even the most grim demonstration.

When we were trapped in the IndyMedia Center while police were brutally beating the people sleeping in the school across the street, we weren't doing anything spectacularly courageous. We were just there. We were, in fact, hiding. I like to think that if we had felt there was anything useful or helpful we could do in the situation, we would have gone and done it, whatever the cost. Lisa and I had certainly spent a lot of the weekend doing what we perceived were useful and helpful things, sometimes putting ourselves in greater danger because of it — her more than me, because she's little and can move fast and has amazing tactical skills combined with a cat's curiosity. But the reality is that during the raid we felt no urge to go try and calm the police (when we couldn't speak Italian) or to throw our bodies between their sticks and the people they were beating — we just hid.

When people tell me I'm brave, the subtext I often hear is "I could never do what you've done." But I was certainly no more courageous than anyone else in Genoa, and the people who were there demonstrating were really no different than any people in any demonstration anywhere. They all had their counterparts in Burlington or San Francisco or Sao Paolo. They weren't some other breed of human — they just happened to be there. Maybe courage is just the ability to rise to the occasion of wherever you happen to find yourself. And I believe most human beings have that ability.

I went to Genoa because of a Tarot reading. I hadn't intended to go. I actually thought flying across the ocean to go to a protest I knew was not going to be peaceful just three months after coming back from the tear gas fest in Quebec City would be a bit excessive, if not neurotic. But as soon as I began meditating on the double spiral vortex we were visualizing to send magical support, I felt a few twinges of desire to be there. I was so sure I shouldn't go that I decided to pull a few cards just to confirm my mature and sensible decision — well, it wasn't even a decision. I wasn't even seriously considering going. Then I looked at the cards, and they said crystal clearly that I should go. I was caught by my own vortex: I'd been invoking positive influences to be attracted there, and I became one of those influences. It took me a day or so to really make up my mind. I asked for a sign. I had meetings set for the next week — within two hours both people had spontaneously called me. I was able to get a cheap flight, four days before leaving. I was going.

You could say that going was an act of faith. I knew I was supposed to be there although I didn't know why. The way I thought about it to myself was, "Okay, Genoa was one of the things I signed on to do in this lifetime. Why didn't I know that sooner?"

Although I've been a priestess of Goddess for more than a quarter century now, a Witch, a teacher, all of that, I often feel that I don't have the same kind of deep, personal faith many people in our community do. To me, the Goddess is not so much a personality as a great force of regeneration acting through the cycles of birth, growth, death, and rebirth. I perceive her as love, but as a great, impersonal force, not a Mommy who will necessarily look after me. Her scale and time frame are so far beyond the human. I'm not sure she grasps pain in the way we do.

I knew that I was serving that force in some way, that I was supposed to be in Genoa, in the IMC that night, although I didn't know why. But to say "I was supposed to be there" implies some larger plan, some Planner. To think "This is in my contract for this lifetime" implies someone I made a contract with, or to. My faith in a personal deity might be shaky, but I have an unshakable faith in doing what I came in to do — or rather, that that's the only thing in life really worth doing, if you can figure out what it is. But of course it's one thing to promise yourself to some mad act when you're wandering in the Silver Isle of Apples in delicious disembodiment, and another to carry out that promise in your all too fragile and mortal body.

When the police came in, we couldn't get out the door so we ran upstairs, with somewhat the same instinct that propels people upwards on a sinking ship. We grabbed sleeping bags to pad ourselves if we got beaten, and hid under some tables, four of us together. Getting beaten, or getting arrested, seemed like a high probability, but I wasn't thinking about it. We knew that down below or across the street, terrible things might be happening to other people, but I wasn't thinking about them. It was as if they'd been sucked down into another realm. I was thinking about breathing and not coughing. We'd run up five flights of stairs faster than I can run, and while I felt calm emotionally I couldn't catch my breath and I couldn't stop coughing. I knew if the police came in my cough would betray not just me but the others. At that point I invoked a Goddess personal enough that I could say to her, "You absolutely have to make me stop coughing." I recall also thinking about all my ancestors who had ever hidden from pogroms. I stopped coughing.

We lay there, and I wasn't so much aware of being afraid. I was grounding, and relieved to be able to breathe slow and silently and deep. At that point, whatever happened was just going to be what happened. If we lay under that table all night, well, we just did. If we got beaten up, well, we just would. I was mostly aware of feeling love. I felt immense love for Lisa and Jeffrey and the young man whose name I can't remember but who lay there with us. I'd met him on Friday, on the street, after the police swept through and beat people badly. He had a wound on the side of his temple and was holding his arm where the police had hit him, but he wasn't as badly hurt as some who had gone to the hospital, only to be arrested there. And tortured in the jail. I felt love for my companions, and I felt the tremendous power of the love and protection and magic I knew was coming to us. Because I'd been on the phone home when the police attacked, I knew my closest friends and my partner knew we were in danger and were sending us love and protection. I knew there were circles and circles of Witches that had us on their altars and were stirring cauldrons and weaving spells, willing us to be in the right place at the right time, with the protection and resources to do the work. That didn't necessarily guarantee our physical safety or freedom — maybe the work would require getting hurt or going to jail. There's bound to be a certain amount of suffering in challenging the rulers of the world, and while I had absolutely no desire or attraction to suffering I was willing to accept whatever came. Or rather, being willing had nothing to do with it. I was just there. Whatever was going to happen would happen. A lot of people loved us and cared about what was going to happen. That was all.

And in the end, it turned into a different kind of a night. The police left our building — it's still not completely clear why. A woman was there who was a Member of Parliament. We simply stared out the windows for hours, watching the scene across the street, where nothing had restrained the violence, watching them carry out stretcher after stretcher in a kind of dead, calm horror. It was as if the wounded and the beaten had slipped into some other dimension where we couldn't follow. I remember when I once nearly drowned, how I felt about the people on land. They were safe, more than that, they were safety itself: if they knew what was happening to me, if I made contact by sight or sound or thought, that safety would reach to me like a rope and draw me back. But we were watching our friends being carried away. A few were walking, hands up, heads averted. We couldn't see the faces of those they carried out on stretchers, couldn't know who they were, who we would miss in the morning. And such safety as we possessed couldn't touch them.

I went to Genoa, I now believe, to bear witness to that scene, to work some small piece of magic on the grim forces gathered there, to bring them out into the light, expose them, undercut their power. But if I deserve credit for courage, it's not for anything I did there — it's for this, now that I'm home and safe: the daily struggle to remain open to love, to the beauty of the ocean, the grasses in the wind, the trees, knowing how fragile we all are, and what it looks like when it's smashed.

WASHINGTON, D.C., AND 9-11

In September of 2001, we were gearing up for another big action in Washington, D.C., at the end of the month when the IMF and the World Bank were planning to meet again. Learning from Genoa and all the previous actions, we were making great efforts to have dialogue among all the different groups involved, and we were expecting the largest mobilization yet in North America.

When hijacked airplanes crashed into the twin towers of the World Trade Center on the morning of September 11, the whole political climate changed. The violence of that day overshadowed anything we in the United States had ever faced before on our home ground. The tremendous loss of life left everyone in a state of shock and grief.

Amidst the grief and fear, we also felt the loss for the global justice movement. Our work suddenly became a thousand times more difficult, and it hadn't been easy to begin with. The possibility of extreme repression loomed large. Bush, who had been unpopular on September 10, positioned himself as a hero and proceeded to push hard for the entire right-wing agenda. A peace movement sprang up as preparations for war increased. The global justice movement faced a range of new challenges, from addressing the issues of war and peace to mobilizing people brought into the movement by the war to look at larger economic issues, to deciding how to negotiate our tactics and strategies in a new era.

The first of these pieces was written before 9-11, the others were written in response to it and to changing conditions.

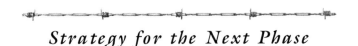

Strategy for the Next Phase

WITH NO GLOBAL CONFERENCE to set agendas, with no top-down leadership decreeing or even coordinating our tactics, the anti-globalization movement has actually had a strategy that evolved organically by some collective unconscious consensus process: to contest and attempt to disrupt every key meeting of every institution of globalization. If we had ever articulated this strategy, we might have said that the goals were first, to shine the light of public scrutiny onto these institutions and trade agreements, and second, to undercut their legitimacy and demonstrate the withdrawal of public consent from their existence and their functions.

In this, we have been amazingly effective. First of all, we have mounted major protests at all these meetings, which is a victory in itself. We've brought the concerns about and the objections to their policies out into the public arena. In many cases, we have actually disrupted the meetings themselves or prevented delegates from attending. Other meetings have been cancelled or curtailed simply because of the threat of our appearance on the scene. In all cases, we have destroyed their function as rituals that subtly reinforce the legitimacy, the status, and the power of the institutions they represent. The powermongers have now been driven out of all major cities, forced to look for remote locations that protesters cannot easily reach. Again, this is a sign of our success. If the WTO cannot meet in any democratic country in the world, its claim to be broadening global democracy loses any legitimacy.

The IMF/World Bank meeting in Washington, D.C., may be one of the last large summits in an accessible location. After Genoa, it's especially important to make it a large, powerful, and inspiring action, to show that our movement can't be intimidated into silence, and to build momentum for the next phase. For it's less likely that in the future, summits and meetings will happen in locations that are easy for us to get to. The WTO is meeting in Qatar in November, the next G8 meeting is in remote Kananaskis, Alberta.

As the meetings move to remote locations and repression against the movement increases, our strategy will also need to evolve. For a model, we might look to the blackberry: it spreads underground and roots wherever a piece of it touches earth. If the first phase of our strategy could be summed up as "Contest the summits!" the next phase might be framed as "Spread dissent!"

Simply put, we're saying: "If you sequester the summits, and still continue with these policies, dissent will broaden, from concern with these specific institutions and agreements to the entire corporate capitalist system itself."

So, if they wall off a meeting place, we consider what we can do with the rest of the city.

If they locate the summit in some inaccessible place, we choose our own turf for a response. That could be in the form of a countersummit, as the World Social Forum in Porto Alegre, Brazil, was a response to the World Economic Forum in Davos. It could be one massive action in a place of our choice. When the WTO meets in Qatar in November, linked regional actions are being planned at stock exchanges and financial districts in New York City, San Francisco, and elsewhere. And of course there are always Global Days of Actions, with smaller local actions in many places.

It's hard to give a local action the excitement and power of the big mass actions. But a local or regional action can truly focus on how global issues affect people's daily lives and on how local issues link to the global. More than that, local actions can strengthen ongoing organizing and build alliances that may cut across barriers of race and class more effectively than the big summit protests.

Issues are always more complex when they're local. You run into your opponents at the grocery store. They have faces. Maybe your kids go to school together. They're harder to dehumanize, and you have to hear their point of view. For that reason, solutions are also likely to be more complex and, ultimately, more intelligent and workable.

Local communities are also better placed to implement solutions. Many elegant solutions to some of our major ecological problems already exist. We know how to generate energy using renewable sources, how to clean sewage using biological methods, how to run diesel engines on vegetable oil, just to name a few. Solutions to social problems also exist: the Grameen banks of Pakistan demonstrate that microlending to the very poor can do more to alleviate poverty than huge World Bank megaprojects.[5] Visit an encampment of the MST, the Movimiento Sim Terra, in Brazil, and you'll see what resettling the very poor on the land can create: communities with pride, health, and an ecological literacy well beyond that of many highly educated people in the U.S.

Local and regional actions may be able to capture some of the excitement and power of the big protests if we link focuses. We might do actions at stock exchanges globally, for example. We might hold a global *consulta*, a day in which we go out into communities to ask people how globalization has affected their lives. We might hold linked actions at the home governmental seats of power of the G8 while they meet in some remote and obscure location. Or pick one corporation and coordinate many levels of action: education, media, strikes, stockholders' actions, and direct actions. Imagine a global campaign that says, "Use Chapter Eleven in NAFTA, sue a government for implementing environmental or social constraints on your profits, and face a consumer boycott, a strike, a stockholders' action, demonstrations across the globe, and protests that shut down your corporate headquarters all at once."

Seattle agreed to implement the Kyoto accords in spite of Bush's refusal to honor the treaty. What if every city and town in the U.S. did the same? That's not only feasible — it's a campaign already underway, with cities that represent 8% of the world's carbon production already signed on.[6] Another aspect of our strategy might be called "Demonstrate alternatives."

We need to continue to mount large actions. They have a power and effectiveness nothing else can equal. But we need to look toward the day when it will not be The Next Big One, but The Next Big Ten, Hundred, Thousand Protests that arise from the rooted day-to-day work of thousands of local communities.

And anyone who has ever tried to dig blackberries out of the garden knows that once they take hold, it's almost impossible to get rid of them. Cut them down in one place, and they spring up across the way. They spread. They grow. So should we.

Hold the Vision

THE WORLD HAS CHANGED in the past week. An act of violence and horror has cost the lives of thousands, and shattered all of our plans and expectations for the future.

We who have been working for global justice now face an enormous challenge. Since Seattle, we've built and sustained a movement in spite of continually escalating police violence and attempts by the media to paint us as violent thugs. Genoa did not intimidate us, and momentum was growing for the demonstrations in Washington, D.C., at the end of the month. Public opinion was shifting, and the whole edifice of corporate rule was losing legitimacy.

The terrorist attacks of last Tuesday could undermine all of our work, at least in the short term. They are the perfect excuse for the state to intensify its repression, to restrict civil liberties, and for anyone who speaks out against blind retaliation to be demonized.

The mood of the country is potentially ugly. People are scared. They're angry. Their sense of power and invulnerability has been badly shaken, and in the U.S., they're not used to it. They're grasping at anything that can restore their sense of power over their lives, and in a violent society, that means punishment, retaliation, war.

And many of us activists are also scared. I know how easily I can sink into fear and despair right now. I'm scared of the repression that might come, scared of being personally targeted, scared of the loss of our liberties, scared, yes, of further attacks. But most of all I'm scared for the movement, which I believe is crucial to our survival as a species.

And yet I also believe that the current crisis can be a great opportunity, if we can only see how to grasp it. Extraordinary times create extraordinary openings and possibilities. Our usual patterns and ways of thinking are shattered. When structures fall, something new can be built.

To do that, we have to behave in extraordinary ways. We need to acknowledge our fears, but not act out of fear. Fear leads to bad decisions and constricted vision, just when we need to see most clearly.

"Hold on, hold on, hold the vision that's being born," our cluster chanted in Quebec City.

It may be that the most radical thing we can do right now is to act from our vision, not our fear, and to believe in the possibility of its realization. Every force around us is pushing us to close down, insulate, retreat. Instead, we need to advance, but in a different way. We're called to take a leap into the unknown.

As a movement, we've often been accused of lacking a clear vision of the world we want. I think we do have a vision, which includes diversity and rejects uniform, dogmatic formulations. But within all its varied forms there's a clear common ground: we want a world of liberty and justice for all. It sounds downright patriotic but if you think about its ramifications, they are revolutionary. And we want a world in which no one has to fear violence, which is the ultimate violation of freedom.

There are many voices right now trying to mobilize people around fear, anger, and blame. As radicals, we have too often tried to mobilize people out of guilt or shame. This is the moment to reinvent our approach, our strategies, and our tactics, to believe in the possibility of moving people to act from hope, to act in the service of what they love.

What would this look like? It would mean embodying the world we want to create in our own movement, and in our actions.

Times of grief and anguish can strengthen our bonds. Right now, we in the movement need each other as never before, and we need to treat each other well, to cherish and care for and support each other and become the community we like to imagine. Our solidarity must go deeper than we've ever known before. Solidarity means listening to each other with respect, and being willing to protect and support people with whom we may disagree on many levels or who might simply irritate us. Solidarity means strengthening our practice of direct democracy, our openness and communication with each other, our willingness to bring everyone to the table and give everyone affected by a decision a voice in making it. It means putting aside our usual internal politicking and maneuvering, and treating each other with openness and trust. This is not simple to do. But in a moment when the ordinary patterns of life around us are shattered, shifting our own patterns of behavior may actually be easier. Perspectives change, and the issues that last week seemed so important now seem trivial.

What would this look like, say, in D.C. two weeks from now? First, we'd have to deliberately drop our assumptions, whether they are that confrontation is always the strongest action, or that nonviolence is always the most moral action, or that direct action is always our strategy of choice, or that a march and a rally with speakers are the ultimate form of politics, and ask what makes most sense? What is most visionary?

I'd like to see whatever we do involve some kind of process of mutual discussion and education around our visions of alternatives. And I'd like to see us think of ways to take that outside of our own groups and into the community, and to bring in voices from the community to teach us about their issues and concerns. That could be a *consulta*, a teach-in, or maybe a learn-in, where we go out into the community and ask people how issues of power and inequality affect their lives, or what their visions are of the world they want. In a time of fear and despair, calling people to consider their visions could be a powerful form of action.

I also think it's important, symbolically and politically, that we make some kind of strong, visible presence in the streets, that we don't voluntarily relinquish the one political space in which we've been able to have a significant impact. But I also think it's important that what we do in the street be appropriate to the moment. A mourning procession, a vigil, or a rite of healing might make sense right now; a standard march with shouted slogans and printed signs would be offensive. But it's hard to predict what the mood or situation of the country will be even two weeks from now. We could be heading into a full-fledged war, and a large march might be a needed and powerful statement.

Direct action is a powerful tool, but like a chainsaw it's not the tool you want in every situation. Direct action points a spotlight on an issue, can directly interfere with an unjust group or situation, and delegitimize an institution or policy. Used at the wrong moment, without a strong base of support, it risks legitimizing the very institutions we seek to undermine.

Many police have just given their lives because they stayed in a dangerous situation helping other people get out. A lot of us in this struggle talk about being willing to die. They just did. Whatever we feel about police as tools of the state, now is not a good moment for a heavy police confrontation. In fact, although generally I'm against negotiating with the police, in this case I'd certainly consider that it might be a wise and even a generous thing to do. As individuals, the police are of a class that doesn't gain from the policies we oppose. Let's not write off the possibility that some of them could be brought to support us.

I want peace, not war. But only calling for "peace" at this moment does not sufficiently address the fear, anger, and powerlessness people feel. I'd like to see us also call for justice:

> Justice for the victims of this week's terrorist attacks.
> Justice, not blind vengeance — meaning that we need to know clearly and certainly who carried out the attacks before we retaliate.
> Justice for the Arab Americans who live among us. They deserve our support and protection.
> Justice for the people of other countries who could soon become our victims.
> Justice for the many, many victims of ongoing terror around the world, and recognition of the part we have played in supporting and forging that terror.
> Economic and environmental justice.

These are my thoughts at the moment. They could change as the situation changes. But mostly I suggest that we all begin a creative thinking process, that we consciously choose to set aside our fears and our depression. I suggest that before we agree to do anything we've done before, we consider at least three creative new alternatives. I think we should show up in Washington, if not in the numbers and the way we expected, then in some other dimension of strength, and hold open the possibility that we can create not just a protest, but moments of public beauty that can transform the world.

Finally, I want to say a word about faith. "Faith" and "religion" are being thrown around and served up to us in ways that are at the moment rather sickening. Religion of any denomination can motivate the worst acts and be a rationale for hate. And yet it's hard to get through times like these without faith in something.

I don't generally like to inflict my spirituality on people who might not want it. But I feel moved to tell you what's getting me through the night, along with the love and support of my community. It's the faith that there is a great, creative power that works through the living world toward life, diversity, healing, and regeneration. That power works in us, in our human love, in our work for justice, in our courage and our visions. We don't need priests or ministers or even Witches to contact that power for us — we each have our own direct line. It exists within us, infinite, unlimited. Ultimately, it is stronger than fear, stronger than violence, stronger than hate. I wish you all deep contact with whatever feeds your soul, and nourishment from whomever and whatever you most love.

Only Poetry Can Address Grief: Moving forward after 9-11

IN THE MIDDLE OF THE ANTI-CAPITALIST Convergence march in Washington, D.C., last month, I found myself nose to nose with a line of police attempting to push the crowd back. I was facing an angry but very short policewoman, so in my case it was actually nightstick to bosom. "Get back, get back!" she was shouting, but our line was not giving ground. I explained to her, calmly and, I thought, quite reasonably, that we were not going to get back because there was nowhere for us to go.

I think of that moment now as a metaphor for where what I like to call the global justice movement is today. We are facing an array of forces telling us to get back, to disperse, to leave the scene. The forces of the state, the media, all the powers that support global corporate capitalism would like to see us go away.

But we have nowhere to go.

We have nowhere to go because the conditions we have been fighting have not gone away. The disparity between rich and poor has not grown less, the attempts of the corporate powers to consolidate their hegemony have not ceased, the environment has not miraculously repaired itself, and our economic and social systems have not suddenly become sustainable. We're on the Titanic; our efforts to turn the course of the ship have just been hijacked, and we're churning full steam ahead into the iceberg.

We don't have the luxury of defraying action to a more favorable moment. We need the movement to keep moving forward.

How do we do that in the face of increased repression and much potential public opposition?

1. STAND OUR GROUND

First, we don't panic, and we stand our ground. Fear is running rampant at the moment, and every effort is being made by the authorities to increase and play upon that fear. While the general public may fear more terrorist attacks, we in the movement are equally or more afraid of what our governments may do in restricting civil liberties and targeting dissent. But either way, fear is the authorities' greatest weapon of social control. When we are in a state of fear, we're not taking in information, we're unable to clearly see or assess a situation, and we make bad decisions. We're more easily controlled.

We can learn to recognize fear, in our own bodies, in our meetings, in our interactions. When fear is present, just stop for a moment, take a deep breath, and consciously set it aside. Then ask, "What would we do in this situation if we weren't afraid?" From that perspective, we can make choices based on reasonable caution, but also on vision.

ii. Acknowledge the Grief

9-11 threw us collectively into a deep well of grief. We have had to face the awful power of death to intrude on our lives, to sear us with pain and loss, to reorder all our priorities and disrupt all our plans, to remind us that we walk the world in vulnerable, mortal flesh.

The political task that faces us is to speak to the depth of that grief, not to gloss it over or trivialize it or use it to further stale agendas. If we simply shout at people over bullhorns, recycling the politics, the slogans, the language of the sixties, we will fail. The movement we need to build now, the potential for transformation that might arise out of this tragedy, must speak to the heart of the pain we share across political lines.

A great hole has been torn out of the heart of the world. What we need now is not to close over the wound, but to dare to stare more deeply into it.

To comprehend that grief, we must look at the possibility that it was present within us before September 11, that the violence and death of that day released a flood tide of latent mourning. On one level, yes, we mourned for the victims and their families, for the destruction of familiar places and the disruption of the patterns of our lives. But on a deeper level, perhaps many of us were already mourning, consciously or not, the lack of connection and community in the society that built those towers, the separation from nature that they embodied, the diminishment of the wild, the closing off of possibilities, and the narrowing of our life spaces. This frozen grief, transmuted into rage, has fueled our movements, but we are not the only ones to feel it.

With the grief also comes a fear more profound than even the terror caused by the attack itself. For those towers represented human triumph over nature. Larger than life, built to be unburnable, they were the Titanic of our day. For them to burn and fall so quickly means that the whole superstructure we depend upon to mitigate nature and assure our comfort and safety could fall. And without it, most of us do not know how to survive.

We know, in our bones, that our technologies and economies are unsustainable, that nature is stronger than we are, that we cannot tamper with the very life systems of the earth without costs, and that we are creating such despair in the world that it must inevitably crack open, weep, and rage. The towers falling were an icon of an upcoming reckoning we dread but secretly anticipate.

The movement we need to build now must speak to the full weight of the loss, of the fear, and yet hold out hope. We must admit the existence of great forces of chaos and uncertainty, and yet maintain that out of chaos can come destruction, but also creativity.

III. DEVELOP A NEW POLITICAL LANGUAGE

Faced with the profundity of loss, with the stark reality of death, we find words inadequate. "What do I say to someone who just lost his brother in the towers?" a hard-core New York activist asks me. "How do I talk to him?"

The language of abstraction doesn't work. Ideology doesn't work. Judgment and hectoring and shaming and blaming cannot truly touch the depth of that loss. Only poetry can address grief. Only words that convey what we can see and smell and taste and touch of life can move us.

To do that we need to forge a new language of both the word and the deed. We on the Left can be as devoted to certain words and political forms as any Catholic was ever attached to the Latin Mass. We incant "imperialism" or "anti-capitalist" or "nonviolence" or even "peace" with an almost religious fervor, as if the words alone could strike blows in the struggle.

Those words are useful, and meaningful. But they're like the cliché that the bad poet turns to. They are the easy first answer that relieves us of the work of real expression.

Lately I'm hearing some of my most political friends say, "I can't go to another rally. I can't stand hearing one more person tell me in angry tones what the answers are."

What if we stopped in the middle of our rallies and said, "But you know, these issues are complex, and many of us have mixed feelings, and let's take some time for all the people here to talk to each other instead of listening to more speeches."

If we could admit to some of our own ambiguities, we might also find that we are closer than we think to that supposed overwhelming majority of war supporters, who in reality may have deeply mixed feelings of their own.

IV. Propose our own Alternative to Bush's War

Defining the September attacks as an act of war rather than a criminal act has only dignified the perpetrators. Going to war has turned us into Bin Laden's recruiting agency, rapidly alienating the entire Muslim world. Bombing Afghanistan has made us look like thugs to the Muslim world (and to everyone else with a heart and sense) and bred thousands of new potential ready-to-die enemies. The bombing, by preventing relief trucks from delivering serious food supplies before winter, now threatens to impose starvation on up to seven million Afghanis.

In spite of what the polls and the media tell us, I don't necessarily believe that the bulk of the U.S. population is frothing at the mouth with eagerness for Afghani blood. The phrase I keep hearing is a plaintive "We need to do something." Bush's program is the only one laid out for us. The attacks were real, and devastating; simply calling for "peace" and singing "Where Have All the Flowers Gone?" does not address their seriousness. If we oppose Bush's war, we need a clear alternative.

Diplomacy does not mean weakness. It means being smarter than the opposition, not just better armed. Diplomacy also does not mean simply issuing ultimatums backed by bombs. It means understanding something of the culture of the people you're negotiating with. It means actually negotiating, offering a carrot as well as a stick, being willing to let the other side come out with something less than total humiliation. If the goal of the war is truly to get Bin Laden, well, the Taliban just offered to deliver him to a third country.

This could be a moment to switch our policy, to negotiate, to work with and strengthen international institutions and the U.N., to begin to deliver massive and meaningful humanitarian aid to the region. Any or all of those acts would increase our long-term security far more than our present course.

V. Expose the Real Aims of the War

We have about as much chance of doing any of the above as I have of being offered a post in the current Administration. All the indications are that Bush wants a war, to establish U.S. hegemony in Central Asia and the East, to forestall an Asian alliance that might oppose our vested interests with interests of their own, to take control of the rich oil resources of Central Asia and provide a safe passage for an oil pipeline across Afghanistan, to deflect from the illegitimacy of his own presidency, to implement the entire right-wing agenda. We need to continue educating the public about those aims and about the real consequences of the war. To do that, we need to talk to people — not just at rallies and teach-ins, but in our neighborhoods, our workplaces, our schools, on the bus, in the street, on talk shows, with our families. It can be easier to march into a line of riot cops than to voice an unpopular opinion where we live, but we've got to do it and to learn to do it calmly and effectively.

And while we're talking about the war, we need to make the connections to the broader issues we were working on before the eleventh of September. The war can be an opening to challenge racism, and to spotlight the U.S.'s historic role of training, arming, and supporting terrorists — including Bin Laden and the Taliban in previous years. In an age of terrorism, does an economy entirely dependent on oil-based long-distance transport really make sense? (Especially as it didn't make sense before, but never mind that.) The Anthrax scares are a perfect opportunity to push for true domestic security in the form of a well-funded, functioning public health system, the availability of hospital beds and medical care, the support for local food producers, the development of alternative energy resources, etc. The right wing has used the attacks and the war to justify their agenda, but with a little political judo we can redraw their picture of reality.

VI. DEVELOP OUR VISION

Despair breeds fundamentalism, fanaticism, and terrorism. A world of truly shared abundance would be a safer world.

The policies of global corporate capitalism have not brought us that world. They've been tried — and found wanting. We need to replace them with our own vision.

The global justice movement has often been accused of not knowing what it wants. In reality, we know clearly the broad outlines of what we want even though we have a multiplicity of ideas of how to get there. I can lay our vision out for you in five short paragraphs:

We want enterprises to be rooted in communities and to be responsible to communities and to future generations. We want producers to be accountable for the true social and ecological costs of what they produce.

We say that there is a commons that needs to be protected, that there are resources that are too vital to life, too precious or sacred, to be exploited for the profit of the few, including those things that sustain life: water, traditional lands and productive farmland, the collective heritage of ecological and genetic diversity, the earth's climate, the habitats of rare species and of endangered human cultures, sacred places, and our collective cultural and intellectual knowledge.

We say that those who labor are entitled, as a bare minimum, to safety, to just compensation that allows for life, hope, and dignity as well as to the power to determine the conditions of their work.

We say that as humans we have a collective responsibility for the well-being of others, that life is fraught with uncertainty, bad luck, injury, disease, and loss, and that we need to help each other bear those losses, to provide generously and graciously the means for all to have food, clothing, shelter, health care, education, and the possibility to realize their dreams and aspirations. Only then will we have true security.

We say that democracy means people having a voice in the decisions that affect them, including economic decisions.

VII. Develop our Strategy

We might begin by acknowledging that we have had a highly successful strategy for the past two years. Since Seattle, what we've done is to oppose every summit, as a means of focusing attention on the institutions of globalization that were functioning essentially in secret, and of delegitimizing them. Systems fall when they hit a crisis of legitimacy, when they can no longer inspire faith and command compliance. Our strategy should continue to work toward creating that crisis for the institutions of global corporate capitalism. In the meantime, in spite of all appearances the government may already be creating that crisis for itself. For ultimately, nothing delegitimizes a government faster than not being able to provide for the physical or economic security of its people.

Now our strategy needs to broaden and become more complex. We need to:

- contest the summits when and where we can, but perhaps with some new tactics that clearly embody the alternatives we represent.
- turn more of our attention to local organizing, bringing the global issues home and making organizing and activism an ongoing, sustained process. And find ways to make that process as juicy and exciting as some of the big, global actions.
- find ways to link local issues and actions regionally and globally.
- start to build the alternatives: alternative economic enterprises based on new models, directly democratic systems of governance such as neighborhood or watershed councils or town meetings, everything from alternative energy co-operatives to community gardens to local currencies. And look for ways to let those alternatives delegitimize the status quo.

VIII. Organize Openly

In times of increasing repression, the strongest way to resist is not to hide, but to become even more open in our organizing and our communications. The more out there we are, the harder it will be to brand us as terrorists. The more faces they photograph at rallies and marches, the less meaningful any single face will be. The more information they collect, the less they'll be able to collate, analyze, and make sense of it all. And if they read my e-mail — they're welcome to read my e-mail. Somebody ought to, and I don't have time to read it all myself. Maybe I could pay one of them a small extra fee to sort it for me and send me a summary of the high points ...

Security culture either has to be so good you can outspook the CIA, or it simply makes you look like you have something to hide and attracts the attention of the authorities. And it makes it extremely difficult to mobilize, educate, and inspire people. Yes, there are actions that depend on surprise, but with a little cleverness we can figure out how to do that in a basically open setting: "And tonight, each affinity group spoke receives a sealed envelope — open it at five a.m. tomorrow and it will give you two alternative beginning points for your march. Flip a coin to decide which one to go to ..."

IX. MAKE OUR ACTIONS COUNT

Political action may well become more costly in the next months and years. That simply means we need to be more clear and thoughtful in planning and carrying out our actions. Most of us are willing to take risks in this work and to make sacrifices if necessary, but no one wants to sacrifice for something meaningless or stupid. We can no longer afford vaguely planned, ill-considered actions that don't accomplish anything — and believe me, I've done more than my fair share of them.

We should never carry out an action that involves significant risks, unless the following five points are addressed:

1. We know what our intention is — are we trying to raise public awareness, delegitimize an institution, influence an individual, end an immediate wrong?
2. We have a clear objective and know what it is — are we trying to close down a meeting, deliver a petition, pressure an official to meet with us, provide a service? What are we trying to communicate, to whom, and how? What would victory look like?
3. We make sure the acts we take, the symbols we use, the focus we

choose, and the tactics we use reflect our intentions and objectives. We resist the temptation to do extraneous things that might detract from our focus.

4. We have an exit strategy. How are we going to end the action? How are we going to get out once we get in?

5. We have ongoing support lined up for afterwards — legal, medical, political support, people willing to offer solidarity if needed.

X. USE TACTICS THAT FIT THE NEW STRATEGY AND SITUATION

All of us are rethinking our tactics in light of the current situation. We often argue tactics on the grounds of morality — is it right or wrong, violent or nonviolent, to throw a tear gas canister back into a line of police? To break a window? We might do better to ask, "Do these particular tactics support our goals and objectives?" and "Are they actually working?"

Those who advocate highly confrontational tactics, such as damaging property and fighting the cops, are generally trying to strike blows against the system. But at the moment, the system has been struck harder than we could have imagined, and is reeling toward fascism, not liberation. In the present climate, such tactics are most likely to backfire and confirm the system's legitimacy.

Many classic nonviolent tactics are designed to heighten the contrast between us and them, to claim the high moral ground and point out the violence of the system. But many of those tactics no longer function in the same way. Static, passive tactics become boring and disempowering. Symbolic, cross-the-line arrests don't seem to impress the public with our nobility and dedication any more, if they are noticed at all. Mass arrests may be used to justify police violence, even when the arrestees are completely peaceful. When the police cooperate in making the arrest easy and low risk, the process confirms rather than challenges the power of the state. When they don't, even symbolic actions are costing heavily in jail time or probation. The price may well be worth it, but there are only so many times in a lifetime we can pay it, so our choices need to be thoughtful and strategic.

We need a new vocabulary of tactics, a vocabulary that can be empowering, visionary, and confrontational without reading as proto-terrorist, that a vocabulary works toward a crisis of legitimacy for the system. We also need tactics and actions that prefigure the world we want to create but do so in a way that has some edge and bite to it.

Here are a few we are already using that could be further developed:

Mobile, fluid street tactics. Groups like Art and Revolution, Reclaim the Streets, the pink blocs of Prague and Genoa, and the Living River in Quebec have brought art, dance, drums, creativity, and mobility to street actions and developed mobile and fluid street tactics. Such actions are focused not on getting arrested (although that may be a consequence) nor on confrontations with the cops, but on accomplishing an objective: claiming a space and redefining it, disrupting business as usual, etc., while embodying the joy of the revolution we are trying to make. In Toronto on October 16, 2001, snake dancing columns of people managed to disrupt the financial district in spite of a very tense police presence. The pink bloc has snake danced through police lines. The Pagan cluster in Quebec City and Washington, D.C., was able to perform street rituals in the midst of dangerous situations, in ways that allowed participation by people with widely varying needs around safety. The Fogtown Action Avengers in San Francisco combined an open, public ritual which distracted the police while a surprise disruption of the stock exchange was carried out by an affinity group dressed as Robin Hood.

Claiming space. Reclaim the Streets takes an intersection, moves in a sound system and couches, and throws a party. A Temporary Autonomous Zone is a space we take over, where we then exemplify the world we want to live in, with free food, healing, popular education, a Truly Free Market where goods are given away or traded, workshops, conversations, sports, theater.

Street services and alternative services. Groups like Food Not Bombs have been directly feeding the homeless for decades. One of the most successful direct actions I've ever been involved with was a group called Prevention Point that pioneered street-based needle exchanges for drug users to prevent the spread of AIDS. In D.C. in September, during the Anti-Capitalist Convergence's Temporary Autonomous Zone and during the Sunday peace march rally, the Pagan Cluster set up an Emotional Healing Space that offered informal counseling, massage, food, water, and hands-on healing. The IndyMedia Centers provide alternative news coverage and a powerful challenge to corporate media. The medical and legal services we provide during an action could be expanded. Guerilla gardeners could be mobilized in new ways. Imagine a convergence that left a community transformed by community gardens, with toxic sites healing, worm farms thriving, and streets lined with fruit trees.

Popular education. One of the values of mass convergences has been the education and training we've been able to provide for each other, from teach-ins on the global economy to climbing instruction. Almost every Summit has had its CounterSummit. Most of these have followed the rough format of an academic conference, with presenters talking to an audience or facilitating a discussion. But many more interactive and creative ways of teaching and learning could be brought into them: role-plays, story-telling circles, councils. We could hold a giant simulation of a meeting, with people role-playing delegations and grappling with the issues on the table, but from the starting point of our own values.

People are hungry to talk about the war, about their fears and beliefs and opinions. The Zapatistas give us the example of the *consulta* — a process of going out to the people to both listen to concerns and mobilize. We might halt the speeches at a rally for ten minutes to let people talk to each other. Or do away with the speeches altogether, and instead ask groups to facilitate smaller group discussions on their issues and tactics, run short training sessions, offer games or dances or rituals. And we could develop ways to create instant Public Conversations as actions and as education. Caravans can bring discussion and education out of the urban centers and could embody alternative energies and possibilities, running their vehicles on vegetable oil, bringing solar panels to power sound systems.

Those are just a few ideas that can stimulate our thinking and awaken our creativity.[7]

XI. RENEW OUR SPIRITS

These are hard times. Many of us have been working intensely for a long time and are now seeing the possibility of our hard-won political gains being swept away. Fear and loss surround us, and many forces are at work trying to make us feel isolated, marginalized, and disempowered. At best, the work ahead of us seems overwhelming.

If we are going to sustain this work and regain our momentum, we need to allow ourselves time to rest, to go to those places we are working so hard to save and be open to their beauty, to receive support and love from the communities we are working for. We need to nurture our relationships with each other, to offer not just political solidarity but personal warmth and caring. Death and loss rearrange our priorities, teach us how much we need each other, and make it easier to drop some of the petty things that interfere with our true connections.

Many activists mistrust religion and spirituality, often for good reasons. But each of us is in this work because something is sacred to us — sacred in the sense that it means more than our comfort or convenience, that it determines all of our other values, that we are willing to risk ourselves in its service. It might not be a God, Goddess, or deity, but rather a belief in freedom, the feeling we get when we stand under a redwood tree or watch a bird winging across the sky, a commitment to truth or to a child. Whatever it is, it can feed and nurture us as well. For activists who have some form of identified spiritual practice, now is a good time to seriously practice it. For those who don't, it might still be worth taking time to ask yourself, "Why do I do this work? What is most important to me? What does feed me?"

The answer might be grand and noble, or it might be small and ordinary, hip hop or sidewalk chalk. Whatever it is, make it a priority. Do it daily, if you can, or at least regularly. Bring it into actions with you. Let it renew your energy when you're down. We need you in this struggle for the long haul, and taking care of yourself is a way of preserving one of the movement's precious resources.

The goal of terrorists, whether of the freelance or the state variety, is to fill all our mental and emotional space with fear, rage, powerlessness, and despair, to cut us off from the sources of life and hope. Violence and fear can make us shut down to the things and beings that we love. When we do, we wither and die. When we consciously open ourselves to the beauty of the world, when we choose to love another tenuous and fragile being, we commit an act of liberation as courageous and radical as any foray into the tear gas.

There is nowhere left to go but forward. If we hold onto hope and vision, if we dare to walk with courage and to act in the service of what we love, the barriers holding us back will give way, as the police eventually did in our Washington march. The new road is unmarked and unmapped. It feels unfamiliar, but exhilarating; dangerous, but free. We were born to blaze this trail, and the great powers of life and creativity march with us toward a viable future.

Spells and Counterspells:
Why Act Now?

THE DAYS ARE SHORT AND COLD, the streets are uninviting. The political climate seems as chilly as the winter winds, and everybody is saying that 9-11 changed everything. Why take action now?

The government, the media, even some of our own allies warn us that public opinion is no longer with us, that repression will be high, that any action we take will be too costly both personally and politically, that we should hold back and wait.

But the WTO, the IMF, the World Bank, and the other institutions of corporate capitalism are not waiting. They continue to meet, to argue for a new round of trade negotiations, to impose policies that result in a widening gap between rich and poor and a staggering global death toll. And as winter nears, the potential rises for massive starvation in Afghanistan if relief trucks cannot deliver supplies because of our bombs.

And so on bad days we hear our own inner voices murmuring, "It's hopeless. We've lost. The forces we face are too strong for us. Give up."

These voices seem reasonable, sensible. But any Witch can recognize a spell being cast.

A spell is a story we tell ourselves that shapes our emotional and psychic world. The media, the authorities tell a story so pervasive that most people mistake it for reality: We're fighting a righteous war against the Source of All Evil, and everyone supports Bush, and corporate control is the only way to be safe and to provide what we need, and to question is Evil, too.

The counterspell is simple: tell a different story. Pull back the curtain, expose their story for the false tale it is. Act "as if":

- Act as if we weren't doomed, as if what we did in the next weeks and months could shift the balance of fate.

- Act as if the movement were coming back stronger than ever, attracting thousands and hundreds of thousands who have had their eyes opened by the war.
- Act as if this movement were the most creative, visionary, inspiring, funny, welcoming, transforming, and truly revolutionary movement that has ever been. As if we had a new language, new tactics, new ways of communicating that could waken the dormant dissent and the sleeping visions in every heart.
- Act as if a whole new public dialogue was beginning outside the boxes drawn by our traditional political lines and our TV sets.
- Act as if all the different factions in our movement were learning how to support each other, how to work in true coalition and act with true solidarity. As if all who should be allies were able to come together and work for our common goals.
- Act as if we were going to win.

November, two years after Seattle, will see the WTO meeting in Qatar. Imagine hundreds of Seattles springing up in the many local and regional actions being planned, opposition rising up all over the world.

The IMF and the World Bank have rescheduled their meeting for Ottawa on November 17 and 18. Imagine the demonstrations now being called against them and against the war astounding the world, confounding the police, shutting down the meetings, and revitalizing the movement.

The School of the Americas Watch is having its annual action that same weekend in Fort Benning, Georgia. Imagine that action getting the attention it deserves, awakening the conscience of the people of the United States to the role our government has played in training state terrorists around the globe.

But won't these actions alienate and polarize people? Maybe, if they're ill-conceived, gratuitously violent, or simply a matter of screaming the old slogans of the sixties over bullhorns. Or if they're timid, apologetic, whining, they may simply leave people bored and yawning. But our silence will not change public opinion, will not educate people or get them thinking again about larger issues. Actions that are creative, vibrant, confident, and visionary, actions that directly and clearly confront the institutions we oppose and pose alternatives can be empowering both to those who take part and to those who hear of them. We need to advance, not retreat, to take the political space we want and claim it. If we silence ourselves, we're tacitly agreeing that our protests are indeed some distant kin to the terrorists' acts. If we insist that our voices be heard, that open dissent is not terrorism but the deepest commitment to democracy, once the inevitable vitriol wears off, we'll find that we've gained legitimacy and shifted the ground of the dialogue. The longer we wait to claim that space, the more rigidified the patterns of oppression will grow. We need to act now, while the future is still fluid, and set the pattern ourselves.

Since 9-11, I've been to more rallies and marches than I can count. I've marched with Gandhian pacifists and white-haired women in wheelchairs. I've marched with dancing, drumming Pagans. I've marched with Socialists and militants screaming about imperialism. I've marched with black-masked anarchists surrounded by riot cops.

And you know what? It's been okay. The police have behaved like police behave, sometimes restrained, sometimes provocative, occasionally vicious — but that's not new. At times we met counter demonstrators, but never more than a handful. And we often received unexpected support. I've seen construction workers flash peace signs at the black bloc.

Of course, our fears aren't just based on fictions. The authorities command real force, real tear gas, real clubs, real guns, real jails. Real people do die, go to prison, suffer. So might we.

But fear makes things worse than they are. Fear limits our vision and our ability to take in information, makes the power holders seem omnipotent, and leads to our suppressing ourselves, saving the authorities the cost and trouble of doing it. And despair leads to paralysis.

The counterspell for fear is courage: facing the possibility of the worst and then going ahead with what you know is right. The counterspell for despair is action in service of a vision. The counterspell for paralysis is stubborn, persistent passion.

Even if we're wrong, if nothing we do does make a difference, courage and passion are a better place to be than hopelessness, cynicism, and fear. If the authorities repress us, that's better than becoming people who repress ourselves. If we see our dreams ripped out of our hands, that's better than never daring to dream at all.

And if we tell our own stories with enough intensity and focus, we'll start to believe them, and so will others. We'll break the spells that bind us. We'll start to want that other world we say is possible with such intensity that nothing can stop us or deny us. All it takes is our willingness to act from vision, not from fear, to risk hoping, to dare to act for what we love.

II

visions

Our Place in Nature

Anumber of years ago, I was in Manhattan being interviewed by a feminist historian who was writing an article on the women's movement. In the course of our conversation, I mentioned that my partner and I were uncertain of our summer plans as we might be facing a short stretch in jail for blockading at Clayoquot Sound up in British Columbia, where we had been protesting the logging of old-growth forests.

My interviewer peered forward and said something high on my list of Least Favorite Responses to Political Action: "Are people still doing that sort of thing?" This was, of course, many years before Seattle, when large street actions were just not happening and protests in the forests were not being covered by the *New York Times*.

When I assured her people were indeed still doing that sort of thing, she leaned back, pen poised in the air, and said, "You know, I think to most New Yorkers the environment is sort of unreal." While I was digesting that thought, she went on, "I mean, we support it, save the whales and all that, but we don't really believe in it."

This conversation made a lasting impact on me. At first, I laughed and felt superior, but as I began to consider her words I realized she had articulated a problem that went far beyond New Yorkers — that was, in fact, a condition shared by lawmakers, corporate executives, decision-makers of all kinds. The environment seems less real than the balance sheet or the latest results of voter polls.

But as I thought longer about the situation, my smugness began to erode. For if I were honest, I would have to admit that to most city dwellers, even most environmentalists, even most Pagans who claim to worship nature, in reality the environment is sort of unreal, something we visit from time to time, or appreciate aesthetically, without deeply grasping that our lives depend upon it. My family and I had been arrested for trying to protect old-growth forest, but the truth is that until our friends took us hiking, we wouldn't necessarily have known old growth when we saw it. How could we? There isn't enough of it left anywhere reasonably accessible for us to have become familiar with it. Like many people, I garden — but the vegetables and fruit I grow are a wonderful addition to the food I buy, not my major source of subsistence. I may worry about the weather, but it rarely determines my income or my daily caloric intake.

We all live in a culture that has more and more made the environment unreal, something exotic we watch on PBS, not the daily fabric of our existence. I began to feel that developing a real relationship with nature was a vital part of both our political and spiritual work.

To do that, we need to be aware of the underlying attitudes that separate us from the natural world. There are, of course, the overriding philosophies that see human beings as above nature and therefore entitled to exploit the natural world for human ends. These philosophies arise both from religious sources and secular worship of profit, and the damage they cause is massive and visible.

But there is another more subtly damaging view of the human relationship to nature, and the damage it causes is perhaps more insidious because this view is often held by activists and environmentalists themselves. That is the attitude that human beings are somehow worse than nature, a blight on the planet, doomed to despoil whatever we touch, and that nature would be better off without us. Now, I admit that a case can be made for this view — nevertheless I think that in its own way it is just as damaging as the world view of the active despoilers. For if we believe that we are in essence bad for nature, we are profoundly separated from the natural world. We are also subtly relieved of responsibility for developing a healthy relationship with nature, for learning to observe and interact and play an active role in nature's healing.

The humans-as-blight vision also is self-defeating in organizing around environmental issues. It's hard to get people enthused about a movement that — even if only unconsciously — envisions its extinction as a good. And people don't act effectively out of feeling bad, guilty, wrong, and inauthentic. As long as we see humans as separate from nature, whether we place ourselves above or below, we will inevitably set up human/nature oppositions in which everyone loses.

There is another view, a view held by most indigenous cultures, by bioregionalists and permaculturalists and many people who live closer to the earth — and that is to see humans as being ourselves as much nature as any old-growth redwood, mosquito, or wildflower. We are, in fact, animals. We are bodies evolved over billions of years to eat, shit, breathe, drink, reproduce, die, and decay like other bodies. In nature, every giant whale and tiny microorganism has a role to play in the balance of the whole. How arrogant to think that we don't!

What might that role be? One hint might be contained in the words of Mabel McKay, Cache Creek Pomo elder and basketmaker: "When people don't use the plants, they get scarce. You must use them so they will come up again. All plants are like that. If they're not gathered from, or talked to and cared about, they'll die."

Could it be that we are supposed to be talking to the plants and animals, interacting with them, accepting the gifts they offer, and using them in ways that further their growth? The Pomo basketmakers, by collecting sedge roots, pruned and thinned the stands of sedge and improved their habitat. The sedge, flourishing by the riversides and on the banks of creeks, helps hold the soil with its roots, preventing erosion. The First People of California pruned, coppiced, harvested, and burned the grasslands and forests in patterns that created optimum conditions for wildlife, for both open meadows and the growth of the great trees. Their interaction with the land was so elegantly attuned that European invaders missed it entirely, believing they had found a wilderness untouched by human intervention (and open for their exploitation), when what they had actually found was more in the nature of an exquisitely cared-for wild garden.

All over this continent, native peoples used fire, prayer, tools, and ceremonies to influence their natural environment. The ecosystems we revere in forest and prairie co-evolved with human cultures. Outside of the highest mountain peaks and the glaciers, no "untouched" wilderness existed here. European preconceptions and racist dismissal of other cultures created the fantasy of the "virgin" wilderness. The very "nature" we see ourselves as blighting was formed by millenia of cohabitation.

Indigenous cultures around the world, including those we draw from in our present-day Pagan traditions, have seen themselves as part of nature. Not all have been successful in keeping the balance: indigenous cultures have hunted animals to extinction, have destroyed forests and desertified cropland. We must not romanticize other cultures, but neither should we close our eyes to what we can learn from them.

The first lesson is that we as human beings do have the capacity to meet both our needs and those of the nonhuman beings around us, in ways that actually increase diversity, habitat, balance, and beauty. If we fail to do so, it is because of a flaw in our attitudes, our observations, our goals, or our actions, *not* our inherent being.

The second lesson we can learn is that nature wants to talk to us. Far from being better off without us, nature would be incomplete without human eyes admiring her and human voices singing praise, human hands tending, pruning, and gathering, and human bellies filled with her bounty. The plants will die if they are not cared about. And especially right now, when so much of nature suffers from human-inflicted wounds, we need human creativity, ingenuity, and sweat to renew the balance our out-of-tune culture has damaged.

DEVELOPING BONDS TO PLACE

All of our ancestors were indigenous to somewhere; that is, they were deeply rooted in one place, living in a culture in which sustenance, spirit, and culture arose from the plants, animals, climate, and resources of that particular land. If we are going to create a new polit-ical/economic/social system, one that truly cares for the environment and for human beings, we may need to become indigenous again, to find at least one spot on the earth we can know intimately.

Come and walk with me in the Cazadero Hills, and I can tell you the names of all the trees. I know where the rare California nutmeg grows, where to find berries in the summer and matsutake mushrooms in the winter, where the gray squirrel crosses the stream running down the big-leaf maple branch and leaping into the redwood, where the ravens court each other with aerobatics after the winter storms. My neighbors, who have lived here longer, know even more.

Because I know these things about my land, I can walk into any forest where the trees are strange and understand something about the relationships going on. I know what health, stress, and recovery look and feel like, and I can be more intelligent in my interventions.

I didn't learn these things in a day, or a week. It takes time to get to know a place. Permaculture, the system of ecological design I attempt to put into practice on my land, has a guiding principle: "Use thoughtful and protracted observation instead of thoughtless intervention." Learning a place takes time because what we need to observe are patterns that only become apparent through time. Not just, "What are the birds in my backyard today?" but "What birds come and go throughout the different seasons? How do their populations change? Are there more this year than last year? How do I know? Is this a one-time fluctuation or part of a larger trend?" And those questions are just the beginning. Indigenous myths and ceremonies reflect thousands of years of careful observation, codified into songs and tales and rituals that tell us what is supposed to be going on, and when.

Observation itself, for most of us, requires a shift in awareness. Most of us don't actually know how to see and hear what is going on around us in the physical world. When we do go out into the forest or the mountains, nature becomes a scenic background to our own thoughts and dramas. If we grew up watching television or riding on the freeway instead of watching birds and animals and walking through the woods, our brains may literally need to be repatterned.

Jon Young, director of the Wilderness Awareness School[8], which teaches these observational skills, tells of a psychology experiment in which two groups of cats were raised in two different rooms. The first room was painted in vertical stripes, the second in horizontal stripes. After a few months, they were both brought into a room full of chairs, with both vertical and horizontal parts. The cats raised in the vertical room avoided the chair legs but bumped into the crossbars. Those raised in the horizontal room steered clear of the crossbars but ran into the legs. They literally couldn't see what their brains had not grown accustomed to seeing. After many collisions, however, they learned.

If we want to repattern our awareness, we need to arrange some regular collisions with nature. The Wilderness Awareness School stresses finding one spot, whether it's in the country or your backyard in the city or a vacant lot beside your house, and spending some time there each day observing what is going on, consciously opening all five of your senses.

When we begin this practice, we can begin to understand something of what it means to be bonded to a place. The dominant culture has no word for or true understanding of this bond. It stresses attachment to people, to family, lovers, and mates as well as attachment to things, to property and commodities and the money that allows us to buy them. Connection to place is seen as unimportant, a sort of aesthetic thing, but really, one place is as good as another.

To indigenous cultures, the bond with place is more akin to the bonds we expect with our mothers or our closest family. Jeannette Armstrong writes from the Okanagan perspective: "The Okanagan word for 'our place on the land' and 'our language' is the same. This means that the land has taught us our language. The way we survived is to speak the language that the land offered us as its teachings ... We also refer to the land and our bodies with the same root syllable. This means that the flesh which is our body is pieces of the land come to us through the things which the land is ... *We are our land/place.* Not to know and to celebrate this is to be without language and without land. It is to be *dis-placed*. The Okanagan teaches that anything displaced from all that it requires to survive in health will eventually perish ... As Okanagans our most essential responsibility is to learn to bond our whole individual selves and our communal selves to the land."⁹

The whole system we call "globalization" is predicated on the destruction of this bond. The global corporate economic system has displaced millions of people. A capitalist economic system needs a workforce of mobile and expendable people, who can be brought to work when the need for production is high, laid off or transferred when its low. And indigenous peoples have an annoying habit of valuing the integrity of their land and culture over the profits that can be extracted from the resources it may command. The whole ideology of "efficiency" and "integration" is aimed at shoring up an economic system in which no region is self-sufficient, in which the resources of the entire globe are available without restraint to corporations that wish to exploit them, and in which the entire world is one huge market open to all. Corporations and enterprises are displaced as well — they are no longer tied or responsible to any local community. They are free to pick up and leave if local regulations become too onerous, or local labor too demanding.

The world we want to create, the revolution we foster, would reroot us back in place. At one of the early meetings of our local land use group, the Cazadero Hills Land Use Council (or CHLUC, pronounced "Cluck"), my neighbor Bob Madrone defined our work as "becoming indigenous." At the first World Social Forum in Porto Alegre, Brazil, in 2001, an indigenous speaker defined what it means to be indigenous. "It's not the color of your skin," he said. "It's not even about being raised in a traditional way. It's about being a guardian of the common treasure of the land."

Brazil's Movimiento Sim Terre

One of the best examples of a balanced human/nature relationship comes from the MST of Brazil. The Movimiento Sim Terre, or Landless Rural Workers' Movement, is the largest direct action movement in the world.[10] Since 1984, they've enabled hundreds of thousands of very poor people to reclaim unused land and start settlements that the government, in time, is forced to legalize.

An MST encampment is the embodiment of reinhabitation. Although the members of the settlement are generally from the poorest strata of Brazilian society, without any formal education, the MST teaches a high degree of ecological literacy.

I visited two encampments in February of 2001. When my companions and I arrived at the first legalized camp with a cargo of bright balls, we were greeted by a pack of delighted children and Tane Rosa, the schoolteacher. Tane Rosa was surprised and happy to learn that I also lived in a rural area. She immediately asked me four questions: "What kinds of trees do you have? What kinds of birds do you have? Do you have any wild animals? What can you grow?"

We walked up to her garden, picked okra for lunch, and she pointed out to me the medicinal herbs and edible wild plants growing alongside the path, just as I would do for her if she came to visit my land.

When we toured the encampment, she pointed with pride at the new coffee planting that would be an example of agroforestry: shade-grown coffee planted under trees that provide fruit and habitat for birds and animals. There are three separate areas of indigenous forest left, and the settlement is planting forest corridors to link them and to provide more wildlife habitat.

In the room we stayed in is a poster that outlines the Ten Agreements of the MST. It reads:

OUR AGREEMENTS WITH EARTH AND WITH LIFE

Human beings are precious because their intelligence, work, and organization can protect and preserve all forms of life.

1. To love and preserve the earth and all natural things.
2. To always improve our knowledge about nature and agriculture.
3. To produce food to eliminate hunger in humanity. To avoid monoculture and the use of agricultural pesticides.
4. To preserve the already existing forest and to reforest new areas.
5. To take care of the springs, rivers, wetlands, and lakes. To fight against the privatization of water.
6. To make the camp and community beautiful by planting flowers, medicinal herbs, and trees.
7. To adequately treat the trash and to fight any threats of contamination and aggression of the environment.
8. To practice solidarity and to revolt against any kind of injustice, aggression, and exploitation against a person, a community, and nature.
9. To fight against the large estates so that everyone can have land, bread, education, and freedom.
10. Never sell the land. The land is the supreme gift for the future generations. Agrarian Reform — for a Brazil without large estates!

"To love the earth, you first must know it, and by the time you do, we'll be able to build a better world," Tane Rosa tells us.

LEARNING TO LOVE THE EARTH

How do we learn to know and love the earth? To begin with, we can each commit ourselves to developing a personal relationship with the natural world, to making that relationship the heart of our spiritual practice and the inspiration of our actions in the world.

Perhaps the best way to begin is simply to step outside and observe. Find some spot that is still at least partly wild. If you live in the city, that might mean a less-tended corner of a park or a vacant lot filled with weeds or an unkempt garden — not a mono-culture lawn under a few clipped trees or a manicured flowerbed, but any place that seems slightly out of control. Spend a few moments each day there, if you can, just looking at the physical reality around you. Not, if you can help it, speculating on how the trees feel or using them as a background for your own meditations or personal work, but actually looking at them, at what insects and birds and animals appear, at how they grow and change over time. Just look, feel, listen, smell, taste. If you get bored, either you've picked a place that's too sterile and controlled to have much going on, or you're not really looking. Notice how your mind gets in there and what your internal dialogue is, but instead of focusing on yourself, focus on what's around you.

Over time, you'll be amazed at how much there is to see, once we open our eyes. And as we relearn our capacity to observe, we'll begin to understand that what we see is real.

THE PRACTICE OF DIRECT DEMOCRACY

Direct democracy, horizontal organizing, nonhierarchical structure — these are all key aspects of our movement. Putting them into practice is an art that requires a shift in our organizational modes as well as in our thinking.

Hierarchy is the model of leadership and organization most people are familiar with and surrounded by from the moment they are born into a modern hospital through their education in a public or private school and beyond, whether their later life includes attendance at a university, a job serving burgers at McDonald's, rising to management at a large corporation, a stint in the military or attendance at the neighborhood church. Although to many of us, hierarchy has negative connotations of disempowerment and lack of freedom, the word actually describes a certain pattern that exists both in nature and in human affairs. A hierarchy is a branching pattern. Go look at a tree and see how the twigs connect to one branch, the branches to one larger limb, the limbs to the trunk.

This branching pattern is extremely widespread in nature. It's the same pattern found in the way that small rivulets combine into brooks, streams, and mighty rivers. It's the pattern of our capillaries, veins, and arteries. Nature repeats this pattern over and over again because it is so useful. A branching pattern functions for collecting, concentrating, and dispersing. It branches out to fill the widest possible space as completely as possible. Notice how a tree fills the maximum volume of space with leaves or needles that can collect sunlight from the largest possible number of surfaces. The energy from the sun is transformed into sugar and then collected and concentrated, and eventually dispersed to feed

169

the cells of the tree and the roots, which in their structure mirror the branches. The roots collect water and nutrients, which in turn are concentrated and then dispersed out to the branches and leaves.

A branching pattern is also a two-way flow. Streams and rivers carry nutrients (and pollutants) from the hills down to the sea. Salmon, swimming upstream, return nutrients from the ocean to even the smallest rivulets — at least they used to. Now they do only in increasingly rare intact habitats.

A branching pattern links the trunk to the furthest leaf in a clear line, but it doesn't allow the leaves to directly feed each other. Salmon cannot leap from the headwaters of one stream to the headwaters of another.

For a branching pattern to be sustainable, the flows both ways must be balanced. The energy collected by the leaves is balanced by the water and nutrients collected by the roots. The trunk, the place of concentration, is merely a conduit that serves this balance.

But in human societies, branching patterns are often used to collect wealth, resources, and labor from one group and to disperse them to another group. Barely enough is given back to insure survival. The value produced by labor is collected from the workers, the leaves of the corporate tree; then concentrated into the hands of various levels of management, and eventually dispersed to owners and shareholders.

In such a hierarchy, power and decision-making flow in opposite directions. Decisions are made by the few in the top echelons and communicated downward to those who have no voice in the decisions. Inequality and imbalance are justified by assigning a higher value to those who are the recipients of wealth and the makers of decisions. They are seen as a different class, a different order of human being, deserving of more, and both political ideology and religions reinforce this view. Even God is addressed as "Lord" or "King."

Hierarchies run on power-over: the entitlement and ability of some groups to control others, extract their labor or resources, and impose sanctions or punishment. Power-over also reflects the degree of privilege each group holds. In our society, men have power over women, white people have power over people of color, the rich have power over the poor, those who fit the norms of society around sexual identity, attractiveness, fitness, age, etc. have higher status than those who don't. Privilege translates directly into wealth and opportunity.

A DIFFERENT MODEL: THE WEB

When we begin to organize around the principle of direct democracy and real equality, we need to look for a different model, a different pattern. It's no accident that the global justice movement has grown along with the Internet and that the most common metaphor for online communication is that of the web. A web implies a pattern of connections that are complex and flexible in ways that a branching pattern is not. In a classic spider web, spokes radiate out from a central point, linked by a spiral of sticky thread. A web can also concentrate information: any point on the web can communicate with the center. But it can also communicate with other points on the periphery. Sitting on the deck during a break while I'm thinking about this, I suddenly realize that I'm staring at three webs, all different. The first is a classic spiral, the second is a dome, held by an intricate arrangement of tension/suspension fibers. And the third seems to have a random, zigzag architecture. All fill space, and their varied forms allow more complex modes of connections.

The World Wide Web is a familiar model of this pattern. It allows multiple forms of communication: one to one, one to a selected few, one to a whole listserve. It allows the posting of information on a website for many to access, and responses can also flow in many directions.

Actions organized in a direct democratic fashion can be patterned in many different ways. One model is for participants to form affinity groups, small groups that support each other, make decisions together, and take on some of the specific roles of the action. Affinity groups send representatives to a spokescouncil, which may be empowered to make decisions or simply functions to synthesize ideas and proposals and to send them back to affinity groups for decision-making. Affinity groups may also combine into clusters or blocs. The organizers are part of working groups which take on specific tasks: communications, media, scenario, etc. They may have their own coordinating council. Their role is to make proposals to the whole body of participants, to hear feedback, and to implement decisions, but it is the whole body that ultimately makes decisions.

The reality, of course, is usually much messier. Actions include many people who are not integrated into affinity groups. Some arrive early enough to be included into mass assemblies, where anyone can come and anyone can speak, without needing to belong to a specific group. In the early stages of an action, before affinity groups form, open meetings allow more direct participation.

Most antiauthoritarian groups work by some form of consensus. Consensus does not mean unanimity; it means that everyone's needs and concerns are listened to and taken into account. Consensus works best as a creative thinking process, when enough time is allowed for open discussion of an issue as well as for synthesis and revision of ideas to occur. At best, consensus fosters an attitude of openness, of respect for each person's position, and of flexibility. Consensus can be time-consuming and frustrating — but so can any decision-making process in which there are real differences to be resolved. Glossing over those differences or allowing one side to simply outvote the other doesn't actually resolve them, and the splits then show up when the group tries to enact its decisions. There are many resources available for learning consensus process, and a skilled facilitator can be a great help to a group.

The model above works for actions, but it may change and develop when a group needs to apply it to the work of an ongoing organization, when people's energy and commitment must be sustained and long-term accountability must be provided.

I've worked with one such group, Reclaiming, for over twenty years. Starting in 1980 as a small collective of five women, we've gone through many evolutionary stages as we've grown and expanded.

Reclaiming began as a tight-knit circle of friends who started teaching classes in earth-based spirituality and Witchcraft together. We were all in the same ritual circle, knew each other well, and saw each other frequently. As we taught each class, we recruited new student teachers for the next, and so our circle began expanding.

Originally, we were an open collective: anyone could come to meetings, get involved in the work, and participate in decisions. We shortly realized the pitfalls of this openness when we found ourselves dealing with an actively hallucinating psychotic at one meeting, or with people who had strong opinions but no interest in the work.

Also, with everyone involved with every decision, meetings were long and often tedious.

We soon shifted to a model of working groups we called "cells," partly as an ironic reference to Communist cells and partly because the word described what the groups did, namely perform specific functions for an overall body: teaching, putting out a newsletter, planning public rituals, etc. Cells had autonomy over their own affairs. A central, closed collective was formed for coordination and to decide on larger issues.

The collective had a tight mechanism for letting in new people: someone would be proposed, and the whole group would have to reach consensus on their admission. We had no mechanism for getting people out, and that proved to be a problem. Over time, the collective grew insular. People didn't want to let new people in and risk getting stuck with people they didn't like. People stayed in the collective when they were no longer actually doing work, and people who were doing work weren't in the collective. Others who might have been interested in joining were entirely mystified by our selection process and had no idea how to get in.

After about fifteen years of existence, we began a long process of restructuring. We collectively wrote a statement of our Principles of Unity. We created a new body called "The Wheel," in which working cells had actual representatives that they chose. The old collective resigned and passed on its power.[11]

In the meantime, however, we had expanded in other ways. For years, we'd been teaching weeklong intensives we called "Witchcamps" in various parts of the U.S. and Canada and Europe. Each camp had inspired local people to begin to teach and organize classes, rituals, and gatherings. Originally, the San Francisco teachers' cell staffed all the camps or chose all the teachers. But as people in other locations developed their own experience and skills, they began to resent the "central control" and to ask for a voice in those decisions. We eventually created a spokescouncil structure for the whole web of Witchcamps. The Spokescouncil consists of a teacher and an organizer from each camp community. It is not empowered: major decisions must go back to the communities for consensus. It meets once a year face-to-face, and once a year online in an extended e-mail meeting.

Teaching teams are now chosen by local selection committees, with input from a smaller group called the "Guidance Council," whose job it is to keep an overview of the whole and to assure cross-fertilization.

In setting up these structures, we've tried to assure maximum freedom, creativity, and autonomy while instituting minimal rules and the least amount of centralized control necessary.

We've found that certain informal roles are useful in our organizations, our celebrations, and our actions. *In Truth or Dare*, I called them crows, snakes, graces, dragons, and spiders.[12]

The task of the crows is to keep an overview, to keep the groups' direction in mind, to look ahead, and see to the big picture. The task of the snakes is to keep an underview, to notice what's not happening, who is not present, what problems are brewing.

Graces invite people in, make people welcome, expand the group. Dragons watch the boundaries, keeping track of the details and guarding against intrusions. And spiders sit in the center of the web, linking and communicating.

At times these roles are formally designated. At other times, they're roles we can each take on. They are all aspects of empowering leadership. When they are articulated, they can be shared and rotated more clearly.

EMPOWERING LEADERSHIP

Leadership is necessary and valuable even in antiauthoritarian, "leaderless" groups. But the empowering leadership needed in such groups is very different from leadership in hierarchical groups. It's not the authority to give orders, issue decrees, make unilateral decisions, or tell people what to do. Rather, empowering leadership is about persuasion, inspiration, and the sharing of power, information, and attention. It's the leadership that steps out in front and says, "Hey, let's go this way!"

Empowering leadership is not based on power-over, on the ability to control or punish others. It draws on a different sort of power that I call "power-among." (In *Truth or Dare*, I called it "power-with."[13] However, since then many people have been using that term for collective power, the power we have when we're acting together.) Power-among could also be called "influence," "prestige," or "moral authority." It's based on respect, on people's assessment that what I'm saying is worth hearing, perhaps because I have more experience or skill or knowledge in a certain area. In most indigenous cultures, elders wield a great deal of power-among because of their greater experience.

Listening to those with greater experience can save a lot of trial and error. If the elder says "Don't eat that plant, my uncle did and he died in agony," we can save a lot of pain by following that advice.

But power-among can also lead to dependency and transmute into power-over. Too much obedience to the words of the elders can prevent experimentation. Maybe Uncle died in agony not from the plant but from something entirely unrelated, and we're passing by a perfectly good food source. In the post-modern world, when situations and constraints change so rapidly, the experience of the past is not always a valid guide to the future. When power-among is recognized and identified, it can be assessed and challenged if need be.

For someone who is moved to take leadership in an empowering manner, power-among is a precious resource, and we do well to think of it as a limited resource. I think of it like I think of the water in my tank in summer that is filled from a spring. Theoretically, it's endlessly renewable. In reality, it fills slowly in August, and it can all too easily be lost if I do something really stupid, like leave a hose on. Once it's gone, it's going to take time for it to recover. If I use too much of it, I diminish the reserves.

Influence in a group is also best used judiciously, and always with respect for others. Never take it for granted. Always listen to the opinions of others with respect. Leave room for others to learn and make mistakes. Overused, influence breeds resentment and dries up.

Empowering leadership means stepping back as much as stepping forward, not doing something you are good at so that someone else has a chance to learn. But stepping back is not empowering if you are sitting silent but are inwardly glowering and criticizing.

George Lakey, a longtime organizer and nonviolence trainer, talks about the value of silently cheering for your students as they practice an exercise.[14] Silent cheering has become one of my ongoing practices as a teacher, trainer, and leader. If I step back and let someone else facilitate a meeting, I consciously cheer them on internally: "Go, Charles, go — hurray, that was a brilliant move, now, yeah, a home run!" Imagine the difference in atmosphere if I'm sitting there thinking, "That was stupid — I would have done that better. Oh no — why did you say that? I should be up there, not him!"

Empowering leadership is not just a metaphor. It means literally supporting others energetically and emotionally, and creating an atmosphere in a group in which that energetic support and respectful attention is the norm. In such a group, people are more creative and smarter and make better decisions, and more energy is generated to do the work.

Power-among is best saved for those moments in which skill and experience are vitally necessary. But do use it when it's needed. When the plants in the garden are about to die, water them — that's what the water is for. When a thousand people are gathered for a meeting after the first day of blockading in Seattle and trying to decide what to do the next day while the police are outside tear gassing the street, the group needs the most experienced and skilled facilitator possible. But that person will meet less resentment in a tense situation if she or he has not previously facilitated every other meeting.

There are several types of leadership we might exercise in a directly democratic group. We might call the first one "issues leadership": proposing actions, directions, tactics, decisions, raising issues, urging the group to take certain directions. The second we could call "process leadership": helping the group find effective ways to make decisions, share skills, and solve problems. Meeting facilitation, training, skills sharing, meditation, and counseling might be some of the ways process leadership is exercised.

In directly democratic groups, when we exercise process leadership we generally try to remain neutral and not exercise leadership around issues. So, if we're facilitating a meeting, we don't argue for a particular proposal. That would concentrate too much power in one voice. If we have a strong action to propose to the group, we don't facilitate that agenda item. If we're embroiled in a conflict, we don't also try to mediate it. When we're training a group, our job is to provide skills and a chance to reflect on experiences that will help people form their own opinions and make their own choices, not to impose our own philosophy or values. Pushing our own agenda would not only be an abuse of our power-among, it would be ineffective and likely cause resentment rather than inspire respect.

If I do a direct action training in which we have time to consider questions of violence and nonviolence, I don't lecture about my own beliefs, no matter how strong they are. Instead, I try to create an atmosphere that models respect, in which people can explore their own beliefs and listen to others.

In hierarchies, leaders often hoard information. If we're trying to create a model of empowerment, people have to have access to the information they need in order to make decisions.

Control of information and monopolies of certain skills are ways in which both power-among and power-over can be maintained.

There can, however, also be a positive benefit to some hierarchies that establish quality control. We can assume that a licensed doctor has a certain body of information, that a licensed mechanic has certain experience and abilities. But part of our work as activists is to spread skills as widely as possible. So, in actions, we train medics to provide care for each other in situations where the officially approved medical teams won't go. Doctors and nurses volunteer to provide their higher level of skill and to train the street medics. When even the Red Cross won't enter a scene because the police are still firing tear gas, when hospitals can't be trusted because activists will be arrested from their wards and tortured, the action medics are literal lifesavers.

IndyMedia, the web-based independent media group that provides alternative coverage for actions and issues, is an example of the power of free access to information. Anyone can post stories. You don't need to be an accredited journalist or a graduate with set credentials. Stories tend to be personal, sometimes biased, sometimes inaccurate. But major media stories are also often inaccurate and biased, and they carry a weight of authority that IndyMedia writers don't. People reading IndyMedia know what the bias is likely to be, and can read critically. If a reader disagrees or knows contradictory facts, she or he can post their own story. IndyMedia journalists rarely have the resources a journalist writing for, say, the *Washington Post* might be able to put into researching a story. But they also don't have to answer to an editorial department with its own biases, which today are more and more determined by corporate interests.

Sharing information, communicating, and networking are aspects of empowering leadership: they help us make links between people, establish connections, weave a rich web of relationships.

Empowering leadership means sharing and expanding skills, passing them on as widely as possible, and making space for others to bring in their own creativity, to take material and make it their own, to do things you wouldn't have thought of, to make their own mistakes but also their own discoveries.

Empowering leadership is not about always having the brilliant idea yourself, but about recognizing and supporting the ideas of others. In ritual, sometimes one person will begin hesitantly humming a new tune or putting words to a chant. A good ritual leader is always listening to the group, ready to join her voice and make that softer melody audible.

Sharing information, sharing skills, supporting the creativity of others, networking, and communicating spread power throughout a group and therefore increase its effectiveness and intelligence.

Through the practice of direct democracy, we can develop forms and models that establish a true contrast to hierarchy and domination. We can learn from our mistakes and experiment, exploring approaches on a small scale that may eventually become a way to organize society on a large scale so that each person has a voice in the decisions that affect us.

BUILDING A DIVERSE
MOVEMENT

In nature, diversity means resilience. A prairie that has hundreds of different plants growing together can resist pests or respond to storms that would devastate a field of identical hybrid corn. In social movements, too, we need diversity in order to thrive.

After Seattle, one of the key articles that circulated widely on the Internet was a piece by Betita Martinez, a Chicana activist and author, called "Where Was the Color in Seattle?" She noted how the young activists were overwhelmingly white, and posed the question: "How can we can build a racially diverse and anti-racist movement?"[15]

In many of the movements I've been in, from the antiwar groups of the sixties and seventies to the feminist movement and the antinuclear movement, this question has been a familiar one. Similar discussions were going on twenty or twenty-five years ago. What often astounds me is how little progress we've made in building racial diversity. Other differences have not continued to divide us so deeply. I remember agonizing conversations in, say, 1979 about whether straight women and lesbians could ever actually work together in the same organization. Today, that's not an issue in most of the groups I work with. Issues still arise, of course, but they don't prevent us from working together.

The global justice movement is not a "white" movement — it's a movement inspired and rooted among people of color around the world, from the Zapatistas of Mexico to the insurrectionists of Bolivia who retook their water supply from privatization. From Africa to Fiji to Papua New Guinea to Thailand to India to the U.S., people of color have been in the forefront of the fight against global corporate capitalism, have faced torture, prison, and death, and have also joyfully pioneered new tactics and new forms of struggle. I have no doubt that stopping the WTO or challenging the IMF is absolutely in the interests of the majority of people of color on the planet, regardless of who does the challenging. But in North America, a large proportion of the direct action movement has been white, and the question of how to build diversity is one of the overriding challenges we face.

There are certain obvious answers and some suggested solutions. As white activists, we can look at our own unconscious racism, at our lack of not just outreach but of real attempts to bring people of color into the central organizing, at our history of not working on the issues that concern people of color and of not recognizing the leadership and organizations of people of color. While the most stunning successes of nonviolent direct action are found in liberation struggles of people of color, direct action poses higher risks for those who are already targets of the criminal injustice system — to face these risks, people need to be convinced that the issues involved are direct life issues. As white activists, we can educate ourselves on the history and contributions of people of color, and learn to become effective allies.

As someone who has been an activist now for over thirty-five years, I often find myself in situations where younger activists are proposing these solutions, often with a kind of outraged wonderment that they haven't been implemented long before. I usually refrain from telling them that most of these solutions have, in fact, been tried. Perhaps not wisely, not well enough or wholeheartedly enough or consistently enough, but I certainly have been part of groups attempting one or another of them for many decades. All of those experiences have been illuminating and valuable, but none of them have effectively changed the demographics of any of the movements that put them into practice.

There's a word that describes the state a group or a movement is in when it is asking the same questions over and over for decades, trying the same solutions, and having the same conversations without visibly changing the situation. That word is "stuck." To get unstuck, we may need to ask some new questions, offer some heretical critiques, and look more clearly at the history of how we got stuck.

To understand, for example, the feminist movement's difficulties in addressing race, you need to understand the context we emerged from.

SOME HISTORY

The Civil Rights movement of the fifties and early sixties was inspired and led by African Americans, but it attracted thousands of white people to participate, join sit-ins and freedom rides, do direct action, and go to jail. Some even sacrificed their lives, along with the many heroes of color. Those who participated saw themselves not as merely supporting someone else's struggle, but as part of a common struggle to make this a more just society. One of the stated goals of the movement was integration, a society where, as Martin Luther King put it, his four little children could be judged not by the color of their skin, but by the content of their character.[16]

But in the African American community, integration had long contended with liberation movements that saw black identity and independence as key. After the assassination of Martin Luther King, the Black Nationalism became ascendent in the Black Liberation struggle. White people were essentially told to get out. In his autobiography, Malcolm X tells the story of a young, blond, Southern white woman so moved by one of his talks that she followed him to New York to ask what she could do to help. "Nothing," he told her."[17] When the Student Nonviolent Co-ordinating Committee (SNCC) became an all-black organization, it encouraged white people to go home and organize their own communities.

There were many complex reasons for this change. The oppressive systems that shape society also shape our personal relations, even within groups that form to oppose them. Undoubtedly within the movement for black liberation, the real relationships between black people and white people had often been subtly patronizing and unconsciously oppressive. Separation aided the development of black consciousness, pride, self-esteem, and self-reliance.

At the same time, many white activists were shifting their focus to the Vietnam War. And many women were beginning to look at their own experiences of oppression within the social movements that were supposed to stand for liberation. Just as unconscious racism was carried into relationships within the movement, so conscious and unconscious sexism characterized the Civil Rights, Black Liberation and antiwar movements. Women saw their organizing work less valued, less rewarded, and less noticed than the work of charismatic men. Ideologies that devalued women were nonetheless seen as radical and liberating. Malcolm X proclaimed that "All women, by their nature, are fragile and weak! They are attracted to the male in whom they see strength."[18] Within the antiwar movement, the visible leadership was almost uniformly male.

The women's movement began a process of consciousness raising, of meeting in small groups to discuss our own real experience. When we began talking to each other about our lives, we discovered a depth and range of women's oppression that hadn't been articulated before.

Women's issues were also issues of people of color, half of whom are, after all, women. But though the leaders of the women's movement included some brilliant and powerful women of color, the most prominent spokeswomen, the women who received the media attention and became the agenda setters, were white.

In part because the renewed feminist movement sprang forth in a time of separation, it became problematic for politically conscious white women to adopt black issues or to offer support to black groups without being seen as patronizing. And we can't deny that some white women may have experienced a conscious or unconscious sense of relief. At last we had an oppression we could call our own! How much more comfortable to explore our own victimization than to confront the ways in which we benefit from the victimization of others.

Women's liberation, gay liberation, and a whole host of new movements developed that focused on social and cultural transformation, on defining, articulating, and challenging oppressions based on some aspect of one's identity. Identity politics generally included some form of separation for the purpose of constructing and consolidating an identity, as well as an analysis of the particular form of oppression, a well-founded distrust of the historical oppressors, a revaluing of history, and the development of new cultures and distinctive styles. To some women, men per se were the problem, much as Malcolm X had named the white devil as the problem. That period of separation allowed groups that had been oppressed to develop self-reliance and self-esteem, and helped individuals grow in a sheltered space, freed of the necessity to constantly confront the oppressor.

Identity politics drew their power and focus from looking at the world through a particular dichotomy: White People vs. People of Color or Men vs. Women.

It was a simplistic but probably necessary phase of political development. Since our oppression as women had been virtually invisible, it allowed us to finally see and articulate what was wrong with our situation. The power of the feminist analysis was to see our oppression as a social force directed against women as a class. It's in the interest of exploiters — whether patriarchal, capitalist, or both — to keep the oppressed thinking that their problems are purely individual and that the solutions lie in individual efforts to change. It's hard to conceive — it's even hard to remember — what a shattering, liberating insight it was in, say, 1970 to finally notice that the painful and debilitating things that had happened to you, from being discouraged in pursuing an education to rape and sexual abuse, constituted social oppression and not just personal failings.

But the focus on separation and self-definition had the unfortunate result of pitting one oppression against another. The dichotomizing of oppression necessarily made it hard for women of color to identify with a movement that downplayed the racism that was a prime feature of their daily existence.

And in the context of separation, building coalitions and diverse movements became extremely difficult. When a significant portion of the women's movement wouldn't speak to men, the black movements wouldn't work with whites, the lesbians and gays could barely work with each other, how could strong alliances grow?

As the Vietnam War ended, cultural transformation more and more took center stage, creating another uncomfortable dichotomy. Marxist theory and reasonable expectations would lead us to believe that the people at the forefront of struggle would be those who had the most to gain: the workers, the most oppressed. But in reality, those on the cultural transformation forefront tended to be people with more privilege and more education. The most radical elements in the liberation struggles of people of color met with intense repression, including assassination and lifelong imprisonment. The unions, traditional sources of economic radicalism, had become more and more conservative. The workers and many nonpolitical people of color tended to be more tied to church and religion as deep sources of community and traditional sources of strength in adversity. Church-oriented people tended to be more socially conservative and less likely to be sympathetic to the wilder cultural experiments of radical youth.

Movements that look toward revolutionary transformation reject many of the values of the larger society. "My anarchist politics were firmly rooted in a politics of rejection, a refusal to participate in a society based on exploitation, oppression, and massive destruction of the environment, animals, and people," writes activist Chris Crass. "My politics were summed up by saying, 'Fuck all authority.' Anarchism is indeed a much more complex body of theory and practice, but this anti-power politic, largely based on rejection, has been a strong undercurrent in anarchist thought."[19]

But for many people in groups that have been for centuries excluded from power and privilege, liberation looks like inclusion, not further self-imposed marginalization. Graduation from a university, getting a good job, moving into professional and prestigious positions within mainstream society could be seen as radical, liberating aspirations for those who historically have been delegated to a lower status. For a person of color, rejecting the system might have simply led back to the familiar ground of poverty and lack of power. And when revolutionary opposition to the system was led by people of color, it was met by extreme repression.

Among predominantly white groups, the focus on cultural transformation and identity politics took precedence over the economic issues that might have otherwise come to the forefront. When Reagan took office in the eighties, much of the white movement turned its focus to opposition to nuclear weapons and, later, militarism and Central American intervention. These were issues that certainly had a bearing on the lives of people of color, whose interests would certainly not have been served by a nuclear war. But that potential disaster did not seem most immediate to communities that were increasingly struggling with economic devastation, the criminalization that accompanied the drug war, and despair on a daily basis and that faced mountainous organizing tasks around those issues.

Within those movements of the eighties, questions similar to that of Betita Martinez began to be asked: "Where are the people of color? Why are we not working on their issues, doing community organizing instead of focusing on issues that, because they appealed mostly to white people, had to be by definition issues of privilege? A sense began to grow in the antinuclear movement that our struggle was not legitimate without the participation of people of color. But after a decade and a half of separation-based politics, following on centuries of racism, we didn't have the contacts, the channels of communication, and the personal relationships that would have allowed us to easily become allies.

When we build movements, our personal relationships are more important than we generally are willing to admit, and especially so when we attempt to cross the divisions that separate us. Here's an example:

In her article on Seattle, Martinez describes how "four protesters of color from different Bay Area organizations talked about the 'culture shock' they experienced when they first visited the 'Convergence,' the protest center set up by the Direct Action Network, a coalition of many organizations. Said one, 'When we walked in, the room was filled with young whites calling themselves anarchists. There was a pungent smell, many had not showered. We just couldn't relate to the scene so our whole group left right away.' Another told me, 'They sounded dogmatic and paranoid.' 'I just freaked and left,' said another. 'It wasn't just race, it was also culture, although race was key.'"[20]

I had a similar reaction when I first stepped into the convergence center. I had come days early, hoping to be able to help with trainings and organizing, but when I walked into the cavern-like warehouse, it seemed to be a writhing sea of pierced, dreadlocked youth (and I mean white dreadlocked youth), all of whom had that faintly hostile, sullen look that cool youth adopt among their peers. I had to go away, have a restorative cup of tea, and gather my middle-aged reserves before I could venture back in. When I did, I immediately found one of the organizers who was an old friend I had been doing political work with for fifteen years. The woman coordinating trainings was another old friend; another of the major organizers was a former housemate. Key people knew and trusted me. I was soon integrated, and it was easy for me to offer my skills and services. But had I not known anyone, I might simply have felt intimidated by the scene, and left. Had no one known me, my offers to help with trainings or meetings might have been met with suspicion or mistrust and left me feeling excluded instead of welcomed.

Without the ties of real, longstanding personal relationships, political alliances are harder to build. There is nothing to help bridge the cultural chasms and gaps of expectations, no history of trust to help smooth the inevitable painful moments that arise when we try to bridge barriers. Oftentimes we also don't know the history, the literature, the art, or the cultural heritage of other groups, unless we have made a conscious effort to seek out those resources that can help us see the world from another perspective.

The era of separation politics was like a rut in the road that was only eroded deeper by the other forces working against true coalition building. Understanding its lingering impact can help us clarify why we have not already built a more diverse movement. But to do so, we need to look both critically at the contradictions inherent in approaches we have tried and proactively at what we can do.

INTERLOCKING SYSTEMS OF OPPRESSION

Racism, sexism, heterosexism, and all of the related systems of prejudice and oppression are, in reality, interlocking and intertwined. They reinforce and feed upon each other, and to end any one of them we have to address them all. All depend on the construct of power as domination: the ability and entitlement that some elite groups have to set conditions, command compliance, control resources, and impose punishment on the many. All depend on isolating the individual, on convincing people that their pain is a result of personal failing rather than part of a larger structure of oppression directed at whole classes of people.

We oppose racism and sexism and all the other related isms not just because we're in solidarity with someone else, but because we realize how all of those syndromes are interconnected. Racism is maintained in part by the deep sexual tensions created by a patriarchal construction of manhood. Manhood is identified with power, and that power is systematically taken away from black men, who are literally and symbolically castrated. These power dramas are enacted on the bodies of women. White men have been raping black women continuously for centuries as an aspect of slavery and a general economic and social oppression. Then that sexual violence is projected onto black men, who are feared and accused of raping white women, and lynched. Racism can therefore not truly be undermined without confronting sexual oppression.

But sexual oppression also is reinforced by racism. Racism leaves the women of the target group doubly vulnerable to exploitation. It separates women from one another. And as soon as one group of women is defined as in need of protection from the sexual violence of some "other" group of men, repression of all women is justified.

That patriarchal construction of manhood — the identification of male sexuality with violence, power-over, and the thrusting piercing weaponry of war — supports militarism, which in turn necessitates the subjugation of women and especially women's sexuality as a possession and prize of war. If that subjugation is to be maintained, heterosexuality and strict gender divisions and roles must be enforced. And the power differentials maintained by this system enforce economic and class divisions as well. Military and prison systems enforce the subjugation of the poor, especially of people of color and the developing world. Poor whites are encouraged to ally with their race against others of their class, women to ally with their race and class against others of their gender.

Any one of these syndromes constricts us all, just as tying a tight band around one leg until it becomes gangrenous will affect one's entire body. So opposing any and all of the isms is a struggle that is in all of our interests if our goal is a world of true liberation for any of us.

The global corporate capitalist system, the latest manifestation of this interlocking system of oppression, is a race thing — it's a continuation of the policies by which the mostly-white North has exploited the mostly-dark South for centuries. And the "lesser developed countries" are that way precisely because of the history of exploitation and resource extraction that have subsidized the wealth of the industrialized world. "Global apartheid" is another descriptive term for this system.

The global corporate capitalist system is also a sex thing — the average worker in the *maquiladoras* and the factories of the Free Trade Zones is a sixteen-year-old woman. Women and children are the majority of the world's poor. Women's bodies are commodified in an international sex trade. Policies that impact health services, education, and the availability of life necessities such as food and water disproportionately affect women, who are the first to go hungry, the ones who walk the dusty roadsides for miles searching for water, the last to receive education.

The inequalities and injustices of global apartheid are maintained by the police and military powers of the state. The threat of force and the use of force keep people from rising up to overthrow the system. But force, to appear legitimate, must be clothed in ideology, embedded in a culture of militarism that glorifies and dignifies war. The patriarchal construct of manhood supports the culture of war. Our public officials are compelled to respond to any real or perceived attack with a show of force or risk seeming weak, ineffectual, womanlike. They respond with as much thoughtfulness and reason as a male dog does when attacked. Negotiation is reduced to a chest-pounding exchange of ultimatums, and force is employed regardless of whether it targets the perpetrators or innocent bystanders and regardless of whether or not it ultimately increases our security. Under the spell of this syndrome, we are also incapable of peering behind the curtain to examine the real reasons for waging a war, which may have less to do with pride and security and far more with oil, money, and consolidating U.S. hegemony.

Racism, sexism, and heterosexism reinforce the dehumanization of whole groups of people, who are then marked as fair game for death or exploitation. In the U.S., the Gulf War is still often referred to as a war with few casualties, which entirely ignores the hundred thousand Iraqi dead who apparently don't count. Attacking the World Trade Towers is a heinous crime, and nothing can justify such pain, death, and suffering. But somehow the pain, death, and suffering of the Afghani people don't impinge on the mainstream U.S. consciousness in the same way because that consciousness has been formed by systems that separate out people who are different from us and define them as lesser or subhuman.

OBSTACLES TO DIVERSITY

Pamela, a young African American woman in my affinity group, comes back from the Convergence Center at the A16 action in Washington, D.C., in distress. "It was weird," she says. "People wouldn't look at me."

Katrina, another African American woman, a longtime activist and organizer and a powerful healer, anchors our healing space in the Temporary Autonomous Zone in the midst of one of D.C.'s African American communities. "I had some great conversations with community people," she says. "But every time I got into a conversation, some young white activist would come up and try to get into the middle of it. Sometimes they made remarks that were so inappropriate that I was embarrassed."

Even in groups that define themselves as antiracist, that want to be welcoming to all people and to broaden their diversity, oppressive behavior still exists. The sexism, racism, homophobia, classism, etc. of the society we grow up in become embedded in our personalities. They lead us to respond to people who are different from us in ways that are often unconscious. They create blank spots where we literally cannot see our own behavior. Trying to examine and uproot those behaviors takes us out onto highly unstable emotional terrain, where shame, guilt, hatred, rage, and grief lie only shallowly buried.

Identity is a complex and uncomfortable question for most of us. Who am I? I was born a woman, a Jew, a white-skinned person whose ancestors obviously dallied in Northern latitudes for a long time. You could call me white, middle-class, and middle-aged. I have chosen to be an activist, an anarchist, a Witch, a writer, a gardener, and a lot of other things.

Each one of these terms I use to describe myself carries with it a load of history, everything from assumptions to entitlements to economic ramifications. They ground me, and yet also constrict me. They describe me, but only partially. If I let them define me, I feel diminished because I am much, much more complex than any of those terms suggest. Moreover, I know these identities both afford me privileges I didn't ask for and make me vulnerable.

They can be used against me, but if I ignore them or deny them, I collude in diminishing myself — because in that complex heritage there are also gifts, riches, and strengths.

When an aspect of my identity is defined by society as "less," I feel especially diminished. I must leave behind some part of me in order to assimilate and fit in — and that part of myself that I abandon may be exactly what I most need in order to challenge the system. That definition creates a wound which can never entirely heal until the conditions causing it change. It's a place where I'll always be sensitive.

When an aspect of my identity is defined as superior, or as the norm, the standard for human appearance or behavior, that definition creates a false picture of the groups defined as lesser. Behind the stereotype lies a void. I literally cannot see people of the target group, or cannot see them as whole persons separately from their identity as members of that group.

In trying to confront that unawareness, people behave badly in fairly predictable ways. Some members of the privileged group — men, white people, heterosexuals, upper-class people — will not see the problem, deny it when confronted, invalidate the perceptions and feelings of the target group, grow defensive, get angry, make predictable excuses and bad jokes, blame the victim, make token efforts at reform, and find new ways to continue the old, offensive behavior. Some will also feel ashamed and guilty — so guilty you can barely stand to be around them — and go overboard trying to please, become wannabee target group members, adopt the hairstyles, slang, foods, and holidays of the target group, and snub other members of their own group while attempting to curry favor with the target group.

Some members of the target group in turn will become defensive, attack people who don't deserve it, blame everything on the ism in question, refuse to see their own problematic behavior, take offense where none was intended, sulk, get quietly hurt and simply leave without confronting the issue, play the race/sex/class or whatever card, make self-righteous judgments, and feel entitled to insult members of the privileged group.

These behaviors often give rise to the following unhelpful syndromes:

The anguished ally syndrome. The person who is most devoted to being a good ally of oppressed people, who goes to the most antiracism workshops or most fanatically works on his or her own sexism, who reads, thinks, meditates, and lives and breathes support for the oppressed, is often the first person to say something offensive under the guise of being helpful. Excruciating self-consciousness mixed with guilt makes it impossible to simply act like a human being, meeting another human being whose color, gender, and ancestry are important but not delimiting factors in the complexity of who that person is. Maya, a character in my novel *Walking to Mercury*, falls victim to this syndrome during an unhappy period in her own life when, immersed in radical politics, she attempts to write a letter to her former best friend and lover who has just had a baby:

"'I hope you're not still mad at me. I'm certainly not mad at you. I guess I've learned a lot and I understand now how the racism of this unjust system has always divided us. I just want you to know that I'm devoting my life to work against the oppression of your people and other Third World people, like in Vietnam. I would like to be your ally in some way. Love, Maya J.'

"This letter did not satisfy her ... the problem was she could no longer simply write a letter from Maya J. to Johanna M., because she was too conscious of writing a letter from a White Person to a Black Person."

Johanna describes in her journal why she can't answer the letter:

"Really it's hard to know what to say to her. At first I was just going to tear the damn thing up. She made me mad! Maya, you asshole, I wanted to say, what have they done to you in Berkeley? Turned you into a pole-up-the-ass ideologue? Lord, how dreary. How dreadfully sad.

"Then I got mad all over again. Child, you talk about racism but this letter is the most racist I've ever known you to do ... Where the hell did I go for you? How did I turn from a person into an abstraction, a Black Person? Ain't I a woman? Aren't I still the girl whose kinky hair you nearly pulled out as we screamed together at the Beatles on the Ed Sullivan show? Didn't we once, twice, touch — heart to heart, hand to hand?"[21]

The Language Police. Part of changing the syndromes of domination is changing our language, learning new ways to think and speak about the issues. Some words need to be simply banished from the vocabulary of people of conscience, and many concepts and images need to be rethought. But often in groups, someone seems to be hovering like a praying mantis, rubbing their hands in anticipation of a mistake they can pounce on. I was once criticized, for example, for speaking of the "victims" of the Nazis — "victim" being a word that disempowers people. However, since I was talking at the time about the dead victims of the concentration camps, the favored term "survivors" didn't actually apply. The Language Police may be consciously or unconsciously trying to establish themselves as antiracist, but their efforts undermine the work of truly challenging oppression. A group in which people become reluctant to speak for fear of making some error in sensitivity becomes dreary and oppressive. Language can be challenged in ways that draw forth more creativity instead of shutting people down: "I wonder how our thinking would change if we used different metaphors, metaphors other than 'darkness' for 'evil' and 'light' for 'good'?" That way the focus can be kept on the larger goal of creating change.

Activist paralysis. After going to Mecca, Malcolm X underwent a spiritual and political transformation. He no longer identified white people per se as the enemy, but instead identified the racist system as such as the problem. He mentioned the young, blond woman so eager to be his ally and now wished he had given her a different answer, had encouraged her to work in her own community, "out on the battle lines where America's racism really is … among her fellow white."[22]

Many white people concerned with diversity have realized that our responsibility is not necessarily to recruit people of color into mostly white groups, but to raise the consciousness of the white community.

Over the years, thousands of activists have gone through workshops on diversity, on unlearning racism, on challenging white supremacy. Many, including me, have gained incredibly valuable insights and new perspectives.

But for a long time now, a disquieting observation has been whispered among trainers and organizers concerned with antiracism and diversity issues. The workshops, the consciousness raising, and the soul searching have not noticeably increased the racial diversity among many of the groups in question. What is worse, a certain percentage of the activists involved seem to come out paralyzed, unable to move forward in the work that they were doing.

Being in the group society defines as superior confers a certain sense of entitlement. One of those areas of unawareness in many men, white people, well-educated people, or middle-class and upper class people has to do with how entitled we might feel to speak, how important we think our perspectives are. In order to make space for the voices of women, people of color, working-class people, indigenous people, and people who have street wisdom rather than formal education, members of more privileged groups need to sometimes step back and shut up. It means not always assuming leadership, setting the group's agenda, or determining its priorities. And if groups want to include people of color and women, they need to include people at the level of leadership, not just as envelope stuffers or street troops.

But for some activists of conscience, these insights become a paralyzing inner dialogue: "If the issues that move us aren't attracting people of color, they must be the wrong issues. If our style of organizing isn't attracting people of color, we must be doing it wrong. We need to take leadership from people of color. If they aren't present to lead us, all we can do is figure out how to recruit them. If we go ahead and act, we're cutting out the possibility that we could bring more people of color into leadership."

But a group that defines its qualifications for leadership by color or gender alone becomes a fertile breeding ground for all the negative syndromes described above. A group that cannot set its own agenda, where people can't work on the issues that call to them or organize in the style that they find most empowering because they are trying to fulfill some other group's priorities, is not an empowering place to be.

The issues a group is moved to work on may not be the immediate priority for local communities of color, but they may still be vitally important issues. Local communities may be overwhelmed by sheer survival and local struggles and may not have energy to put into struggles around global trade agreements or financial institutions. Organizers of color may already be overwhelmed and overworked and not have time to attend new meetings or take on new issues. Or they may need longer lead times to mount long-term educational campaigns and not be able to respond to the urgency of the next scheduled summit.

But the global struggles are vitally important to people of all colors around the world, and to lay them aside would not be ultimately in the interests of any of the oppressed. We can frame local struggles in a global context and link global issues to the local campaigns that touch on immediate community needs. In fact, the local struggles reflect the impact of the global issues — they *are* neoliberal policy made manifest. Thus "privatization" becomes the closing of a local hospital, a WTO ruling on gasoline additives becomes increased cancer and asthma rates in a low-income community.

The direct action wing of the global justice movement is able to swiftly mount powerful, risky, confrontational actions in response to moves by the global power holders, actions that are vitally important. At the same time, we can build toward the long-term broadening of the movement by rooting our analysis and our organizing in local struggles, knowing that even if this work is successful, it may not immediately change the look of the next action.

NURTURING DIVERSITY

The global justice movement has to be a diverse thing, if only because the one great advantage we have in the fight against the greatest conglomeration of political, economic, and military power ever amassed on the planet is our human creativity, and we certainly can't afford to waste the talents and vision of any one of us, let alone of women, people of color, poor, and working people, who make up the vast majority of humans on the planet.

Understanding our recent history and the interconnections of the isms can help us see how to move forward. We can nurture the diversity that already exists within our movements, and expand it by consciously deciding how we frame the issues, by expanding our learning, by doing our own deep work, by making our groups and actions welcoming, and by building alliances and coalitions.

Framing the issues. The global corporate capitalist system impacts us in many different ways. For the more privileged, this may happen through the diminishment of space for alternatives, for a true public culture, for a real depth of inquiry and creativity. Or it may happen through the diminishment of wilderness, ecological diversity, or environmental health, or through the lessening of possibilities for a full, vibrant life.

But for the less privileged, the system hits full in the face with guns, bombs, torture, and the prison systems that maintain the authorities' control. Or it hits through starvation and disease. Environmental destruction may mean a literal loss of land through droughts or hurricanes or rising ocean levels, loss of a traditional seed source, a livelihood, a culture, and a heritage. The commandeering of resources may mean the destruction of ancient sacred lands and ways of life — in effect, genocide.

How we frame the issues affects who is inspired to work on them. The global justice movement needs to be loudly and clearly identified as antiracist and antisexist. Or, to get out of the "anti, anti, anti" syndrome, as a movement *for* economic, racial, and gender justice.

The global justice movement needs to draw the connections between economic hegemony and military hegemony. Indigenous peoples in their fights for sovereignty are in the forefront of the global justice struggle, and the movement in North America and in Europe needs to acknowledge their importance and be guided by their perspectives.

Expanding our learning. We can seek out works by people from backgrounds different from ours, learn the history that is not taught us in school, read the literature, learn the language, dance the dance. Oppressed groups necessarily learn a lot about the culture of the oppressors — otherwise they won't survive. People of privilege do not need to learn about the cultures of the oppressed in order to function. But if we want to build bridges and broaden our connections, we do need to make a conscious effort to expand our perspectives, and doing so will give us more ground for understanding and communicating.

Doing our own deep work. Issues of race, gender, and identity involve our core selves. To really change our groups and our unconscious behavior means to examine the construction of our selves in ways that go beyond political analysis and engage deeper powers of spirit and healing. Confronting our identity means coming to terms with our family — and all the pain and discomfort that may be present in our family history. It means looking at our own wounds and at the ways in which we have wounded others.

One of the powerful collective tools we have for doing such work is ritual. For many years, I've worked with a Multicultural Ritual Group that addressed many of these issues within Reclaiming, our spiritual/political community. In one of the rituals, we led people in a drum trance back across a bridge to the land of the ancestors. As people stepped out on the bridge, a chorus of voices cried out, "Stop!" We had to listen to the voices of the Unquiet Dead, those who told us, "I sold my sisters and brothers into slavery." "I loaded the Jews onto the cattle cars." "I raped." "Hear us, face us, embrace us," they cried. "We exist in every heritage, every bloodline. We are your ancestors, too."

As we proceeded, we were stopped by another group of voices: "I led my sisters and brothers into freedom." "I hid a family in my attic, at the risk of my life." "I taught my children our language." "Hear us, face us, embrace us," they cried. "We exist in every heritage, every bloodline. We are your ancestors, too."

In fact, there is no one alive whose ancestry includes only Pure Victims or Noble Hera/os of Resistance. Nor is there any group of Purely Evil Oppressors. Every one of us is born of both oppressors and oppressed. Facing those contradictions within ourselves, our families, our heritages is some of the beginning work we need to do to open up to more diversity in our communities. It is also the work we need to do to heal our own wounds and become whole human beings.

In the Multicultural Ritual Group, we found that the most powerful tool we had for holding our own contradictions and bridging our differences was to simply sit and tell our personal stories. As a group, telling our stories helped us bond and know each other.

Many political groups are not open to ritual. Sharing our stories does not have to be framed in a ritual context. The feminist movement of the late sixties and the seventies called it "consciousness raising." Out of the small groups that met to talk about our real life experiences, we developed the feminist agenda for organizing. A similar process could be an extremely valuable political tool today. Encouraging people to form small groups, to discuss not just race but their own real experiences of the economic and political realities, might move us beyond the barriers.

Making our political culture welcoming. Many years ago, a group of us from the Bay Area taught the first Witch Camp in Germany, an all-women's camp. I was the only Jew among us. I had worked in Germany before and knew that it was a deeply uncomfortable place for me, but I managed to put that unease aside until the day we were planning an ancestor ritual as the evening's work. Somehow we couldn't plan and couldn't plan and couldn't plan the ritual. Time wore on, until finally, ten minutes before the evening session was due to start we sat down to meditate together and ask why the work was so difficult. Suddenly the answer was clear to me: I didn't want to be there. I felt guilty, as if I were betraying my ancestors by consorting with the enemy, and I was in a state of frozen terror. We had never discussed the Holocaust; I had no idea if the women we were teaching ever thought about it or cared about it.

Once I acknowledged what was going on, we were able to do the ritual. But the real opening came the next day, during a camp discussion. One woman spoke about her difficulty reconciling her Christian heritage with Witchcraft. Suddenly, for me the circle was ringed with ghosts — the spirits of all the Jewish women who might have been there but had never been born because their mothers and grandmothers were killed in the Holocaust. I began to cry, and we began openly talking about the Holocaust for the first time.

Remembering that discussion, I can say that what helped me was hearing the German women acknowledge their own pain, the shame and guilt they felt for events they did not cause, hearing that yes, indeed, they struggled with these issues all the time, that some of them were involved in

Jewish/German dialogues, that there was one other Jew in that group of ninety. Then I could move from fear and victimization to compassion for the loss the German people suffer in being cut off from what is good in their heritage. I didn't need answers, comfort, or solutions from the women — indeed there are no answers to the pain of genocide. But I needed to know that the pain of my people was not forgotten or denied, and that the women were struggling with the questions.

I imagine a person of color coming into a political action might feel something of the same spectrum of emotions: Who are these people? Are they descendents of slave owners, land-grabbers, exploiters? Have they dealt with it? Are they safe to be around? Is there anyone like me here? Am I consorting with the enemy, betraying my own community? And can I make a difference here? Will I be listened to, will my viewpoint and experience be respected?

In fact, these are some of the very questions that may be brewing inside any newcomer in some form. We all come into a new group wondering, Who are these people? How do I know that I can trust them? Will they accept and understand my differences? Will I be welcome here? Will I be able to make a contribution?

Pamela might like to walk into the Convergence Center, and feel seen, as the warm, funny, brilliant, and beautiful woman she is, not just as a Black Woman, or as Validation On the Hoof. Katrina might like to be able to have a conversation with another black woman without it becoming a proving ground for white activists to show how nonracist and concerned they are. They might both like to feel that positions of responsibility and leadership are open to them, but not necessarily be burdened with providing direction for a group they haven't yet committed to. If the group vests them with trust and power, they might hope it's because their gifts and wisdom are recognized, not because a visible black face is needed to make the group look good.

Some of the conflicts that arise when we work multiculturally come from our underlying assumptions about what is respectful. In white culture, generally the way you show respect is to offer something, to do or say something. The underlying assumption is that you are a person of value, that your ideas and creativity have worth and that if you don't share them you are being stingy or withholding, that you are entitled to be heard. If there are rules, you'll be told what they are.

But in other cultures, including most indigenous cultures, the way to show respect is to shut up, to look and listen until you figure out what's going on. As an intelligent, observant person, you have the responsibility to figure out what the rules are, to notice what is and isn't being done, and not to do anything until you've discerned what's appropriate and what's not. No one will tell you — that would be an insult. Jumping in and offering your opinion or your story before you've worked out what's appropriate would be the height of arrogance.

When you enter a new group, especially a diverse group, it's wise to stop and look and listen before eagerly volunteering or pontificating. Notice how people interact, who speaks and who doesn't, how deference is expressed, what is and what is not being done or said.

The things we can do to make our groups and actions welcoming to people of color are mostly the same things we need to do to make them welcoming places to all people. In fact, most of them are simply good manners. Now I know that manners are not high on the anarcho-punk agenda, but if we want to build bridges across barriers of difference, if we want to show respect for others, there are some fairly simple, tried and true things that work:

Look people in the eye. (Of course, in some cultures, this is an insult, so sharpen your sensitivity to body language cues and notice if you are causing discomfort.) Smile. Greet people and make them feel welcome. Pay attention to everyone in a group or a conversation, not just to those you identify as most important. Give everyone a chance to speak. Give respectful attention to every person's ideas. Don't interrupt. Don't jump into other people's conversations unless you're invited. Sense other people's personal boundaries, and respect them.

Katrina taught me a simple exercise that can also be helpful in changing our group culture: Think of a group that has more social power or privilege than you do. Close your eyes and imagine walking into a meeting full of those people. It's on an issue that's important to you, and you have a viewpoint that you vitally want to be heard.

What would they have to do to make you feel welcome? To make you feel that your ideas could be heard and respected?

Open your eyes. Write those things down and share them with the group. Now do them for everyone who comes to your group.

There are many things we can do to make our events more diversity-friendly. But the most important thing we can do is to really be a community willing to openly struggle with these issues. We don't have to have answers, or achieve perfect political correctness. We've certainly made mistakes, and we will undoubtedly make more. But we can clearly and visibly be asking the questions.

Building alliances and coalitions. To diversify our movement, we need to be good allies of a broad range of diverse groups and peoples. Many low-income groups are necessarily focused on the immediate local issues that most directly impact their lives. When groups focused on the global picture adopt and support these issues, we not only expand our base but learn to address the real complexities of the global issues.

- Being a good ally means developing personal, not just political relationships. It means getting to know people in the fullness of who they are, going out for coffee or a beer, hanging out, inviting people to dinner, not just to meetings.
- Being a good ally means raising the issue of diversity in groups that are not yet thinking about it, noticing who is included and who is not, challenging policies or practices that result in de facto exclusion.
- Being a good ally means sharing resources, media attention, opportunities to speak and be heard.
- Being a good ally means interrupting oppression, challenging racist or sexist remarks, not leaving it up to the target group to always be the ones to defend themselves.
- Being a good ally means offering support for the issues and concerns of others, without abandoning your own.

In the end, the diversity of our movement will be reflected not so much in who turns up for any given meeting, but in the web of alliances we can build. ChuckO, one of the organizers of the Anti-Capitalist Convergence in Washington, D.C., expresses this view in an e-mail to the listserve:

"Liz, we've learned a few things about that diversity thing. There are a few people out there who are dissing the ACC — they say we are just a bunch of smelly, young white activists. If you look at the faces that come to ACC meetings, they are mostly white. But if anybody judges us on those terms, they are subscribing to the tokenistic methods that have characterized Left recruiting for years.

"What we've learned is the importance of creating relationships with *allies* in the community. These allies can include groups, organizations, institutions, issues, and even individuals. When you create a relationship with an ally, you are not asking them to contribute members to your group, which may have a bigger agenda that would overshadow their specific concerns. A relationship with a community ally is a more egalitarian one. The methods of nurturing this relationship vary, but sometimes they are as simple as providing resources and support for the community group's project. Sometimes this means having your meetings in a community institution, instead of at some local university.

"The Anti-Capitalist Convergence has been engaged in building these community relationships all summer. In a sense, this work has been one of the ACC's biggest successes. We've been doing lots of work on the D.C. General Hospital situation ..."

ChuckO goes on to describe the work the ACC has done on issues of local health care, on the closing of the major public hospital in D.C., and on local housing issues. Support for these issues included organizing rallies and marches, a hunger strike and lockdown at the hospital, recruiting a brilliant anarchist artist, Seth Tobocman, to do a flier for the hospital, and bringing people to public meetings and demonstrations.

When groups working on global justice issues are willing to bring their courage, commitment, and dedication to community struggles and can respect local leadership and issues, when white activists can do the hard work of self-education and transformation that leads to the sharing of power, when women activists and activists of color are willing to risk trust, we can begin to build those bridges that can cross barriers. When we identify the interlocking systems of oppression as our opponent, we can begin the work of true transformation that can liberate us all.

(I am especially indebted to Katrina Hopkins, Pamela Harris, Margo Adair, Bill Aal, and Chris Crass for their contribution to this chapter.)

CULTURAL APPROPRIATION

I n today's diverse and changing world, we can experience and learn from a multiplicity of cultures and spiritual traditions. Out of the encounters between East and West, the developed world and the indigenous world, out of the revisioning of history and the re-envisioning of the sacred that arose from the women's movement, new rituals and spiritual traditions have arisen and old ones have changed form. The edge where different systems meet is always fertile ground, in culture as well as in nature. But for that meeting ground to remain nurturing to all traditions, issues of entitlement and authenticity need to be addressed.

Cultural appropriation as a concept arose from the Native American and First Nations communities, who grew angry at people taking rituals, chants, myths, and sacred objects out of their context, diluting their meanings, and sometimes profiting off them or dishonestly claiming authority and expertise they hadn't earned. To too many European Americans, the traditions of Native Americans seemed sadly but safely dead, and therefore free for the taking. The cultural appropriation debate was a way the indigenous community could shout loudly, "Hey, WE'RE STILL HERE! We're not dead, we're alive and still practicing these traditions — and we, not you, will determine how they grow and develop and change. You took our land, you murdered millions of us, now keep your hands off our ceremonies! And besides, YOU DON'T KNOW WHAT YOU'RE DOING! You're taking the form without the culture, the acclaim without the accountability, the symbols without the knowledge behind them, and you're screwing them up. Go practice your own traditions — or create them, but hands off ours."

In Reclaiming, the community of people I work with who link earth-based spirituality to political activism, we were both looking for the earth-based roots in our own varied but mostly European heritages and creating new rituals. We were never claiming to be Indians or to be performing Indian ceremonies. Nevertheless, the Pagan community as a whole was for a time included in these charges. Pagan rituals and Native American ceremonies share enough similiarities — the concept of the circle, the four directions, the reverence for the earth — that it could easily look like we were trying to do Indian ceremonies and just not getting them quite right. But of course, we could not practice an earth-honoring tradition on Turtle Island without being shaped by and incorporating elements of the indigenous cultures.

Because Reclaiming folks tend to be sensitive, politically conscious people, we listened to what indigenous voices were saying. We put away our smudge sticks and purged our chants of anything questionable. We became more acutely aware of how our different cultural interpretations might cause pain or harm to others. As an example, in Reclaiming we have a long-standing tradition of writing parodies of our most sacred chants. It's part of what keeps us sane and humble. One time I had taught a group of students a chant I learned from Yoruba Priestess Luisah Teish, and later that day was horrified to hear them singing a not-very-nice parody of it. Had someone from her community heard it, it would not have sounded like loving self-mockery, but like racist trivialization of something sacred. A Hopi clown can ritually mock the ceremony he is part of — but were a stranger to jump in and do the same, it would be a hostile and destructive act. We can make fun of our own sacred symbols, but not of somebody else's — especially when we belong to a group that has historically been the oppressors and the somebody else has historically been the target of our oppression.

As the cultural appropriation debate spread to include other traditions, we in Reclaiming became more and more careful about what symbols we used and what deities we invoked. In practice, this meant that our rituals became whiter and whiter. The issue of what sacred powers, myths, and symbols we have the right to work with became very confusing. Does our entitlement depend on our ancestry? If so, then how do I as a Jew have the right to call on the Irish Goddess Brigid any more than the Pueblo Spider Woman? Am I limited to Asherah and Shekinah? Do I have the right to play the doumbec, the common Middle Eastern drum, because presumably somewhere back in the lost mists of time my ancestors came from the Middle East? Then what about Mary Ellen Donald, my drum teacher, who, to my knowledge, has not a drop of Middle Eastern blood in her body, but plays all the instruments better than I ever will. Must she be limited to the kettle drum or bodhran? Can I claim Freya because the Germans killed my people, or the Baba Yaga because presumably, somewhere in their sojourn in the Ukraine, at least one of my ancestors may have been raped by a Cossack?

In practice, we tended to feel entitled to anything European along with whatever we could claim some remote blood connection with. However, we Reclaiming teachers also do work in Europe — where actual Europeans tend to see themselves as German or Irish or Welsh and not something as generic as the new Euro currency. The women in our German Witch camp loved working with the Baba Yaga, but they didn't identify the story as representing their heritage; they were looking for German stories, and if they had found a story from North Germany, the Swabish and Bavarian women may not have identified it as theirs. At one English camp in Glastonbury, we worked with a Welsh story from maybe fifty miles away, and were constantly asked, "Why aren't you doing a story from here?"

Questions of entitlement can make us as obsessed with our ancestors as any keeper of the roster of the Daughters of the American Revolution. At a certain point, we have to stop ourselves and say, "Hey, is this the road we want to go on? Weren't we working for a world of freedom, where we could honor the ancestors but not be cut off because of our race or culture from realms of human knowledge or endeavor?"

In the midst of my own personal wrestling with these issues, I encountered an old, wise woman in trance who simply shook her head and said, "Forget about your ancestors, child, it's the children that I care about!"

As I write, three of my Goddess daughters are up in the loft giggling over the Harry Potter books. Their ancestry includes English, Irish, African, Jewish, Native American, and probably many others, but two of them look "white" and one looks "black." I know that in spite of all our efforts to eradicate racism, their lives will be shaped differently because of that fact.

I wish for Florence a world in which she will never for a moment see her skin color or the texture of her hair as anything but beautiful, where every opportunity she craves will be open to her, where prejudice, racism, and slavery will seem as incomprehensible and archaic as the metallurgy tools of a Bronze Age culture. I want her to know that she is the Goddess, and that the Goddess is black, brown, red, yellow, fat, thin, old, and young.

If I want to create that world for her, I need to make sure that she sees images of the Goddess that resemble her. I don't have the luxury to ask, "Do I have the authority to put African Goddess images in my home?" I need to have them, for her sake, and to know something about them if I am to fulfill my responsibilities to her.

But what about Allison and Lyra? I want them, too, to see themselves as the Goddess, as beautiful, as able to do anything they want. And I want them to know that the Goddess is also black, brown, red, thin, fat, old, and young, and that deity comes in all genders and forms. Is it not equally important that they grow up surrounded by a multiplicity of figures and images?

And is it not important for the grown-up children we are to also see a multiplicity of images of deity? First, so that we truly know that we are welcome in this community, whatever our heritage may be. But also so that we who live in a deeply divided, racist world, remind ourselves, again and again, in sacred space that deity comes in all colors and that all of us are valued.

How do we do this without falling back into superficiality and cultural appropriation? And without losing or diluting traditions and connections that are dear to us?

These are not simple questions, and I have no pat answers to give. But here are some guidelines we might begin with:

Be honest. Don't pretend to be what you're not or to speak with an authority you haven't been granted.

Make room. Make room for people to express their heritage, to sing in their own language, and to call on the deities and symbols they are deeply connected with.

Define ourselves differently. Or maybe refuse to define ourselves. The new spiritual traditions arising are like jazz or rock music, a synthesis of many influences.

Deepen our knowledge. Truly learn and study the traditions that call to us. Take lessons on that drum and learn about the rich musical heritage it comes from. Don't just pick a name out of a book — devote real time and effort to developing an in-depth knowledge of both a deity and its surrounding culture. Moreover, learn about the history and support the present-day struggles of the people.

Ask permission and give credit. This one isn't always easy because we don't always know who to ask permission from or who has the authority to speak for a tradition. But sometimes it's clear — if someone teaches you a song she or he wrote or tells you a story, ask permission to pass it on and give credit where credit is due.

Interrupt oppression. Speak out when you hear insensitive, racist, sexist, homophobic remarks. Don't put the burden to confront attacks on the target group. If a culture has fed you, defend it.

Give back. If we are fed by symbols, stories, or deities of a particular people, we have an obligation to give back something to that community and to participate in their real life, present-day struggles. This might mean doing political work, or supporting particular events, or teaching what you know in that community, or visiting a friend in the hospital and entertaining him with a tale from his own culture he doesn't know. It might mean giving back money: if you hit platinum with your recording of a Latvian folk song, you tithe back to that community.

In practice, because everything is interconnected, giving back also means working on the global economic, social, and environmental issues that affect us all.

Focus on the children. If we are nurtured and inspired by a tradition, we can worry less about who our ancestors are and start thinking of ourselves as the ancestors of the future, taking on responsibility for the lives and well-being of the children of that culture and for creating the world we want all the children to grow up in.

"Many Roads to Morning:"
Rethinking Nonviolence

In the ancient Scottish ballad "Thomas the Rhymer," True Thomas is stolen away by the Queen of Elfland who shows him a vision of three roads. The narrow, thorny road of righteousness leads to heaven. The broad, broad road leads to hell. But the third road, the green road, leads to Fair Elfland, the unexpected place that breaks through all the categories, the place of magic, poetry, and inspiration.

During the heated and oft-repeated discussions about violence and nonviolence that arise in the movement, I often think of that ballad. Nonviolence might be called the thorny road of righteousness. The broad road, the road of violence, sometimes seems the only alternative.

But neither violence nor classical nonviolence will win this struggle. To truly transform this system, we need to move beyond the violence/nonviolence dichotomy.

If, for a moment, we set aside the moral and spiritual reasons for why we might reject violence, we must realize that a strategy based on violence can't win simply because we are outclassed. The weaponry gap has increased a thousandfold since the days when the peasants of the French revolution rose up against their overlords or the Russian proletariat overthrew the Czar. Throwing rocks, even Molotov cocktails, against the heavily padded, armored, shielded, tear gas-wielding and rubber bullet-firing riot cops may feel like a strong act, but it is essentially symbolic more than effective in countering their violence.

Moreover, to organize in the way we would need to use violence effectively, we would have to become what we are fighting against. We would need a hierarchy, a chain of command, leaders, and troops. Armies have been organized in just this way for thousands of years because it is the most effective way to solve the problems of armed warfare: the sheer logistical problems of moving masses of people from point A to point B without the enemy knowing what you're doing, of co-ordinating attacks and elaborate strategies, of motivating people not just to fight, but to kill.

When a movement embraces armed struggle, it loses its ability to organize openly. There are many places in the world in which open organization is not an option, and armed struggle is already a daily reality. But in the U.S., Canada, Europe, in the privileged North, the base of support for violent revolution does not currently exist.

And after 9-11, the base of support for any kind of action is shaky. At the moment, the police look like heroes, and many of them did act heroically, giving their lives to help others escape the burning towers. Heavy confrontation, in this climate of fear and shock, is more likely to win support for the system than to galvanize opposition.

But beyond the strategic reasons listed above, there is a deeper reason for being extremely wary of violence as a political tool. If we wage this fight on the terms of violence, we risk a hardening of the spirit that will taint whatever world we create once we've won. We risk replacing one brutal system with another in which the most ruthless ultimately rise to power.

But classical nonviolence — the nonviolence of Gandhi and King as it has evolved over the last thirty years in North America in the anti-nuclear, post-Civil Rights, peace, environmental, and solidarity movements — is not capturing the imaginations of many of the more radical and dedicated activists, who challenge a lot of cherished assumptions and sacred icons of the movement. They are worth listening to because they are smart, committed, and courageous and because they provide the driving energy and radical edge of the movement for global justice.

Who are the challengers? Of course, they represent a broad range of age, experience, and political philosophy, but on the whole they tend to be young, to be aligned with antiauthoritarian and anarchist visions, and to challenge not just a particular trade agreement or unjust war, but the whole structure of capitalism itself. They mostly work outside of formal organizations. In North America, the groups they do form are direct action oriented. They include CLAC, the

Anti-Capitalist Convergence that came together for the Quebec City action in April of '01, and the ACC — the Anti-Capitalist Convergence formed in Washington, D.C., for the September '01 actions. And they don't advocate violence, but rather a diversity of tactics.

Diversity of tactics, in part, means flexibility, not being locked into strict guidelines. It means support for every group to make their own decisions about what to do tactically and strategically. It acknowledges the struggles of groups in the Third World, where armed struggle is a current reality. And at times, it means tacit support for property destruction or for clashes with the police that would generally not be supported by strictly nonviolent groups.

The more extreme tactics are generally identified with the much-maligned black bloc, the masked, black-clad bands that can cause both the police and the pacifists to tremble. They have perfected the art of looking like archetypal Anarchists: dressed in black, hooded, faces concealed, gas masks at the hip, they look dangerous and menacing — mindless violence personified. But in reality, they have clear principles for their actions, and most often consider themselves to be acting protectively toward other demonstrators.

An anonymous woman, calling herself Mary Black, explains her approach to action: "At demonstrations I attempt to use black bloc actions to protect nonviolent protesters or to draw police attention away from them. When this is not possible, I try to just stay out of the way of other protesters."

The black bloc is not a group or an organization, but a tactic, an approach to an action, that stresses group unity, mobility, and confrontation. The masks are, in part, a way of protecting activists who are possibly going to engage in illegal activity. But they may also be worn by those who simply want to express solidarity with other activists. The anonymity they embody is also a principle.

Here is Mary Black again: "The black bloc maintains an ideal of putting the group before the individual. We act as a group because safety is in numbers and more can be accomplished by a group than by individuals, but also because we do not believe in this struggle for the advancement of any one individual. We don't want stars or spokes-people. I think the anonymity of the black bloc is in part a response to the problems that young activists see when we look back at the Civil

Rights, antiwar, feminist and antinuclear movements. Dependence on charismatic leaders has not only led to infighting and hierarchy within the Left, but has given the FBI and police easy targets who, if killed or arrested, leave their movements without direction. Anarchists resist hierarchy and hope to create a movement that is difficult for police to infiltrate or destroy."

Generally speaking, the North American militants are more likely to consider themselves essentially nonviolent or to act in support of nonviolent demonstrators. In Europe, with its different history and political culture, militants more strongly support fighting the police as a political tool. Sven Glueckspilz, a German activist, reports on his experience of the militants in Genoa:

"The political goal of the militants was reached already on Friday. It had been proved that only by military force could a summit of the people in power be done and defended, and that the GNPO [global justice] movement has a strong militant option. An opposing movement only then has a chance of getting political strength when the people in power have to fear this option of militancy. No politician and no big banker will be impressed by five hundred thousand peace demonstrators as long as there is no doubt they are going to stay nonviolent all the time. Only the possibility of radicalization makes a movement dangerous and by that strong."

We could argue that hundreds of thousands of people in the streets do make a difference, even when they are entirely pacific. Daniel Ellsberg, former government official and later antiwar activist, tells the story of how the Fall '69 mobilizations against the Vietnam War made Nixon change his plans to use nuclear weapons against Hanoi and Haiphong because "there were too many people in the streets." The people in the streets, of course, never knew of their impact.

But no one who has marched, blockaded, vigiled, organized, and otherwise been politically active for decades can deny the sense of frustration and powerlessness that often follows a mobilization that receives little public attention and seems to have little impact. Mary Black describes why she sees property destruction as a viable tactic:

"I started my activist work during the Gulf War and learned early that sheer numbers of people at demonstrations are rarely enough to bring the media out. During the war I spent weeks organizing demonstrations against the war. In one case, thousands showed up to demonstrate. But again and again, the newspapers and television ignored us. It was a major contrast the first time I saw someone break a window at a demonstration and suddenly we were all on the six o'clock news.

"As a protest tactic, the usefulness of property destruction is limited but important. It brings the media to the scene and it sends a message that seemingly impervious corporations are not impervious. People at the protest, and those at home watching on TV, can see that a little brick, in the hands of a motivated individual, can break down a symbolic wall."[23]

When dissent is ignored, when peaceful protest seems ineffective, when critics of the system are marginalized and ignored, escalation of the level of conflict can seem like the only alternative.

The issue of property destruction is a complex one. What property, where, and in what context? The window of a corporate chain store, or of a local corner store? A police car, or a private car? A battered old VW, or a Mercedes? Tearing down a fence erected to contain protesters, or burning a bank? Strict pacifists have been known to hammer on the nose cones of missiles and pour blood on draft files.

How do we define "violence?" From twenty years of preparing people for direct action and facilitating discussions, I can tell you that no two people define "violence" and "nonviolence" in exactly the same way. Is it violent to attack inanimate objects? Who is responsible if attacks on property stimulate or justify police brutality against protesters?

When People's Global Action, an umbrella group that links global justice actions around the world, met in Bolivia in September of '01, they changed one of their hallmarks of unity from "PGA supports nonviolent direct action" to "PGA supports actions that maximize respect for life." "Nonviolence" meant too many different things. In Europe, it mostly meant not attacking people. In the U.S., it was often interpreted to mean not attacking property. In Chiapas, the Zapatista rebellion began as an armed struggle that attempted to minimize the use of violence, and then turned itself into a political struggle.

Nowhere can the lines between violence and nonviolence be drawn absolutely. My intention here is not to provide definitions and answers, but to outline a different framework in which to think about the questions. To do that, the full critique of nonviolence must be examined.

CRITIQUES OF NONVIOLENCE

Some critiques of nonviolence arise from misunderstandings or misrepresentations. Jaggi Singh, himself a strong proponent of a diversity of tactics, nevertheless takes issue with a black bloc recruiting poster that "shows a Gandhi figure getting run over by a D.C. cop's motorbike. The caption reads 'Gandhi is dead, because he didn't strike back! Support your local black bloc!'"

"You can disagree with King and civil rights pacifists of the 50s and 60s on many fronts, but they were our comrades, and they were for the most part courageous," Jaggi counters. "Cheney, Goodman and Schwerner, and hundreds of others, including Martin Luther King, are not dead because they 'didn't strike back,' but because of racism and white supremacy. Martin Luther King or Gandhi are not the problem, but the people who mystify them today. Pardon the history lesson, but Gandhi is not dead 'because he didn't strike back,' but because he was murdered by fascist Hindus. The political descendants of those same fascists are alive-and-well in today's India."[24]

If King and Gandhi died by violence, so did Malcolm X, Che Guevara, many of the Black Panthers, and thousands of other revolutionaries who waged armed struggles. Violence does not necessarily add to a revolutionary's life expectancy, and physical survival is not the measure of success of a movement.

Nonviolence is also accused of being safe, passive, middle-class. Poor and working class people and people of color, it is said, don't have the luxury of avoiding violence.

But nonviolence is not about avoiding violence; rather, it's the refusal to inflict violence. In reality, nonviolence has been the tool of choice of precisely those people who face overwhelming violence in their daily lives. King and Gandhi were both people of color, mobilizing their own communities. Organizing in the segregated South, the Southern Christian Leadership Conference chose to use nonviolence because any violent resistance would have immediately been suicidal.

Ward Churchill, in his influential essay *Pacifism as Pathology*, describes as pacifism "Jewish passivity in the face of genocide ... grounded in a profound desire for 'business as usual', the following of rules, the need to not accept reality or to act upon it."[25] Aside from being a distortion of the historical reality of Jewish resistance, this argument confuses compliance and nonaction with pacifism.

Pacifism is not passivity, nor does it mean avoiding violence or risk. "Nonviolence is a way of life for courageous people" was one of Martin Luther King's key points.[26] The essence of passive resistance is the refusal to obey unjust laws, the willingness to act and to risk, to disrupt business as usual, not through violence but through noncompliance. Pacifism also does not imply an unwillingness to defend oneself or one's family from a violent attack. Pacifism is the refusal to use violence for political ends.

Pacifism is a life philosophy, a deep, personal commitment. But many people who are not pacifists engage in nonviolence strategically.

Strategic nonviolence is definitely not passive. Gandhi's basic strategy was to stay on the offensive. The art of structuring a nonviolent campaign is to constantly create dilemmas for the opposition. As George Lakey describes it, "This form of direct action puts the power holders in a dilemma: if they allow us to go ahead and do what we intend to do, we accomplish something worthwhile related to our issue. If they repress us, they put themselves in a bad light, and the public is educated about our message."[27]

The lunch counter sit-ins practiced during the Civil Rights campaigns against segregation are a classic example of a tactic that creates a dilemma for the opposition. "If they were served, racism took a hit. If they were either attacked by civilians or arrested, racism also took a hit. The sit-inners didn't even need the signs they brought in order to make their point. The power holders were repeatedly put in a dilemma: whatever they did resulted in lost ground for the status quo," Lakey explains.[28]

Strategic nonviolence withdraws consent from the structures of oppression, refuses compliance, and eventually delegitimizes them. It involves not obedience but civil disobedience, the conscious and public breaking of an unjust law.

But it is also true that what nonviolence has become in practice is often something much less inspiring than the Civil Rights campaigns. Too often, nonviolence has come to mean stale, static tactics and orchestrated arrests, often prenegotiated with the police. Such actions may have their place: they can be a step into another level of risk for some people. But for those who challenge the authority of the police and the state, such actions are not deeply empowering.

Moreover, nonviolent actions are often characterized by strict guidelines that focus on telling people what not to do and on controlling the behavior of the activists. Monitors, marshals, or "peacekeepers" control the crowd, on the theory that "we have to police ourselves, or the police will do it for us." But those who question the very concept of policing and control in society are likely to resent the "movement police."

Part of the way nonviolence functions is by heightening the contrast between protesters and police, between the movement and the larger society. The violence inherent in the unjust social structure is dramatized and brought to light. The calm, pacific demonstrators are contrasted to the brutal police. Ideally, the protesters look enough like the general public that the public can identify with them. They appear to be good, noble people, who claim the moral high ground.

Again, in the Civil Rights movement the contrast was clear. The public saw brutal, racist cops beating neatly dressed, nonresistant, black youth and their white supporters.

But many of today's younger activists are not going to look like the Good Guys, no matter what they do. Their hair is in dreadlocks, their eyebrows, tongues, chins, and private parts are pierced, they're covered with spikes, studs, and tattoos, and their clothes are unwashed and torn. They've chosen the look to express their utter rejection of society as it stands, and they aren't going to change it for a demonstration. Even if they did, if one of them put on a suit and tie, he would simply look like an extremely uncomfortable shaved punk in a suit and tie. The look, the posture of rejection, is part of who they are at this point in their lives, and part of what gives them their strength, energy, and commitment as activists.

The Civil Rights movement drew a lot of its strength from the church. King and many of the leaders were ministers, and many of the activists drew on a deep religious faith. They could appeal to a public steeped in Christian values and predisposed to see martyrdom and sacrifice as admirable.

But the activists of today, especially the more radical anarchists, are not Christians. They are mostly devout secularists, raising the cry, "No

Gods, no masters!" Or they are active or intuitive Pagans, believing in the sacredness of the earth, of nature, of the erotic, with a sprinkling of other religions and spiritualities. A drama that echoes that of the noble Christian martyrs thrown to the lions is much harder to pull off when the suffering is being done by those who challenge traditional values rather than proclaim their adherence to God.

Certainly many Christians and other religious groups are deeply involved in the movement. Religious groups have staked out their own campaigns: the School of the Americas Watch, for example, is heavily supported by radical Catholics. Activists at the School of the Americas have built a strong movement in spite of heavy jail sentences for completely pacific demonstrations, to focus attention on the military school where the U.S. government trains torturers and state terrorists for Third World countries. In the anti-globalization movement, traditional religious groups have supported the marches for debt reduction of Jubilee 2000 and most of the legal protests, but, aside from the Pagans, not been a strongly visible presence in organizing the direct actions.

The Civil Rights movement in the South also had a broader audience to appeal to in the liberals of the rest of the country, who could distance themselves from the overt racism of the white segregationists and feel identified with a noble struggle for justice. When the Black Liberation movement moved north, and white liberals were challenged to look at the more subtle racism of their own communities, the moral drama was not so clearly delineated.

MORALITY PLAYS

In today's world, morality plays are harder to stage and tend to ring false and unconvincing. The activists, as I've noted, don't necessarily look like the good guys. The media tend to ignore peaceful protests or pick out the one moment of conflict or violence to highlight. And the public is less likely to view arrest numbers as evidence of commitment and dedication, and more likely to accept the police and media view that they are evidence of troublemakers needing to be corralled.

In fact, the classic dramas of nonviolence begin to seem as overly simplistic as the melodramas of the early silent screen. They play now to a post-modern world where the Right Wing attempts to frame issues in terms of clearly drawn lines between good and evil, and the work of progressives is to address complexities and ambiguities.

Moreover, they play to an audience that is less likely to see suffering and sacrifice as marks of character and worth. For people to stand quietly while being beaten, it helps to be motivated by a deep religious faith, a belief that the suffering itself has a transcendent value, or a belief that your act is about to accomplish something, that people will see it and be moved to your cause. You have to have, in the back of your mind, the thought that people seeing the video of your action or hearing about it will say to themselves, "What brave and noble and moral people — I should join their cause."

The act loses its appeal, however, if you suspect that what they will really be thinking is more along the lines of "That was a stupid thing to do — are they suicidal?" In a culture where profit has become the true God, self-sacrifice can seem incomprehensible rather than noble.

Critics of nonviolence also take issue with the self-righteousness of many advocates of pacifism. "Some of the most authoritarian people I've come across in activist circles are pacifists," Jaggi Singh says.[29]

To be fair, I've met plenty of authoritarian leftists and self-righteous advocates of militant revolution. But it is true that some of the staunchest adherents of nonviolence are often Not Real Fun People. They're too good. You want a little bit of the devil in a person — you want to think that they might sometimes get enraged, throw things, get so overcome with passion and fervor that they might do something really unwise and unstrategic. Overpowering goodness becomes insufferable.

When nonviolence becomes a morality play, the assumption is that "our goodness and suffering will attract people to our cause." The reality may be quite different. People who are angry at the system may not be attracted to a movement that suppresses rage. It may be that the "general public" can actually see themselves mirrored more in an angry protester who throws a rock at a cop than in an overly earnest figure who responds to every assault with an unearthly calm.

But anger and rage are not the only emotions left out of the morality play. Rowan, a nonviolence trainer I worked with in London, talked about the split between the "worthy" pacifists and the "sexy" anarchists. This worthy/sexy dichotomy may go deeper, may touch on the roots of the Gandhi/King formulation of nonviolent philosophy.

Does Gandhi's Sex Life Matter?

Gandhi and King were not the only influences on the development of movements grounded in nonviolence. In the United States and in England, Quakers have long been in the forefront of struggles for social justice. Their religious pacifism influenced the course of liberation movements from the antislavery campaigns of the 1800s to the antinuclear campaigns of the 1980s.

Women pioneered many of the tactics used by Gandhi and King. Alice Paul revitalized the suffrage movement in the U.S. when she brought back from England the tactics of direct action. In England, suffragists demanding women's right to vote chained themselves to lampposts and broke shop windows in an earlier version of the property-damage controversy. They filled the jails and went on hunger strikes, withstanding enormous suffering when they were forceably fed. In the U.S., women marched, chained themselves to the White House fence, and challenged President Wilson over the hypocrisy of fighting for democracy abroad while denying it to women at home.

Nevertheless, it is Gandhi and King who again and again are cited as the authors of the nonviolent philosophy, whose pictures are carried in demonstrations, whose works are quoted. Many pacifists call themselves Gandhians; I know of no one, not even any woman, who calls herself a Paulian or Pankhurstian or Ella Bakerian or Rosa Parksian. It may be a measure of the internalized sexism even among people in the movement that we still look to men as moral authorities and erase the contributions of women. But for that very reason, we need to examine their legends and legacies.

For Gandhi nonviolence was not just strategic, it was deeply moral, and it went far beyond eschewing violence. *Satyagraha*, truth force or soul force, was an energetic force that could only be marshaled by long and deep preparation, much as certain yogis employ special techniques and diets in order to command special powers. It was part of a way of life that required forms of self-discipline few of today's activists are interested in undertaking: most notably, giving up sex altogether. While no one I know of is proposing abstinence as a requirement for joining a direct action campaign, for Gandhi it was indispensable.[30] *Satyagraha* could not be mobilized without *brahmacharya*, a comprehensive self-discipline that included sexual abstinence. And not just abstinence outside of marriage. Gandhi actually went beyond the Pope in viewing even marital sex as a sign of lack of self-control. A man's progeny were living proof of his inability to control his lusts.

Satyagraha, for Gandhi, was also not about low-risk cross-the-line actions. He waged *satyagraha* campaigns infrequently, and each campaign required a pledge from his followers to be willing to die before giving up. Gandhi used all his moral authority and the weapons of guilt and shame on his followers to get them to live up to his ideals.

And Gandhi was no antiauthoritarian. He was a Mahatma, a religious leader in an authoritarian religious tradition that included a level of veneration and obedience unlikely to appeal to most of us today. His near deification by many pacifists lies firmly within that tradition. Jaggi Singh describes seeing "some protesters smugly [carrying] portraits of Gandhi above their heads. The portrait was accompanied by a quote that I can't exactly remember, but it was a Gandhian platitude about not following his personality, but his deeds." He notes "the irony of them holding the portraits while the quote exhorts the opposite kind of behavior ...".[31]

King was also a religious leader, a minister, functioning in a milieu in which ministers were venerated and strong leadership was expected. King held a deeply religious, Christian moral commitment to nonviolence. In the Birmingham campaign of 1963, the very first pledge required of activists was to meditate on the life of Jesus every day and to pray. Three of the ten pledges involved Christ.

But King was also a fallible mortal being who, we now know, carried on a long-standing secret extramarital affair. We can't begrudge him the comfort and solace he must have needed to sustain the tensions and dangers of his work. But we can point out that he follows the pattern of male spiritual and political leaders from New Age gurus to Jim Baker to Clinton, who publicly preach a strict sexual morality while privately indulging their own needs and desires.

Does Gandhi's sex life matter? Does King's? On the one hand, no, their flaws shouldn't undercut our respect for their philosophy, their courage, their real contributions to human liberation and political struggle.

But from a woman's point of view, from an anarchist viewpoint, and from the perspective of earth-based spirituality, yes, it does.

Gandhi's rejection of sexuality, of the body, leaves us firmly in the world view of patriarchy, split between body and spirit, venerating Gods that transcend the flesh, and suffering the inevitable degradation of those of us who bring that flesh into the world. That world view is a comfortable fit with Christianity as well (although certainly within both Christianity and Hinduism, strands can be found that do value nature, the erotic, and women).

The revolution we need to make includes a profound change in relationship to our experience of being a body. One of the insights of ecofeminism, the convergence of the feminist and ecology movements, is that our destruction of the environment is allowable because of the deep devaluation of nature and the body in the underlying religious and philosophical systems that shape our worldviews. And the devaluation of women — the violence, rape, and destruction perpetrated on female bodies around the globe — is also supported by the same philosophical and religious systems that identify women with nature and the body, and assign them both low value. The devaluing of the earth also supports the devaluing of indigenous peoples and cultures. Subcommandante Marcos, spokesperson for the Zapatistas who fight for the rights of the indigenous cultures of Mexico, consistently refers to his compañeros as "people the color of earth." Oppressed groups are also identified with sexuality, darkness, lowness, and "animal drives"; those associations are used to show that they "deserve" their state as slaves, servants, colonized people.

That essential mind/body split is the basis of all systems of domination, which function by splitting us off from a confidence in our inherent worth and by making integral parts of ourselves — our emotions, our sexuality, our desires — bad and wrong.

When we **are** bad, we deserve to be punished and controlled. Punishment systems lie at the root of violence. Marshall Rosenberg, a teacher of nonviolent communication, describes how violence is justified by the split between the deserving and undeserving: "You have to make violence enjoyable for domination systems to work ... You can get young people to enjoy cutting off the arms of other young people in Sierra Leone because of the thinking that you are giving people what they deserve. Those people supported that government. When you can really justify why people are bad, you can enjoy their suffering."[32] And so we see people who deplore the violence of the attacks on the World Trade Towers, who empathize and suffer with the victims, gleefully demanding that we bomb Afghanistan back to the stone age because the Afghanis have been defined as deserving of punishment.

As human beings, we always have a somewhat problematic relationship to our body. The body is the source of pleasure — it is life itself. But it is also the source of pain, need, discomfort, and deprivation, and ultimately it suffers death. A liberated world, a world that could come into balance with the natural systems that sustain life, a world that values women, must also value life, embodiment, physicality, flesh, sex.

NONVIOLENCE AND SUFFERING

Both King and Gandhi believed in the transcendent value of suffering. Now, a certain asceticism is helpful if you are asking people to risk physical discomfort, injury, imprisonment, or even death. A belief in the value of suffering is a useful thing to have when you are voluntarily putting yourself in a position in which you are likely to suffer.

But embracing suffering is problematic for women, who have always been taught to suffer and sacrifice for others. Conditioned to swallow our anger, to not strike back, we have not had a choice about accepting blows without retaliation. Nonviolence puts a high moral value on those behaviors, encourages men to practice them, and develops them as a political strategy. Yet women's empowerment involves acknowledging our anger, owning our rage, allowing ourselves to be powerful and dangerous as well as accommodating and understanding.

And from the perspective of an earth-based spirituality, which values pleasure, the erotic, the beauty and joy of this life, suffering is sometimes inevitable but never desirable. We can learn from it; if we are truly going to change the world, we probably can't avoid it — but we don't seek it or venerate it. Instead, we share it as much as possible through solidarity with each other.

One of Gandhi's strong principles was that we accept the suffering and the consequences of our actions, that we don't try to avoid or evade punishment but welcome it. That position creates a powerful sense of freedom and fearlessness. If we accept the inevitability of punishment, if part of the power of our action is to voluntarily go to jail, we move beyond fear and beyond the system's ability to use our fear to control us.

But often the way this principle plays out is that the focus becomes the arrest rather than the action. And few of us do what Gandhi would have done: demand the highest possible penalty for the action. If we did, our acceptance of the punishment would not have the same political impact it did for Gandhi.

Filling the jails can be a powerful political statement, and a jail witness can be an important political tool, inspiring and challenging others to take more risks. But when the jails have expanded to become a prison industrial complex hungry for more human fodder, a strategy of going to jail can also be seen as feeding the system rather than challenging it.

There's something to be said for doing a strong action and getting away with it. There's even more to be said for conceiving of an action that does not derive its impact from an arrest, but from what it actually is and does. And if we do choose an arrest strategy, let's do it for a purpose we've thought about and clearly defined, not just by default.

AUTHORITY AND VIRTUE

The underlying moralism in Gandhi's formulation of nonviolence is a subtle thread, but it encourages other moralisms that contribute to the worthy/sexy dichotomy. If we hold a punitive relationship to the body's needs, we assume a posture of internal violence toward the self that extends to other strong emotions and passions. And we become judgmental toward others, rigid in our thinking and viewpoints. Any behavior that does not fit our model is seen as "violent," and violent people are seen as deserving of punishment. So our very "nonviolence" puts us into an authoritarian, dominating mode.

Gandhi and King both exemplified religious authority and top-down styles of leadership. They were good, benevolent father figures (although how good they were to their own children is another issue), but dependence on any sort of father figure is not a route to empowerment for women, nor for anyone who wants to function as a liberated, full human being. Anti-authoritarians rightly criticize that model of leadership as keeping us all childlike, released from true responsibility for our lives.

Nonviolence does not have to be practiced in an authoritarian manner. The Quaker tradition of consensus and nonhierarchical organization is a counterbalancing force in nonviolent movements. The Quaker-influenced Movement for a New Society, which introduced affinity groups, consensus, and horizontal power structures to the antinuclear movement in the seventies and eighties, pioneered an open and empowering model of organizing.

But at times the Quaker influence in the nonviolence movement also contributed to the drift toward morality plays. Quaker pacifism involves a process of deep discernment, of constant self-questioning, of asking, "Are my actions in alignment with my values? Does my conscience allow me to participate in this act or comply with this procedure?" This process of deep self-examination imparts a clarity and purity to actions, and can serve as an important inner compass.

But if the main measure of an action's success becomes how closely it allows us to conform to our personal moral values, we can lose sight of whether or not it is actually effective. When our actions again and again are ignored or seem to have little immediate impact on the wrongs we protest, we can unconsciously give up hope of actually winning.

There are many different modes of a politics of despair. We usually associate that phrase with the secret, militant cells of the seventies that carried out political bombings and robberies in a last desperate hope that the extremity of their acts would spark a revolution. But it could equally be applied to those who act simply to be virtuous in the face of doom and lose sight of the possibility of victory. Such actions may be admirable and inspirational. But our time and attention can become focused on the minutia of moral choices in an action: Should I stand up or sit down when the police come? Should I walk with them or go limp? Should I voluntarily place my hand on the pad to be fingerprinted or make them pick it up and place it there? It's not that those questions shouldn't be asked, they can be valuable in helping us define our goals and limits. But when we don't go beyond them to ask, "What is the objective of this action? How does each of my choices further that objective?" then we undercut our chances of being effective. And they reinforce the system's focus on individuals as isolated actors instead of encouraging us to ask, "How do we collectively take power?"

DIALOGUE

"Nonviolence seeks to win friendship and understanding" was another of King's key principles, along with "Nonviolence seeks to defeat injustice, not people. Nonviolence chooses love instead of hate."[33] Each of these speaks of the importance of contesting a system as opposed to targeting individuals, of leaving people room to change. King did expect to win, and in part he chose nonviolence because he looked ahead to a time when segregation would be ended, when blacks and whites would need to live together peacefully. An armed struggle, even if successful, would have left a legacy of bitterness and renewed hate.

For King, negotiation was key to the success of a nonviolent direct action campaign, and one of its goals. As he wrote in his "Letter from a Birmingham Jail": "Nonviolent direct action seeks to create such a crisis and establish such creative tension that a community that has constantly refused to negotiate is forced to confront the issue … the purpose of the direct action is to create a situation so crisis-packed that it will inevitably open the door to negotiation."[34]

But extending the hand of friendship and dialogue can also undercut the effectiveness of an action. Institutions such as the IMF and the World Bank routinely use "dialogue" to establish their legitimacy, to make them look like they are open to criticism when in fact they are not. At times, negotiation can resolve a wrong and open a new direction. But such negotiations incorporate mechanisms for accountability on both sides. Sham dialogue, "win-win" solutions that do not redress real wrongs, can simply reinforce the power and legitimacy of the system.

Systems are maintained by individuals making choices, and to undermine those systems we ultimately need to win the support of individuals. Nonviolence encourages us to speak to the person, not the role, to hold out the hope of real communication even with an enemy. But winning friendship and understanding can be interpreted as "making nice," spending more time chatting up the prison guards than talking to your fellow activists, giving flowers to the police chief who has just made himself look good by "negotiating" a voluntary arrest while in the meantime protesters are being beaten and brutalized behind the scenes. Individuals in roles that serve certain structures behave very differently than they might outside of those roles. King was actually quite realistic about the possibility of changing the system by winning over individuals: "History is the long and tragic story of the fact that privileged groups seldom give up their privileges voluntarily. Individuals may see the moral light and give up their unjust posture, but ... groups are more immoral than individuals."[35] For individual change to result in systemic change, pressure must continue on the groups those individuals represent.

THE PRICE OF VIOLENCE

Nonviolence, at its worst, can indeed be a thorny road of righteousness, venerating martyrs, idealizing suffering, repressing real anger and passion in favor of a sugary sweet pseudo-niceness. But to end our critique here would be a shame because nonviolent direct action at its best can also be powerful, confrontational, courageous, and effective. If we can remove nonviolence from the domain of the morality play, we find insights and tools that are desperately needed.

For even before 9-11, the path of increasing militancy, confrontation, and police brutality was beginning to look more like the broad, broad road to hell. In Sven Glueckspilz's words:

"The price [of militancy] is the splitting within the movement ... The moderate and the radical wings are too far apart from each other, there is no way of doing their own thing side to side on the same streets. Militants are naive if they claim the possibility of reciprocal respect. Our militancy has very concrete effects on other ones. It is true that police encroachments happen even without street fighting. But it is also true that police violence increases heavily after street fighting and doesn't hit only the militants. Police take brutal revenge, often on spectators and the inexperienced (while the militants know best when to retreat)."

The tension between the pacific and the militant wings of the movement is, in some ways, what gives it its strength, edge, and staying power. But it can also be manipulated to tear the movement apart. Here is Sven again:

"The GNPO (global justice) movement can only then get stronger (or survive) if it stands this tension. Otherwise it will inevitably be split in a radical wing, going to be isolated, dragged down and smashed, and a reformistic wing, going to be fobbed off by lip services, corruption and lies. To stand the tension it is necessary that every faction has the chance to do its own actions. This also means that non-violent groups should have the possibility to demonstrate the way they want without being hindered by our militant actions and the following police actions. Militant actions, if organized, have to take care that other people are not affected seriously. If police attack, they should have no chance to blame us for it."[36]

How Systems of Violence Function

To hold that tension, to find our way to actions that can be empowering, effective, and survivable, we need to find that third road. And we need ways to restrain the violence of the system, which is potentially ruthless and lethal.

To understand how violence functions, we need to step out of a moral framework and look systemically at how systems of domination function. Such systems are characterized by the concentration of resources and the fruits of labor to benefit the few. They involve top-down decision-making: bosses who give orders and issue directives that others must obey. And they require a philosophical underpinning that accords some people more value than others.

I define "violence" as the capacity to inflict physical pain, harm, or death, the capacity to punish by restricting freedom and limiting choices, the capacity to withhold vital resources or rewards, and the capacity to inflict emotional and psychological damage, to shame and humiliate.

Systems of domination, no matter how powerful they seem, are unstable. They are inherently unsustainable, because to be sustainable any system or organism must be based on balanced, cycling flows of energy and resources.

Domination systems maintain themselves by the actual and threatened use of force and violence. They require enforcers willing to inflict violence. No gun shoots by itself — a human hand pulls the trigger, a human mind makes the choice to do so.

The use of force, however, is costly. No system of domination can afford to use force to control every aspect of its functioning. Instead, it engages our fear and our hope. We comply with its decrees because we fear punishment or retaliation if we resist. Or because we hope for some reward, some benefit. We might win the lottery, after all.

Systems of domination limit our imagination. They present us with restricted choices, and then make us believe that those are the only choices available.

Violence is unleashed by several factors. Dehumanization is key in encouraging and justifying violence. When we see our opponent as a category rather than a full human being, when she or he is defined as deserving of punishment, we lose our sense of restraint. This is how racism, sexism, homophobia, classism, etc. maintain systems of domination. People of color, punks, anarchists in dreadlocks, visibly poor people, all who fit a stereotype of prejudice are at greater physical and legal risk in an action as well as in daily life.

When we feel we are being attacked, when we perceive a threat to our well-being, we are more likely to strike first. A global strategy to counter our movement, even before 9-11, has been to portray us as threatening terrorists and the police as "saviors" of the people.

Other factors can also remove inhibitions to violence. Approval for an act of violence by figures of respect — teachers, church leaders, politicians — approval by the authorities, and the perception of the legitimacy of the act by the public make violence acceptable. A lack of potential witnesses or of repercussions loosens the web of restraint. Drugs, alcohol, and other substances that relieve inhibitions also remove restraints to violence. And group pressure can be a powerful force. Men who alone would never molest a woman can be pressured into joining a gang rape. Once a group consciousness sees brutality or atrocity as acceptable, it becomes easier for individuals to participate and harder to resist.

Nonviolent direct action, indeed, any action, depends on a subtle web of restraint to keep the violence of the system at bay. That web includes basic human empathy and reluctance to kill or harm. Many studies have shown that even in wartime, the average soldier must be specifically trained to overcome inhibitions against killing. Although some police are brutal, many are not, and some can be swayed even in the tension of an action to act humanely.

Fear of repercussions — personal, political, and legal — is another restraint on violence. So is the presence of witnesses and media. We often see the police using restraint on the street during the action, and then brutalizing and intimidating prisoners in jail where they cannot be seen. Public opinion, fear of censure, law, and the structures of accountability that are built into the system also can restrain abuses of power.

NONVIOLENCE AND SELF-DEFENSE

Militant activists often talk about the right to self-defence. They may be unwilling to agree to nonviolence guidelines, for example, because they wish to reserve the right to defend themselves against brutal police.

Again, there is no absolute line that separates self defence from aggressive violence. Is throwing a tear gas canister back into a line of police violence, or does that simply mean returning it to the people best equipped to withstand its toxic fumes? Is it violent to kick out at a cop who is attacking you with a billy club? To grab a comrade out of the police's grip and escape down an alley?

But a systemic understanding of violence tells us that real self-defense involves tightening the web of restraint. To understand whether a defensive move will work, we need to look at the entire context.

A helmet, for example, may provide physical protection against police clubs. But if a helmet makes a protester appear to be looking for trouble, it may loosen the web of restraint. A barricade is a barrier to a police charge, but if the police fear that attackers are sheltering behind it, it may actually increase the overall tension and danger.

In some actions, guidelines forbid the wearing of helmets or the building of barricades. But an empowering approach to an action would encourage people to make their own choices, rather than legislate their behavior. Situations change, and effective actions are often unscripted and unpredictable. I would once not have considered bringing a gas mask to an action; after Quebec City, it was tops on my wish list for a fiftieth birthday present.

In preparation for one action, a group called Masquerade creatively addressed the tension between self-protection and an increasing image of militarism by buying up hundreds of gas masks to decorate with rhinestones, sequins, and color. In their communique, they stated: "We at the Masquerade Project want to make sure that our sisters and brothers have the protection they need — and we also think it's time for an aesthetic intervention on the front lines of the movement for global justice. So we're organizing the D.C. Masquerade: raising money to buy and fabulously decorate hundreds of gas masks for free distribution at the IMF/World Bank protests in Washington.

"Black may be timelessly chic. But we long for more color, more élan. We believe our movements should reflect the world we want to create. And for us, that's a world with loads of color, sparkle, variety, and individual creativity ... Wearing a gas mask doesn't have to mean adopting a grim paramilitary uniform: Leave that to the police who will be defending the institutions of the global elite.

"We're using bright paints, rhinestones, sequins, glitter, and trim to transform the masks we'll be giving away into splendid and sassy creations."[37]

After 9-11, they donated the masks to the volunteer rescue workers at the World Trade Towers.

TIGHTENING THE WEB OF RESTRAINT

Identifying the web of restraint should not lead us to blame protesters for police violence. It does mean acknowledging that we can in many but not all circumstances have some impact on how the police behave. Police violence has been high since the very first morning in Seattle, escalating to the use of live ammunition against protesters in Goteburg, Papua New Guinea, Genoa, and Argentina. But even in the midst of the battle zones of Quebec City, Prague, or Genoa, demonstrators were at times able to de-escalate the level of conflict and win concessions from the police. And, at other times, police brutally beat and arrested completely nonviolent demonstrators.

We can also work to tighten the web of restraint long before the day of the action itself. We can do effective outreach and education so that the public understands the goals and tactics of our action. We can make alliances and build coalitions with groups that can increase public pressure and potential political repercussions for the authorities.

Legal actions and media campaigns can hold public officials accountable for past acts of violence. In the wake of 9-11, laws have been passed that remove restraints on police power. We can work to repeal those laws and we can contest their implementation in court. Group solidarity during and after actions can also assure that brutality costs the authorities politically.

WHAT IS DIRECT ACTION?

Along with restraining the violence of the state, to be effective we need to understand what direct action is and what it does. Direct action is not any particular tactic or activity, nor does it necessarily involve breaking a law. It's anything that directly confronts oppressive power, prevents a wrong or interferes with an unjust institution, or that directly provides for a need or offers an alternative. Feeding the hungry can be a direct action, as can providing clean needles for drug users to prevent the spread of AIDS or providing shelter for battered women. Blockading the WTO, disrupting the financial district to protest laws that target the poor, or Rosa Parks refusing to sit in the back of the bus — these are all examples of direct actions that interfere with or refuse to comply with a wrong. When direct action involves openly breaking an unjust law, it becomes civil disobedience.

Direct action is an important political tool, but like with any tool there are certain jobs it does especially well. It can be a powerful spotlight, illuminating problems or injustices that have been secret or unnoticed. It raises the social and political costs to those in power of continuing their practices. It can help build a movement; it can empower, radicalize, and educate people. And it ultimately can delegitimize an unjust system by withdrawing our consent and participation.

Of course, it can also polarize and antagonize people, raise the costs of activism, disempower, discourage, and terrify people who take part, and confuse everybody else. Like a crowbar, it's an extremely useful tool that can be destructive if used at the wrong moment or in the wrong way.

Direct action is a tool that needs to be used together with other tools, with a whole campaign that might include research, education, the building of organizations and coalitions, attempts to use the legislative or court systems to address a problem, negotiations, and symbolic actions.

Direct action can be used to pry apart the subtle ties holding the system together. Those who organize and who take the risks of action are the tip of the crowbar that inserts itself into a crack in the system. But the weight, the heft that pries the nails loose, is the larger base of support we've created.

Through direct action, we can destabilize the systems of control and undermine the mechanisms that maintain them. We can achieve this by doing the following:

Raising the costs. When we cease complying out of fear, we force the system to actually enforce its decrees. This is costly in terms of money, materials, and the undermining of public support. We force the system to reveal the underlying violence that supports it.

Undermining compliance. The police, the army, the prison guards are not generally of the class that actually benefits from the current economic and political system. When their willingness to serve as enforcers is undermined, the system falls. And their compliance in turn rests on the cooperation of masses of other people whose labor, creativity, and time are commandeered to serve the system.

Creating a crisis of legitimacy. Ultimately, unjust systems fall when they lose their legitimacy. When the overall tacit and overt support for a system is lost, it cannot stand. When people become hopeless about improving their condition, they can become despairing and apathetic. But when they are no longer invested in the status quo, they can also be moved to take action against it. When the system goes too far, it sows the seeds of its own collapse.

A CRISIS OF LEGITIMACY

If we define our strategy as aiming to create a crisis of legitimacy for the system, we take a step along that third road. We can also see more clearly the immense challenge that lies ahead of us in the wake of the 9-11 attacks.

People in fear are likely to run for the nearest shelter, for what seems familiar, safe, controlled — and that is generally the structures that support the status quo. So after 9-11 it has been extremely easy for governments to shore up their power, to institute restrictions to freedom that would have been unthinkable six months ago, and to implement key pieces of their agenda of hegemony. And it is enormously more difficult to delegitimize a system that people are clinging to for some small sense of security.

But the system carries within it its own instabilities. For nothing undermines the legitimacy of a system like failure. At the moment, ongoing anthrax scares are being used to keep people scared, distracted, and compliant. But in the long run, if the state is unable to assure people's basic security, it starts to lose its authority.

The attacks of 9-11 both coincided with and exacerbated an economic downturn. The downturn had to come because the prosperity of the Clinton years was based in part on false premises. Yes, technological innovations and the Internet did spur some real growth and productivity, but they set off a bubble of speculation that was entirely removed from reality and had to crash. And that was on top of an economic system that is inherently unsustainable because it is based on a premise of unlimited growth in a world of limited resources.

When the current economic system can no longer deliver the goods, when people no longer feel confidence in their economic future, the legitimacy of the system is also called into question. A smart progressive movement would begin now to build alternative structures, strengthen community, seek ways to provide true security, and develop alternatives ready to be put into place when parts of the current system crumble. Imagine if we had networks of self-managed enterprises that could absorb laid-off airline workers, for example.

A NEW ROAD

We can lovingly critique Gandhi and King, and still acknowledge the many valuable insights and aspects of their work along with their immense contributions, courage, and gifts. But it is time to move out of their shadow. They would be the first to agree that social movements need to constantly change and evolve.

We also need to move out of the other 19th-and 20th-century shadows: revolutionaries armed and unarmed, Great Men (and one or two women) and Great Books and Revolutionary Martyrs, Marx and Mao and Bakunin and all the rest of them. Again, all have made contributions we can learn from and acknowledge, but we cannot let them confine our thinking to their categories and assumptions.

We need to turn away from both the narrow, thorny road and the broad road and look for that hidden green path that leads somewhere else. To find it, we need a *satyagraha*, a truth force that speaks for the truth of the body as well as the soul, that does not assume a punitive relationship to the body's needs, that openly proclaims the inherent value of the body's drives and desires.

That form of action goes beyond the dichotomy of violence and nonviolence. The word "nonviolence" keeps us still thinking in terms of violence. For the moment, I'll speak of that third-road activism as empowered or empowering direct action, for it contains within it a critique of power. Here are ten principles upon which it might be based:

1. **Empowerment.** Empowering direct action aims to transform the structures of domination and control and to radically change the way power is conceived of and operates. We say that domination, control, and violence represent only one sort of power. But another type of power exists as well: power-from-within, empowerment, our ability to create, to imagine, to feel, to make choices. When we act together in an empowered way, we develop collective power. Through personal and collective empowerment, we can fight against, dismantle, and transform the systems of domination that perpetuate oppression. Empowerment implies courage. The more we can move beyond fear, the less control the system has over us. Courage can be found through individual faith — not necessarily in a God or religious tradition, but faith in human capacities for change or in nature's infinite creativity.

2. **Life, body, and connectedness.** Empowering direct action maximizes respect for life. We embrace life, the body and its needs and desires, our strong emotions and passions. We understand that all of life is interconnected and that empowerment arises from our connections to the web of life. Every act we take affects the whole. All systems of oppression are also interconnected. We might choose to focus on one issue at a given time, but we must ultimately dismantle the whole system of domination.

3. **Radical imagination and prefigurement.** Empowering direct action envisions and prefigures the world we want to create. We don't locate the revolution in some mythical future — we are the revolution, now. Our means must be consistent with our ends because the end is present in the moment, along with the begin-

ning and the sustaining middle. Our strategies, tactics, and organizations are the foundation of our new social structure. We value creativity, bringing art, music, dance, drums, magic, ritual, masks, puppets, drama, and song into action. We refuse to be boring, tedious, dreary, or doctrinaire. Instead we embody the joy of liberation. We refuse to accept the dominators' picture of the world. Instead, we dare to dream what has never been before, to think the unthinkable, and then to create it.

4. **Hope.** We replace the false hope of individual advancement offered by the system with a vision of a free, just, and abundant world. We embody that vision in how we organize, how we treat each other, in the symbols we choose and the actions we take. Part of our work as activists is to develop the skills, tools, and resources to make that vision real, and to make it so desirable, so inspiring, that the pale hopes the system offers cannot compare.

5. **Solidarity.** We know that the structures of domination cannot be undermined without risk. Through solidarity, we share the price of our resistance and attempt to mediate the violence of the systems of oppression. While we may incur suffering as a result of our actions, we don't embrace suffering for its own sake. Our goal is to alleviate suffering, and our solidarity extends to all who suffer under political and economic repression.

6. **Choice and intention.** Empowering direct action understands that every situation offers choices to be made. We do not let structures of force limit our choices, nor do we let fear control us. Instead, we know what our own true intention is and remain focused on it. We learn to stay centered in the midst of chaos and to retain our ability to make conscious choices in any situation. We pose new choices and craft dilemmas for our opponents. We learn how to de-escalate tension and potential conflict in order to expand our options in any situation. We fight against institutions, structures, and acts of domination, but we hold open the possibility that the individuals caught in those systems can change. We craft our strategies and tactics to make change easier for our opponents.

7. **Inclusiveness and diversity.** Empowering direct action values diversity and seeks to expand our movement and to increase opportunities for people of diverse backgrounds, needs, and life

situations to take part. We respect our own differences, needs, cultures, life circumstances, politics, and views as well as differences of gender, race, class, sexual orientation, age, physical challenges, and others. The patterns of oppression also exist within us and within our movement, and we are willing to transform ourselves as well as the structures we oppose.

8. **Direct democracy and horizontal organizing.** Empowering direct action creates ways of organizing and acting that allow all people involved to have a voice in decisions that affect them. We create the minimum structures necessary for our actions and organizations. Decisions are made from the bottom up, not from the top down. We encourage everyone to take leadership in the sense of stepping forth and proposing directions for the group, but we allow no one to direct or control the group.

9. **Dialogue.** Empowered people will not all think alike. Our movement contains a great diversity of ideas, visions, strategies, and principles. We honor these tensions and engage in ongoing discussion and dialogue to further our collective growth. We recognize that decisions made without adequate discussion will not hold.

10. **Freedom and passion.** Empowering direct action values passion, emotion, freedom, spontaneity, and surprise. We honor rage as a sane response to oppression and as a potential creative power. We embrace the erotic, the life of the body, the sensual, the earthy, the dark. We are willing to love deeply and fearlessly, and we fight not just against what we hate but also for what we love.

A DIFFERENT VOICE

Empowering direct action understands the power of language and symbols. We are conscious of what voice we speak in. There is a power and clarity in defining what we're against, but there is another sort of power in naming what we're for, what we want.

The voice of what Doris Lessing calls the "Self-Hater" — the shaming, blaming, judgmental voice of authority — cannot move people to freedom because it is the voice of our internalization of the systems of domination. We need to recognize it, on the Right and on the Left and when it echoes in our own minds, and avoid using it. Instead of telling people what not to do in an action, we clearly formulate our intentions and ask for support. Instead of blaming the middle class for its love of comfort and lack of revolutionary zeal, we need to undertake the much harder task of awakening our mall-prowling, SUV-driving compatriots to a possibility so liberatory that it will compensate for the loss of all that feels familiar and safe. If we want to move people to empowerment, we need to find a different voice, to speak in poetry, not in rhetoric or blame. We might listen to Subcommandante Marcos, trickster poet of the Zapatista insurgence:

> Indigenous brother, sister —
> Non-indigenous brother, sister:
> We are here to say that we are here. And when we say "we are here," we are also naming the other. Brother, sister, who is Mexican or not. With you we say "we are here" and we are here with you.
> Brother, sister, indigenous or not:
> We are a mirror. We are here to see and be seen, for you to see us, for you to see yourself, for the other to see himself in our image. We are here and we are a mirror. Not reality, just a reflection. Not light, but just reflected light. Not the road, but just a few steps. Not the guide, but just one of many paths which lead to the morning.[38]

An empowering direct action understands both the power of symbols and the need for confrontation. Every action tells a story, and we carefully craft the tale we want to tell. We steer away from the old tales of martyrdom and virtue. What we're saying is "Look! A new force is rising up in the world, so creative, so vital, so full of life and passion and freedom that no system of control can withstand it. And you can be a part of it. Yes, you'll face great risks and danger, but you will have friends with you, amazing, wonderful, mythical, magical comrades all around the globe. And you will be part of creating the most amazing transformation the world has ever seen."

We find every way we can to enact that story. At times, we may literally create the alternative: the medical clinic, the school, the garden. At times, we may stage a symbolic or real confrontation.

George Monbiot wrote in the *London Guardian* after Genoa:

> It is simply not true to say that Carlo Giuliani died in vain.
>
> By contrast to the hundreds of thousands of people who, like me, spent their working lives making polite representations, he was acknowledged by the eight men closeted in the ducal palace. They were forced, as never before, to defend themselves against the charge of illegitimacy.
>
> This discovery is hardly new. I have simply stumbled once more upon the fundamental political reality which all those of us who lead moderately comfortable lives tend occasionally to forget: that confrontation is an essential prerequisite for change.[39]

Empowering direct action looks for ways to embody our vision in the face of power, to get in the way of its workings, to interrupt its consolidation with our embodied alternatives. This requires great creativity. Symbols are powerful, and symbolic actions can also be effective. But empowering direct action aims at being more than symbolic; it looks for ways to interfere. with and delegitimize the operations of injustice.

For an action to be empowering, we need to know clearly what our intentions and objectives are, long-range and short-range. We choose our tactics to support our objectives.

Monbiot goes on to quote "the great Islamic activist Hamza Yusuf Hanson [who] distinguishes between two forms of political action. He defines the Arabic word 'hamas' as enthusiastic, but intelligent anger. 'Hamoq' means uncontrolled, stupid anger."

We honor anger, but attempt to act with intelligent rage that communicates a message and stays focused on our intention. We don't let our rage control us, but rather make conscious choices on how to use the tremendous source of energy it represents.

The movement has already been experimenting with new forms and formulations that may be the first steps along that path that leads to the morning. Reclaim the Streets throws a party in an intersection and takes back urban space. The fence at Quebec City is contested with a carnival: a catapult lobs teddy bears over the chain links. The White

Overalls create moving barricades of inner tubes and balloons, padding themselves up to walk through police lines. The Pagan Cluster moves as a Living River through the streets. The pink bloc dances through the tear gas of Genoa. The Zapatistas deplore the necessity of carrying arms and issue mystic communiques. Protestors snake march through the streets of Toronto, outflanking the police while avoiding clashes. Gas masks are covered with glitter and rhinestones.

All of these actions embody some of the principles outlined above. They change the categories and challenge our expectations. They favor mobility, surprise, and creativity over static, predictable tactics. They may involve the risk of arrest, but getting arrested is not the goal and protesters may actively seek to avoid it. They maximize respect for life in its fullness: erotic, angry, joyful, loving, wild, and free. And they are only the beginning of the experiment.

For we don't need to be limited to the thorny road nor to see the broad road to hell as the only alternative. Even the third road is only one of the many paths that, as Marcos says, lead to the morning. No matter how we stumble in the cold of the night, the sun must eventually illuminate a new way that we can walk with joy and courage in our bodies of earth and flesh and desire.

WHAT WE WANT:
ECONOMY AND STRATEGY
FOR THE END TIMES

What does the global justice movement want? What is our vision, our picture of an ideal society and economy? When we say "Another world is possible," what kind of a world are we talking about?

The global justice movement is diverse. It ranges from union leaders who want to secure a fair share of this economy for their members to old-line Marxists, to anarchists, to indigenous communities struggling to preserve their traditional lands and cultures. No one picture of the world can describe all the different viewpoints. No one vision may actually serve this tremendous diversity. And how could it? How could the aspirations of an urban office worker in Chicago be the same as that of a Mayan farmer in Chiapas? Why should we think that one form of economy or social organization should serve all?

Nevertheless, there are certain commonalities, deep principles and imperatives, that I believe are shared across the broad range of the movement. Here are nine points that attempt to define that common ground. Some branches of the movement might feel these principles don't go far enough; they envision a society transformed in more far-reaching ways. I am not trying to describe an ultimate ideal here, but to articulate what I see as the points of minimum agreement in the broader global justice movement.

1. We must protect the viability of the life-sustaining systems of the planet, which are everywhere under attack.

The current global corporate capitalist system is unsustainable. It is based on a premise of unending growth, in a world of finite resources. It produces enormous quantities of wastes, pollutants, and toxins, and depends on the common resources of air, water, and land to absorb them, thereby externalizing its true costs onto those who suffer from its impacts.

1. *We must protect the viability of the life-sustaining systems of the planet, which are everywhere under attack.*

2. *A realm of the sacred exists, of things too precious to be commodified, and must be respected.*

3. *Communities must control their own resources and destinies.*

4. *The rights and heritages of indigenous communities must be acknowledged and respected.*

5. *Enterprises must be rooted in communities and be responsible to communities and to future generations.*

6. *Opportunity for human beings to meet their needs and fulfill their dreams and aspirations should be open to all.*

7. *Labor deserves just compensation, security, and dignity.*

8. *The human community has a collective responsibility to assure the basic means of life, growth, and development for all its members.*

9. *Democracy means that all people have a voice in the decisions that affect them, including economic decisions.*

A system of sustainable abundance would mean that the true social and ecological costs of each product are accounted for rather than being externalized. Our first priority would be to end pollution at its source, not just to mitigate or clean it up. We would immediately begin a shift to the development and use of renewable resources and clean, renewable energy sources. We would protect biodiversity, habitat, and the diversity of ecosystems. We would ban potentially disastrous experiments such as the introduction of genetically engineered organisms. We would drastically reduce carbon emissions and attempt to forestall global warming. We would ban nuclear weapons.

These ideas may seem impractical or utopian, but in fact the technology already exists or is in development to do most of them. In their book *Natural Capitalism: Creating the Next Industrial Revolution,* Amory and Hunter Lovins and Paul Hawken discuss many examples of companies who have put these principles into practice and found them actually profitable even under the current system.

2. *A realm of the sacred exists, of things too precious to be commodified, and must be respected.*

"Sacred" may mean places that have special meaning to indigenous cultures or local communities, ecosystems such as old-growth forests so irreplaceable and beautiful that to exploit them is a desecration, aspects of culture and the human heritage that are vitally important to a society, and the basic life resources such as water that we all need to survive. This principle implies that there should be a limit to commerce, however it is organized, that Jesus had a point when he chased the moneylenders out of the temple, that a social and cultural space must be reserved outside the marketplace, however the market is organized.

3. *Communities must control their own resources and destinies.*

Both natural and human resources are best preserved and allocated by the communities where they are found. Outside ownership and exploitation do not lead to shared abundance. Communities can only be secure when they have control over their own food, water, energy sources, and other life support systems. Outside institutions such as the IMF and global trade agreements should not be allowed to dictate policies that override the democratic decisions made by communities.

Certainly not all communities are enlightened, and local communities are capable of exploiting their own resources in destructive ways. But communities also have a vested interest in the long-term health of their environment and the sustainability of their resources. Complex negotiations between the needs and rights of individuals, communities, and the larger society will always be necessary under any system that recognizes all levels of rights. If this principle were followed as part of a whole system defined by all these nine points, excesses would be kept in check.

4. *The rights and heritages of indigenous communities must be acknowledged and respected.*

Indigenous communities are nations with a right to sovereignty over their lands and the right to protect their cultures and traditions. International agreements among "nations" must include a voice for indigenous people; they must be on an equal footing with other nations.

5. *Enterprises must be rooted in communities and be responsible to communities and to future generations.*

The purpose of business, however it is organized and administered, is to serve the community. Businesses and enterprises need a specific community that they are accountable to; they need to be rooted in a place and must not be infinitely free to chase around the globe seeking the lowest labor prices and the most lax safety standards. Accountability extends to future generations: enterprises cannot liquidate their assets, clearcut their standing old growth, mine their soil, or exhaust their resources to satisfy a short-term need for profits. Businesses are responsible parts of a whole economic ecology that needs to last into the long-term future.

6. *Opportunity and support for human beings to meet their needs and fulfill their dreams and aspirations should be open to all.*

All forms of discrimination, all false privileges based on gender, race, class, age, ability, place of origin, sexual orientation, etc. should be abolished. This principle leads directly to a world of greater abundance, for we would no longer stifle the creativity and innovation of much of the human race.

7. *Labor deserves just compensation, security, and dignity.*

People who labor deserve to be paid enough to live with dignity, to enjoy safe working conditions, to have maximum control over their work lives, to be treated with respect, to enjoy job security, and to have security in case of illness or injury. Child labor, slave labor, and prison labor as well as pay standards below a living wage are unacceptable.

8. *The human community has a collective responsibility to assure the basic means of life, growth, and development for all its members.*

As a community, we bear a responsibility for each other. At times, disease, injury, emotional breakdown, or sheer bad luck may plague us all. We need to help each other bear our burdens and weather the rough passages in life, and to do so graciously not as charity but as an aspect of our human solidarity, in ways that respect and empower those in need. A strong public health system is part of our basic security. Public support for education determines the level of awareness of those citizens who will one day enact laws and elect representatives. A community is an organism — we must support its overall health and functioning if any part is to function well.

9. *Democracy means people having a voice in the decisions that affect them, including economic decisions.*

In a representative democracy, we have some voice in choosing who will make decisions for us. In a direct democracy, we have a voice in the actual decisions themselves. Of course, on the scale of a nation as large as the United States, a purely direct democracy would be impractical. But this principle implies that we attempt to organize on scales in which people can have a voice in many of the decisions that impact their lives, and that we extend the principle of democracy to some nontraditional areas. Most businesses are currently organized on a top-down decision-making model. Democratic enterprises would encourage input from all levels and would favor self-management, worker ownership, and community input.

DIFFERING ECONOMIC VISIONS

While I think the global justice movement does have areas of broad agreement as described above, the devil is in the details. We would undoubtedly have much disagreement on how best to implement them, on what an ideal system might look like.

Some, such as the Lovinses, Hawken, and Korten, favor a democratic or "mindful" market economy, relieved of the worst abuses of the current system, counting the true costs of what it produces. They maintain that the rewards for sustainability will be inherent in the system once we remove the supports for the current destructive practices. Hawken talks about a Restorative Economy, which would not only prevent further ecological abuses but encourage further earth-healing.

Michael Albert and Robin Hahnel's Participatory Economics identifies four qualities of a beneficent economic system: equity, solidarity, diversity, and participatory self-management. Albert and Hahnel picture a world in which labor is fairly rewarded and fairly distributed, where work is divided into balanced job complexes that combine the sorts of tasks by which people are traditionally empowered and the tasks by which they are not. Decisions are made not by the market but by democratic councils that determine needs and capacities, and people are rewarded for effort and sacrifice, not necessarily for talent or skill.[40]

Gen Vaughn's Gift Economy is perhaps the most truly radical. A feminist, she sees communication as gift-giving and exchange as an alienated form of communication. She reminds us that the gift of life nurturing mothers — and fathers — give to children is perhaps the basic economy of life. An economy modeled on the nurturing values that women have embodied might pose the ultimate challenge to patriarchal capitalism.

Bioregionalists favor local sustainability. Anarchists speak of networks of self-managed communities. And, of course, every type of Socialist preaches every variation on state support and control of some areas of production and private control of others.

Any of these systems could be adapted to the nine principles listed above. Again, in a diverse world we may need a spectrum of systems to fully fit each unique set of circumstances. And anyone who has ever tried to work collectively or to help run a cooperative enterprise knows that much experimentation will be needed to develop the skills and processes needed for a new form of social organization. Our visionary political efforts might best be directed not toward putting in place some preconceived system but toward creating the conditions in which that experimentation can begin.

The Role of the Economy

Drawing on the nine principles above, if we were to seek a commonly agreed-upon definition for what an economy should do, we might be able to agree on the following:

> *The job of the economy is to produce security and abundance for all, equably, efficiently, and sustainably, in a way that furthers human freedom and mutual solidarity, that strengthens our bond to place, and that protects the interests of future generations.*

Security means that people can look forward to maintaining a reasonable standard of comfort, health, and beauty in their lives, and do not have to fear for their families' survival.

Abundance means we value pleasure and beauty as well as survival. Abundance is more than survival; it means bread and roses, enough resources to allow us to indulge our creativity and curiosity, time for play as well as for work.

Equably does not mean that all people are rewarded exactly equally, but that all are fairly rewarded, that some forms of work are not overvalued while others are undervalued, that vast gaps in income and opportunity do not exist.

Efficiency, the watchword of the global power mongers, takes on a new meaning: the use of the least amount of nonrenewable energy and resources possible to do the job.

Sustainably means that our enterprises can continue on indefinitely because they are based on renewable energy and resources and the waste products they produce can become resources as well.

Solidarity means that we support each other through the vicissitudes of life and that no one has to bear the brunt of misfortune alone.

A name for this economic system might be *Restorative Economic Democracy. Restorative*, because its task is to heal the wounds and excesses left from our current system, to restore habitat, diversity, abundance, and hope. And *democracy*, to imply participation in decision-making at every level.

GENERATING ABUNDANCE

Any model we create must be based on real abundance, on the productivity of the natural and human resources involved. No one is eager to trade in this system for a life of privation and grim sacrifice under the control of the Commissars. But how do we generate abundance?

I'm not an economist, which may be an advantage. Hazel Henderson claims that economics is a form of brain damage. I am a gardener, and I attempt to garden in line with ecological principles, some of which are articulated in a system called "permaculture," developed by Bill Mollison and David Holmgren, that lays out some ground rules for applied ecological design. It may be that gardening and ecology have more to teach us about abundance than the current dysfunctional economic theories.

There are five basic ways to generate abundance:

1. **New inputs of energy.** In a sustainable system, the energy we use would be renewable, ultimately deriving from that free gift of solar energy that every day arrives on the planet. The sun drives the wind and the tides, sustains plant growth, and ultimately provides nearly all the energy in use on the planet. Oil and coal are the stored solar inputs of the past and are not renewable in any human time scale, so their use should be extremely costly.

2. **New inputs of materials and labor.** Again, in a sustainable system renewable and nontoxic materials would be favored; nonrenewables would become extremely expensive. Our current system replaces human labor and energy with oil-based energy; a sustainable system might reverse that trend and find empowering and productive ways to use the renewable resource of human labor.

3. **Recycling.** Abundance in natural systems does not depend on how much of a substance comes into the system, but on how many times it is used before it passes out. Human economies also thrive when every dollar that enters a local economy is cycled through many, many times before it leaves. Abundance can be created not necessarily by generating more cash but by finding ways to recirculate the money and the value it represents.

   In nature, waste is food. Every byproduct of a process becomes the source of some other process. Decay breeds fertility. We could design our production processes so that every part of a product either can be reused or reprocessed or can decay naturally into fertilizer.

4. **Creativity and innovation.** Creativity is perhaps our only unlimited resource. Creativity thrives in conditions of freedom, dignity, hope, and respect. Societies that oppress whole groups of people, that limit the opportunities of women or people of color or the poor, cut off their potential human resources and ultimately impoverish themselves.

   In nature, the edge where two systems meet is often the most creative place. The tide pools, where the ocean meets the land, teem with life and diversity. Of course, each system must be large and intact enough to function well. A forest that is so cut up it becomes all edge cannot provide viable habitat for many creatures.

In human society, the edge where different cultures, social systems, and worldviews meet is often an extremely creative edge. The cultural edge where African and European musical traditions meet, to take one example, generated jazz, blues, soul, rock & roll, rap, and hip hop. Cultural hegemony, the superceding of indigenous cultures and local traditions with one global McDonald's/shopping mall/superstore, destroys edge and diversity and undermines our potential for the creative innovations that could increase real abundance.

5. **Efficiency.** Efficiency really means doing more with less, as Buckminster Fuller said. If we can accomplish the same ends using less resources, we have freed them up to produce more abundance. Permaculturalists talk of "stacking functions" — making sure that every element of a system serves more than one function. So I might plant comfrey under my apple tree to keep the grass down, draw up nutrients from the soil, provide mulch, and give me a valuable healing herb. So, too, in an economic system, each element should fulfill more than one need. The city of Arcata, California, for example, treats its sewage by running it through designed wetlands, which not only process the sewage but also provide habitat for birds and animals as well as an area for local recreation and a tourist destination.

The old economic model is based on the image of the frontier: there is always somewhere new to go, there are always new sources of materials and energy to explore and exploit. But we have now come close to the end of those resources. The model of endless expansion is leading us to the cannibalization of the very systems that support life on earth.

But possibilities of expanded abundance still exist, even when we acknowledge the limitations on finding new sources of resources and materials in a finite and well-exploited world. A restorative economic democracy generates abundance by shifting to the use of the resources that renew themselves, such as the sun's energy, and by improving our efficiency, through conservation and better use of what we have. Recycling and recirculation of inputs are another source of abundance. And finally, human creativity and ingenuity are an unlimited resource when we provide the conditions in which they can flourish.

Security and Stability

Human beings also long for security, for the assurance that they can look forward to a benign future. No one wants to spend their old age penniless and homeless or see their children go hungry or lack opportunities. Responsible adults are assumed to base their economic and career decisions on their concern for security rather than on their wilder dreams and desires. Our current economic system does not meet that need. Jobs are no longer secure; the cost of living rises faster than wages. Real estate speculation drives up the price of homes and land, and the economically marginal are made homeless. A restorative economic democracy should meet our need for security.

In an ecosystem, security or long-term stability comes from the following:

- **Diversity.** Diversity gives a system resilience. A forest composed of many different kinds of trees will resist a pest better than a tree plantation of genetically identical cloned Douglas fir. Of course, diversity has limits: a mango won't grow in a Canadian maple grove. But a secure economy needs diversity. It cannot be based on only one source. Third World countries are often forced to depend on one major export; as a result, when world prices fall or a bad year reduces the harvest, they are devastated.

- **Redundancy.** Permaculturalists design more than one element to meet every need. So, if food is a need, we have more than one source in the garden. If the tomatoes fail, we can still eat squash. In an economy, we also need more than one source to provide income.

- **Balance.** The limiting factor in any system is that which is in shortest supply. A stable system remains within its limits. I plant my garden according to the small amount of water I know will be available in August, not according to how much I have on hand in the spring at the end of the winter rains. A stable system lives off the extra energy provided by the sun, it doesn't deplete its essential resources. It limits its growth and expansion to what can be fueled by that free solar energy. A stable system does not use more resources than it has.

- **Change.** "Stable" does not mean "static." Real stability is dynamic: it responds to changes in circumstance and returns to equilibrium. A truly stable system is open to change and provides ways in which changes can be integrated.

So a restorative economic democracy is not one huge monolithic structure, but a mosaic of interlocking systems that foster diversity, edge, and exchange.

PATTERN THINKING

The first principle of permaculture design is to use "thoughtful and protracted observation rather than thoughtless intervention." Another key principle is to think in terms of systems, to look at patterns rather than isolated objects, to design connections and flows rather than single elements. Putting these principles into practice requires a shift in our way of thinking. Instead of going out and digging up my meadow for a garden, I might wait, watch, notice the patterns of the sun and wind, notice what plants are already growing and thriving. Instead of eagerly perusing the garden catalogs and saying, "I want an Abraham Lincoln rose! I want a purple buddleia!" I have to think about what roles each will play in a system and what other functions they might serve. I might decide on a rugosa rose that needs no spraying and that will give me rose hips as well as flowers. I might plant the buddleia in a hedge to grow into a windbreak, feed the butterflies, and give me cut flowers, or I might decide a native shrub would serve me better. I'd be mentally juggling a dozen needs as well as my site's constraints, planning how I might move fertilizer in or, better yet, integrate a fertility-providing element into the system, how I might move the harvest out, where a pond might go, or a worm bed.

I would start small, planting one bed, continuing to watch and observe and experiment, to notice what flourishes and what dies. I'd think long and hard before I made a major change in the landscape. I'd include the garden in the design process, by listening to what it is communicating back to me.

DESIGNING AN ECONOMY

Could we approach the design of an economy the way a permaculturalists designs a garden? The World Bank, the IMF, the WTO, and the other institutions of globalization are essentially in the economy design business, but they proceed very differently. They start large, funding huge interventions with little or no input and often against strong opposition by the people most affected. They apply one economic model to all situations in spite of decades of evidence that it doesn't work toward the stated goals of reducing poverty and improving living standards in the Third World. They pay no attention to sustainability, to equity, to fostering human creativity among the oppressed, or to the other principles expressed above.

But what would it look like if they did? Let us imagine the World Bank, in a sudden shift of consciousness, decided to transform itself into the Bank for Restorative Economy, Agriculture, and Democracy, or BREAD. Their goal is to transform the stagnant and depressed small Third World country Impoveria into a thriving and hopeful place. In doing so, they will apply the principles above as well as some of the principles of ecological design.

They begin by instituting a process of community dialogue and *consultas* for free discussion of the goals and visions and needs of the Impoverians. Out of these community councils, representatives are chosen who will guide the economic design process.

Aiming to follow the permaculture design motto of "thoughtful and protracted observation rather than thoughtless intervention," the Design Council takes time for information gathering. What is thriving in the Impoverian economy? What resources exist, human and natural? What needs are not being filled? What things are in the wrong place? What connections could be made?

The Design Council decides to fund a series of small projects around the country rather than the massive hydroelectric dam favored by the previous incarnation of the bank. It institutes a microloan program modeled after the Grameen Banks of Pakistan, which make tiny loans to the poor and give support and education to help their enterprises thrive. They look for promising local initiatives to support.

Mountainous Impoveria, currently a desert after decades of war and drought, once had a thriving squii nut economy. The squii nut, grown for its oil, provides the shady habitat in which the sweet kulu berry thrives, and kulu wine is the Impoverian national drink. But many of the groves were cut down during the civil war that just passed.

And the costs of transportation have become so high that people working the groves that remain, in the far mountains, cannot afford to bring the nuts to market.

BREAD brings ten local youth to a training program where they learn to convert diesel trucks and buses to run on vegetable oil. BREAD also helps with the purchase of two buses and five used trucks. Back home, the youth form a cooperative and train others. They convert the used vehicles and run them on the slightly rancid squii nut oil that has piled up from previous years of unsold harvests. The prime oil is extracted from a first cold pressing of the nuts; for this year's harvest it is carefully bottled, trucked to market at virtually no expense, and the profits are invested in improvements to the press, new seedling trees, and kulu berry plantings. A second pressing extracts oil that is not used for cooking but is perfectly suited for truck fuel. As the plant and the transportation cooperative grow, the bus is used to transport workers to do cooperative planting, pruning, harvesting, and processing. Soon they are also producing kulu berry wine, much in demand in the capital, with Impoverians who have emigrated overseas, and with a small international market. (It's an acquired taste.) More labor is needed, and many of the local young people who had migrated to the capital in search of work are able to return home. As the groves expand, the trees conserve moisture and attract rain clouds, so the climate begins to be restored. The waste pulp of the squii and the kulu is returned to the fields as fertilizer, and rich crops of grain improve the quality of the local diet. Local people now grow vegetables and fruit for sale locally to the workers. A small guesthouse is opened where people from the dusty capital can come to relax in the fresh mountain air.

Similar small-scale projects all over Impoveria begin to transform the economy. Local communities begin to meet their own food and energy needs and to provide surpluses that can be sold outside Impoveria to bring in some foreign exchange. An Impoverian engineer makes a small but dramatic improvement to the squii press that can be transferred to olive and wine presses, and the Italians pay high royalties for it in foreign currency that can be used to seed a new training program in solar panel design and construction. The rise in income level measured in money is not huge, but the rise in the quality of life, in the levels of health, nutrition, education, and satisfaction happens so fast that after ten years Impoveria votes to officially change its name to Abundia.

This scenario is not difficult to imagine. It doesn't require the resources of the World Bank; much more modest resources would do. Similar projects are actually underway all over the globe. For them to succeed, aid and input from the institutions of international globalization would be helpful but they're not necessary. What is necessary is the removal of those institutions, the end of their current policies. If Impoveria has to devote all of its resources to paying off foreign debts, if it cannot provide for its own needs, invest in its own future, develop in its own mode, and set its own priorities, it cannot thrive.

In fact, a real-life version of Impoveria's transformation occurred in a small, experimental community called Gaviotas on the Columbian llanos, the remote interior plains. Setting out in the 1970s with the support of an enlightened government, its scientists and engineers developed solar panels that could function in a foggy climate, water pumps so efficient that children playing on seesaws could keep their school's water tank filled, and many amazing technological and social innovations. At one time, they were providing water pumps and simple technology to supply pure drinking water to over six hundred villages in their area. They ran a modern hospital that could provide culturally sensitive care for the indigenous community. Their story, told in Alan Weisman's book *Gaviotas: A Village to Reinvent the World*, demonstrates both the potential of an ecological approach to social transformation and the tragedy that ensues when war, drug trafficking, and, above all, the economic policies of privatization and militarization interfere.

HOW WILL THE TRANSFORMATION HAPPEN?

Let's assume we know at least the broad outlines of the kind of system we want. And let's also assume that we are working toward a situation in which we can end the worst abuses of the current system and open up room for experimentation and innovation. An enormous transition still needs to be made. How we imagine that transition, what we call it, and how we work toward it depends on how we see the current system.

Do we perceive the current global economic system as essentially benign and viable, a good ship that just needs a course correction? Do we want to toss out the current captain and crew and take over their jobs? Or do we perceive the ship as badly designed from the get-go, needing to be torn apart and rebuilt from hull to mast?

And do we see the current system as sustainable, as a sound ship speeding gracefully through open water? Or do we see it as unsustainable, an ocean liner churning full speed ahead blind through the icebergs?

Our answers to those questions — what we think will happen — will determine the strategies we adopt. Here are a few possible scenarios for the future:

BUSINESS AS USUAL

How will the transformation happen? Looked at with a cold, purely rational eye, the most likely scenario is that it won't — that the global authorities have already so consolidated power that at most all our efforts will force a few token reforms. The rich will continue getting richer, the poor poorer, and the chasm between them will grow, while environmental exploitation proceeds unchecked.

Of course, a truly rational eye, especially one trained to even the tiniest degree in ecological literacy, sees that this system is unsustainable. There are a few subtle hints around us — like the melting of the polar ice caps or the disappearance of most of the ocean's plankton, enough to indicate to sensitive souls that, yes, Virginia, the environment is real, it's not just something brought to us on the Discovery Channel. And it can only be pushed so far. For that matter, people can only be pushed so far — which brings us to another scenario.

THE TITANIC

At first this scenario looks much like Business as Usual. Those above decks keep dancing to the orchestra while the poor swelter and starve below, until we hit the iceberg of environmental and/or economic collapse (although nuclear war should never be discounted as a possible dramatic denouement). This collapse could be total: we so disturb the oxygen-generating balance of life on the planet that we can literally no longer breathe. Or it could be serious and irreversible in a thousand different ways that still leave room for survival.

As the Native American proverb says, "If we don't change our direction, we're going to wind up where we're headed." Unless we succeed in making major changes fast, this is where we're headed. It might be worth renting the movie, fast-forwarding through the love scenes, and noting how, in the end, the rich get the lifeboats. And then consider that when the ship is the earth, there ain't no rescue ship to take us away, nor any safe land to go to.

The less exciting version of this one could be called Gradual Attrition. Collapse could come not through one dramatic event, but through an ongoing slow leaking away of our capacity to sustain life and viable culture on the planet. Another name might be Frogpot — from the observation that a frog dumped into boiling water will jump out, but a frog in a pot of cool water that is gradually heated will stay in and get cooked.

Alas, many factors indicate that we are indeed trapped in some version of this scenario.

FASCIST TAKEOVER

Since 9-11, another scenario cannot help but present itself. If groups as ruthless as those who took down the World Trade Towers succeed in enough attacks, they could push us firmly into the arms of a consolidation of top-down power, whether of the right-wing state variety or of the terrorist groups themselves. Whatever brand of domination they represent, whether foreign or homegrown, that scenario does not bode well for women, for the earth, or for liberation in the world in general.

ENLIGHTENED EVOLUTION

Given that the crash into the iceberg is really not in anyone's best interests, those who hope for enlightened evolution believe that the system can be changed gradually through a combination of enlightened decisions by those in power and through pressure, guidance, and example, using our existing democratic systems. This model assumes that what is most important is to provide the alternatives, build the models, invent the new life-friendly technologies, and demonstrate that ecological sanity is actually more profitable. And it comes from the awareness that a major disruption of the system will cause major suffering — and, as always, that suffering will fall hardest on those with the least resources.

Much of the environmental movement, the bioremediationists, many of the bioregionalists, the "natural capitalism" folks, such as Hawken and the Lovinses, and many of the NGOs have at times espoused this scenario. And I have to admit that for me, a fifty-year-old woman who has seen a lot of revolutions fail to produce happy results, this would be the number one choice. It would cause the least amount of suffering to everyone involved, leave the smallest residue of hostility and resentment, and provide the smoothest transition. Slow evolution generally provides better and longer-lasting results than fast transitions and abrupt changes in direction — unless, of course, you are riding on the Titanic.

The heartbreaking thing about this model is that it could have worked. Had Clinton done what we originally elected him to do, had we left the Sandinistas alone, had the IMF not imposed structural adjustment on the Third World, had we kept tax credits for alternative energy, had we invested a fraction of the money spent on nuclear power on solar power, had we not overthrown Allende ... the "what ifs" go back and back. We could be a lot further along the road to a world of social justice and environmental sanity than we are. And it still could work, but all indications currently are that it is unlikely to be tried.

This model assumes that our democratic institutions are faltering but still functional. But recently we've had too many indications that they are not — the Bush coup being one wake-up call. Another is the response to the attacks of 9-11, the immediate, unquestioned call to arms, the restrictions of civil liberties, the devastating bombing of those who had no direct connection with the terrorists, and the cover-up of the underlying oil interests behind our policy. The level of violence directed against the global justice movement, from the first morning of the Seattle blockade to the over 4700 canisters of teargas fired in Quebec City to the murder and brutal beatings of protesters in Genoa is another indication. Rather than voluntarily embracing change, we now seem to have political and economic power holders who are intent on resisting it at all costs and silencing those who clamor for it.

The problem with changing the system from within is that systems — whether they are organisms, ecosystems, or corporations — try to maintain themselves. Individuals within the system may strive to do good, whole corporations may dedicate themselves to fair and green practices. But they still function within an overall system that is working to consolidate power and remove restraints on the worst abuses.

Systems do change, but they change in response to changing conditions, to stimuli coming from outside. Ice melts from the outside in. Our job is to create the external conditions that force change and shape those changes in the direction we want.

REVOLUTION

This is the model of sudden, convulsive change. The change may be long in preparation, but its impact is abrupt rather than gradual. Moreover, this model says that existing institutions are not functioning and must be replaced or radically revised. The Captain must be overthrown so we can turn the ship around. Or maybe we need a new ship altogether, built on a different plan — maybe one that doesn't have stifling steerage quarters in the hold and luxuries above.

Even in evolution, the evidence now shows that change is not a seamless, gradual process but one of sudden, dramatic shifts. Small incremental changes reach a tipping point.

Revolution can be violent or nonviolent, or the result of empowered action that negotiates new territory. The issue of how best to wage the struggle is a huge one, and because I have already addressed it in this book, I want to focus on other questions here.

There is more than one model of revolution. The old left version is to remove the current crew, generally by a revolt of the below-steerage passengers against the crew and the privileged dancers above, to take over their jobs and resources, and to assume control of the ship of state. Then, of course, reforms can be made and new courses can be set.

The critique of this approach to revolution is that it leaves unchanged the underlying architecture of the ship as well as the model where a few control the direction of the many. The Who song of the seventies comes to mind, with its refrain "Meet the new boss — same as the old boss!"

Unless you murder all the privileged, some will remain in virulent opposition to the new regime. And the massive massacre that is required to cleanse the new state of pernicious influences becomes an extremely nasty thing that undoes any movement toward true human liberation. The people willing to carry it out inevitably are more concerned with consolidating their power than with empowering others. The French revolution, the purges of Stalin, and the excesses of the Chinese Cultural Revolution are all examples.

Other models of revolution — anarchist, Zapatista, ecofeminist, and as yet unnamed — are more concerned with the basic structure of the ship than with who is at the wheel at any given moment. There are, of course, a number of challenges: How do you tear down the ship when you are riding on it and there's no place else to go? How do you mobilize the people below decks and feed their belief in the possibility of change? How do you reconcile the privileged to the loss of their special status? And perhaps even more of a challenge is to envision the blueprint of the new ship, and to imagine how we might construct it while swimming in cold water amongst the debris of the old, and the odd shark.

THE FUTURE IS NOW

Revolutionaries are fond of ideals and often work from some internal model of a realized society located in some distant future, when the state will wither away or when we will all live cooperatively with no need for control or violence. Magic teaches us that it is good to have an ideal, a vision. We can direct energy toward that vision without needing to foresee every step along the way. But a vision can also be an illusion, and the future has a way of receding and receding into never-never land. If we are too focused on an ideal future without grappling with the real present problems of moving toward it, then "revolution" becomes another word for "Heaven": the distant promise that makes up for a grim reality here on earth.

But what if this is it — what if that distant "then" is actually "now"? What if this is the future we've been waiting for, the end times, whether for good or ill? The apocalypse, as millions of Christians and Muslims believe. The deluge of the Hopi prophecies, the end of the Mayan calendar, or simply the limits of our ecological leeway for waste?

What if we ceased to locate the revolution in the future, and embraced it now? Revolution is what we are, not what we will become; what we do, not what we will do someday. An unfolding, evolving, enlivening experiment, something we continually reinvent as we go along, a living process happening now.

Rather than trying to envision the ultimate ideal and arguing about it, we could admit that there may indeed be many paths to the morning, to quote Subcommandante Marcos again. That there may be many viable and liberatory models of society and economies that might not all come from the same mold. That our task is to define "not the road, but just a few steps."

What those steps should be will still depend on how we see the current system: as desirable or undesirable, sustainable or unsustainable. If we see it as desirable and sustainable, we may want to fix its worst excesses or improve its functioning. If we see it as desirable but unsustainable, we need to change its course immediately. If we see it as undesirable but sustainable, we need to bring it down.

My own position is that the system is both undesirable and unsustainable, and the strategy I want to explore begins from that premise. The questions that arise are these: "How soon will the crash come? Do we wait for it, work to prevent it, or help it along?"

The argument for preventing the crash or at least mitigating its effects would be that the crash falls hardest on those who have least resources.

The argument for speeding it up would be to make the system fall while there is still some ecology left to save.

In the movie *Titanic*, there's a scene after the ship has hit the iceberg where the chief engineer, the captain, and the officers review the blueprints. The ship is designed to stay afloat if four bulkheads have been breached. But five have been breached. The ship will sink.

However much we might want to tear the ship apart and rebuild it on a new plan, we must first deflect its present course at least enough that we don't breach all five bulkheads. For if the ship sinks, we all sink with it, reformists, revolutionaries, and reactionaries alike.

And we might also think in terms of lifeboats, think about what we can put into place to help sustain us through the crash and give us a base for rebuilding.

The life-sustaining system of true freedom and abundance will not come from slapping down a new, fully formed model to replace the current one, but from a process of experimentation and evolution and development. So rather than asking, "What is the new ideal and how do we put it into place," we might ask, "How can we best create conditions and open up spaces where that experimentation can take place? How do we buy time for it to unfold?"

Of course, much experimentation is already happening, has been happening for decades. Alternatives in everything from organizational models, governance, agriculture, energy sources, healing models, and spiritual practices to waste treatment abound. Our task now is to move them out of the margins so that they pose a living challenge to the ethos of oil dependency and top-down control.

The role of confrontation is to create the external conditions that cause change, and the role of alternative-building is to set the direction of that change. We deflect the ship by contesting its current course and shining a light on the looming iceberg. We dismantle its architecture by delegitimizing the structures that uphold it. We support the aspirations of those in steerage who dare to dream of a different ship. We provide alternative models of how that ship might be configured, how space and resources might be allocated, and how decisions about its course might be made.

The Movement as Ecosystem

Radicals often spend much time and energy arguing with each other over what the correct form and aim of struggle should be, who we should associate with, whether we are being co-opted by mere middle-class reformists or led astray by impractical extremists, what lessons we should take from the past. Revolution is not an exact science: we can learn from the past, but we can't rerun any given action or insurgency in a different mode as we could a laboratory experiment. We inevitably draw different lessons from the same events.

But if we were to apply some of the principles of permaculture to the design of the movement, we might see that a movement is like an ecosystem. It needs the full spectrum of diversity. It needs white-haired women in wheelchairs singing "Where have all the flowers gone" and it needs black-clad masked youth calling for class war. Revolutionaries and reformists fill different niches. Unless the niches of reform are filled, revolutionaries can't exist, can't mobilize a base of support for broader and more radical change. And unless there is some group willing to push the edge of the comfort zone, willing to engage the system at a higher level of confrontation, the reformists have no clout.

And we might see that reform and revolution march along together for quite a while yet. For however we value or critique that ship, our immediate task is to change its course and prevent, if we can, a crash so devastating that the life systems of the earth will be irreparably damaged.

To do that, we must

- prevent the extension and consolidation of power by the globalizers,
- contest new treaties and trade agreements, laws, policies and practices that extend corporate control,
- delegitimize and dismantle the current institutions, and
- introduce alternatives on whatever scale we can.

In these efforts, both reformists and revolutionaries have important roles. The NGOs, the academics, the writers, thinkers, analysts, and lobbyists can mount cogent arguments against current policies, influence legislation, provide the research that is the basis for the movement to formulate its positions, engage in high-level dialogue, and, at times, succeed in winning reforms that actually mitigate suffering and lessen the damage of the system.

The radicals can mount direct actions that spotlight the system's abuses, attack the legitimacy of its institutions, interfere with its ability to do business, and provide living examples of alternative ways of organizing.

The creators of alternatives can find ways to make their experiments more visible and more known and to push for their adoption on a larger scale.

And we might all shift roles from time to time. The work of creating the alternatives is satisfying and soul-nourishing. The work of contesting the current structure is sometimes exciting, but often hard, grueling, and dangerous. Radicals can have their spirit renewed by working on alternatives. Researchers and academics can be energized and radicalized by occasionally taking to the streets.

The permacultural art, of course, is to make our every action serve more than one function. Our organizing a direct action to interfere with a summit meeting can itself be a model of an alternative form of governance. We can seek for ways to let our positive alternatives undermine the legitimacy of the current ways of doing things. An encampment for an action could be a model of ecological design. Every successful solar installation is an argument against the need for oil dependency.

Much debate goes on in the movement about whether to focus our efforts globally or locally. We need to do both. The global institutions can most effectively be countered on a global scale, with international coordination and solidarity. But on a local scale, alternatives are much easier to implement. By their very nature, the alternatives that lead to a restorative economic democracy will be small-scale and rooted in community.

There's a story about an organizer who was widely known for being effective and getting things done. One day a student asked him how he was able to accomplish so much. He smiled and said, "I just do the easy things first."

There are relatively easy changes that can be made within the existing system that will alleviate some suffering or solve a problem, and they should be made. An anarchist slogan speaks of "building the new society in the vacant lots of the old." We can look for spaces within the current structure in which to craft lifeboats — the alternative structures that can meet basic needs in new ways — and to try out new ways of doing things, which can provide us a base from which to organize a larger social transformation.

Today, as I write, San Francisco has just voted to fund municipal bonds for solar power and almost voted to take our utilities back from the private corporation that has brought us financing crises and rolling blackouts. Sebastopol, near my home in Sonoma County, has a Green City Council and Mayor. Through a process called Sustainable Sonoma, citizens meet in small groups to envision an ecologically balanced future for the city.[41]

The city of Porto Alegre, in Brazil, uses a participatory budget process where citizen councils take part in setting priorities and deciding on spending.

A campaign is currently being waged to get cities and counties to voluntarily sign on to the Kyoto treaty and to reduce their emissions, regardless of Bush's policies.[42]

In our area, Watershed Councils have been formed for most of the major rivers to bring together stakeholders from across political boundaries — environmentalists with loggers and gravel miners, farmers with residents — to work out issues affecting the health of the watershed.

The Movimiento Sim Terre in Brazil occupies unused land and forms settlements of the very poorest displaced people that embody ecological sensitivity and real abundance.

Local currencies can provide a mechanism for recirculating money and value within a local community and for nurturing local enterprises. Community land trusts can take property out of the speculative market. Alliances between city activists and farmers can begin to create "food-sheds" for food security. Cooperative and collective structures can be tried out and new practices developed. And many, many other creative alternatives already exist. We can seek them out, learn from them, organize around them, make them real. The technology already exists to make the transformation.

Our problems are not insurmountable — solutions already exist to most of our major ecological problems. Now we need the political will and power to put those solutions into place in a just and equable way.

To make those changes, we need a change in our way of thinking. We need to learn to see patterns, to think in terms of flows and connections rather than isolated objects, to plan for and design the connections rather than focus on the things they connect. This sounds simple but it is actually quite difficult to practice even on the scale of a garden, let alone the world. But we need to do it. It is the direction of our cultural evolution, and it will give us the perspective we need to see not only where we want to go, but how to get there.

And so the revolution unfolds. We don't have to wait for it, we can be it, live it now. Another world is possible, and necessary, and here. We are its co-creators, its dreamers, its defenders, its midwives, guiding it to light, bringing it to birth.

Spirit and Action

> *"We the indigenous are not part of yesterday;*
> *we are part of tomorrow."*
> — Subcommandante Marcos

For thirty years and more, I've been walking that edge where the spiritual meets the political. For me, the two have always been integrated. My spirituality is rooted in the experience of the earth as a living, conscious being, and names this world, nature, human life, sexuality, and culture as sacred. And so I feel compelled to take action to protect the earth and to work for a world in which human freedom and creativity can flourish.

The edge where two systems meet can be a place of great fertility in nature. But edges and borders can also be sites of enormous conflict. Spirituality can bring life and vibrancy and imagination into activism — but the mixture of religion and politics can also fuel the most extreme and destructive acts and lead to systems of great repression. Shouldn't progressive people rightly be wary of mixing the two? Of letting go of a sound, rational basis for our actions?

We should be rightly suspicious of religion when it means a belief system, a dogma, a set of standards for determining who are the Worthy People and who are the Others. The root meaning of the word "re-ligio" — "relinking" has more to do with connection than with discrimination. Still, it's far too formal and systematic to convey what I'm talking about. Language is always a problem, because the English language doesn't have the word I want, a word that doesn't split "spirit" from "matter" or "nature" but integrates the sacred and the mundane, the high and the low, the dark and the light — a word that conveys the sense of living in an animate and generous universe. I am left with the word "spirit" or "spirituality" by default.

The type of spirituality I embrace is one that encourages us each to have our own relationship with the greater creative powers, that teaches us not what we should believe but how we can learn to listen, that sees spirit embodied in nature, and that honors the body, the earth, and the everyday. While we draw from the past and respect the wisdom of the ancestors, we are not trying to live in yesterday or abandon the post-modern world, but rather to find those practices and modes of awareness that can lead us into a viable future.

In some places, among indigenous people or among my neighbors in the Northern California hills, the integration of the spiritual and the political is understood and expected. In other areas, in Europe with its history of disastrous Nazi meldings of the two, among hard-core mil-itants or Marxist intellectuals, linking the two may seem like a strange and dangerous idea.

Why bring ritual, magic, spirituality into action? Why mix up a clear, clean militant critique of the world with woo-woo, mumbo-jumbo, New Age fluffy stuff?

The first reason is that a part of our humanity needs symbols and myth and mystery, yearns for a connection to something broader and deeper than our surface life. That part of us is powerful and dangerous: it can call us to the most profound compassion or justify the worst intolerance, lead us to sacrifice for the greater good or to commit mass murder in the name of our ideals, open us to a wider experience of life or imprison us in a narrow moralism, inspire our liberation or function as an agent of our repression. Progressive movements are understand-ably wary of it, for we have all seen the religious impulse fuel hatred and holy wars and justify extreme oppression. But we ignore it at our peril, for if a movement of liberation does not address the spiritual part of us, then movements of repression will claim that terrain as their own.

The events of 9-11 showed us how deep our need for expression and communal connection in moments of deep pain really is. When normality is shattered, when we face death and loss, when we encounter great fear or great hope as we do in activism, we need some framework within which to find meaning in our experiences.

Fundamentalisms of all sorts, whether religious or political or academic, appeal because they provide a coherent system of meaning. We need alternative ways of thinking, feeling, and understanding that lead to tolerance, compassion, and freedom. And we need to express them in ritual as well as in rhetoric if they are to touch the aching wounds of the soul.

The struggles of indigenous peoples are in many ways the soul and inspiration of the global justice movement. To really understand those struggles, to truly support them, we who are not indigenous must at least be able to imagine what it is like to live in a bonded relationship to place, in a deep integration with the land, the plant and animal life, the wind and sun and seasons, the spirits and the ancestors and the powers that go beyond the rational. The expression of that integration in myth and story and ceremony is what sustains and nourishes a culture and a people.

The experience of the women's liberation movement taught us that to change something as deep as our experience of gender meant challenging all the symbols and icons of the culture, including the religious symbols. In the words of feminist thea-logian Carol Christ, "Symbol systems cannot simply be rejected; they must be replaced. Where there is not any replacement, the mind will revert to familiar structures at times of crisis, bafflement, or defeat."[43]

I admit that I do experience the world as alive and speaking. Forces and energies that have yet to be described by science are real to me. The birds, the trees, the rocks, the winds, the land itself have voices, and part of my work in changing the world is to listen deeply to them. The ancestors are present, and aid me in my work. When we cast a web of magical protection for an action, I can feel its power.

And I would rather live in an animate world. I believe we are likely to create a healthier, more dynamic, freer, and more balanced culture if we perceive ourselves as living cells in a living body imbued with an underlying consciousness than if we perceive the world as dead, exploitable matter.

The tools of magic — the understanding of energy and the power and use of symbols, the awareness of group consciousness and of ways in which to shift and shape it — are also the tools of political and social change. Dion Fortune's definition of magic as "the art of changing consciousness at will" is also a fine definition of transformational political praxis. We construct our world through the stories we tell about it, and the practice of magic is the art of cultural storyshifting, the conscious dreaming of a new dream.

A demonstration or a direct action is a ritual, a conscious use of symbolic and real actions to direct energy toward an intention. An understanding of the way symbols move energy and of the patterns of energy flow can help us make actions vibrant and transformational rather than repetitive and dreary. When we are met with intense repression, the tools of consciousness change can help us stay grounded, calm, and focused, able to make a conscious choice about what we want to do. So magic is extremely useful in activism.

Without a spiritual base for my activism, without regular practices that renew my energies and my sense of hope, and without a community to share them with, I might long ago have succumbed to frustration and despair. Political work is hard. Results are rarely immediate and sometimes barely evident. The forces we contest are immensely powerful. To carry on for a lifetime, we need faith in something, whether it is the perfectibility of human nature, the ultimate withering of the state, or the belief that the universe is on the side of justice, as Martin Luther King said. My connection to the earth helps me believe that loss can lead to transformation, that decay can be food for something new, that all energy moves in cycles, that the universe is filled with immense creativity which is stronger than violence, and that hate is ultimately not as powerful a force as love.

There are many possible names for my form of spirituality. I sometimes use the more inclusive terms "earth-based spirituality" or "feminist spirituality" rather than a word like "Witch" — a word that most people don't understand; a word that may label you as either evil or ridiculous; a word that is likely to cause people to discount what you say.

To move beyond our usual categories of thought, we need words that shock and confuse and shake up our usual thinking. Like any system, a system of thought needs pressure from outside to spur change. Words like "Witch" and "magic" and "spells" keep us from getting too serious, from thinking too much of ourselves. The use of the term "Witch" to describe myself was a political and spiritual choice I made long ago. Political because I felt that to challenge the deep misogyny in our culture, the ingrained fear of women's power, the identification of strong women as evil, we had to make visible those underlying thought structures and challenge them, and the word "Witch" does that. I've used the word as a conscious identification with the victims of the Witch persecutions, and in solidarity with all the shamans and healers of indigenous cultures who have been persecuted as Witches. But to be honest, I've used it mostly because it was the word that intuitively felt right.

There are risks and penalties in every choice. Calling myself a Witch publicly was not always the safest thing to do, but twenty-five years have taught me that our fears can inflate the power of our opposition. There have been moments of harassment, doors that have been closed, but overall what has surprised me is the amount of openness, the welcome I've received in many religious communities, the shift in consciousness that has indeed begun slowly to take place.

These are choices I have made. They are the right choices for me, but I am not suggesting that they are right for everyone, or for anyone else. We each need to find our own way along this borderland, to identify the deep values that we hold and the ways in which best to express them and work for them. When we know what we stand for and are willing to risk ourselves for, what the standard is by which we measure our actions and choices, what is most deeply important to us, and what most profoundly nourishes and inspires us, we know what is truly sacred. All we need to do, then, is to put our life energies and time and creativity at its disposal, however we name or describe it. Then the great powers of the universe, inner and outer, seen and unseen, move in alignment, and as agents of embodied love we are fed and sustained.

ENDNOTES

1. Some resources are the Global Exchange website (www.globalexchange.org), the Public Citizen website (www.citizen.org), and the Council of Canadians website (www.canadians.org).

2. The statistics are from David Korten, *When Corporations Rule the World* (West Hartford: Kumarian/San Francisco: Berrett-Kohler, 1995), p. 8, p.108.

3. Davison Budhoo, "IMF/World Bank Wreak Havoc on the Third World," in Kevin Danaher, ed., *Fifty Years is Enough: The Case against the World Bank and the International Monetary Fund* (Boston: South End Press, 1994), pp. 21-22.

4. For David's own account of this event, see Miller, David. "I Didn't Know God Made Honky Tonk Communists" (Berkeley: Regent Press, 2001).

5. Jessica Matthews, "Little World Banks," in Kevin Danaher, ed., *Fifty Years is Enough*, pp. 183-185.

6. Cities for Climate Protection Campaign, see www.iclei.org

7. The New Road Map Foundation has begun sponsoring Conversation Cafes to encourage people to talk about issues in public places. See www.newroadmap.org and www.conversationcafe.org. For resources on Permaculture, see www.permacultureinstitute.com.

8. See the Wilderness Awareness School website at www.natureoutlet.com.

9. Jeanette Armstrong, "Keepers of the Earth," in Theodore Roszack, Mary E. Gomes, and Allen D. Kanner, eds. *Ecopsychology: Restoring the Earth, Healing the Mind* (San Francisco: Sierra Club Books, 1995), p. 323.

10. The website for the Movimiento Sim Terre is www.mstbrazil.org.

11. The principles of unity can be found on the Reclaiming website; www.reclaiming.org.

12. Starhawk, *Truth or Dare: Encounters with Power, Authority, and Mystery* (San Francisco: Harper & Row, 1988), pp. 276-285.

13. Starhawk, *Truth or Dare*, pp. 8-10.

14. George Lakey works with Trainers for Change in Philadelphia. See www.TrainingforChange.org.

15. Elizabeth (Betita) Martinez, "Where Was the Color in Seattle? Looking for reasons why the Great Battle was so white," *Colorlines Magazine* (Spring 2000), at www.colorlines.com. 2000), pp. 74-81.

16. Martin Luther King Jr., *I Have a Dream: Writing and Speeches that Changed the World* (San Francisco: HarperSanFrancisco, 1992), p.104.

17. Alex Haley and Malcolm X, *The Autobiography of Malcolm X* (New York: Ballantine, 1999), p. 292.

18. Alex Haley and Malcolm X, *The Autobiography of Malcolm X*, p. 96.

19. Chris Crass, "Looking to the Light of Freedom: Lessons from the Civil Rights Movement and Thoughts on Anarchist Organizing," at www.tao.ca/~colours/crass8.

20. Elizabeth (Betita) Martinez, "Where Was the Color in Seattle? Looking for reasons why the Great Battle was so white," *Colorlines Magazine* (Spring 2000), at www.colorlines.com.

21. Starhawk, *Walking to Mercury* (New York: Bantam, 1997), p. 235, p. 241.

22. Alex Haley and Malcolm X, *The Autobiography of Malcolm X*, p. 383.

23. Mary Black's and Sven Glueckspilz's posts were circulated to various e-mail lists, but to my knowledge are not currently posted to any website.

24. Jaggi Singh's critique can be found at www.tao.ca/~colours/gandhi. He is currently working on a longer critique demystifying Gandhi.

25. Ward Churchill, *Pacifism as Pathology: Reflections on the Role of Armed Struggle in North America* (Winnipeg: Arbeiter Ring, 1998), p. 36.

26. Martin Luther King Jr., *I Have a Dream*, p. 87.

27. George Lakey, "Mass Action Since Seattle: Seven Ways to Make our Protests more Powerful," at www.TrainingforChange.org. See also his article critiquing Churchill.

28. Ibid. ?

29. ?Jaggi Singh's critique can be found at www.tao.ca/~colours/gandhi. He is currently working on a longer critique demystifying Gandhi.

30. Homer A. Jack, ed., *The Gandhi Reader: A Sourcebook of his Life and Writings* (New York: Grove Press, 1956), p. 140.

31. ?Jaggi Singh's critique can be found at www.tao.ca/~colours/gandhi. He is currently working on a longer critique demystifying Gandhi.

32. Marshall B. Rosenberg, "Anger and Domination Systems", a workshop on non-violent communication given by Dr. Rosenberg in England in May of 1999. See www.cncv.org.

33. Martin Luther King Jr., *I Have a Dream*, p. 86.

34. Martin Luther King Jr., "Letter from a Birmingham Jail," *Why We Can't Wait* (New York: New American Library/Penguin, 2000), p. 68.

35. Ibid. ??

36. Mary Black's and Sven Glueckspilz's posts were circulated to various e-mail lists, but to my knowledge are not currently posted to any website.

37. For the Masquerade Project, see www.masqueradeproject.org.

38. Speech by Subcommandante Marcos, EZLN, March 11, 2001, in the Zocalo of Mexico City (trans. Justin Podur).

39. George Monbiot, "Raising the Temperature," *London Guardian*, 24 July 2001.

40. Michael Albert, *Thinking Forward: Learning to Conceptualize Economic Vision* (Winnipeg: Arbeiter Ring, 1997), p. 25.

41. See Sustainable Sonoma's website: www.sustainablesonoma.org.

42. Cities for Climate Protection Campaign, see www.iclei.org

43. Carol Christ, "Why Women Need the Goddess," in Charlene Spretnak, ed., *The*

Politics of Women's Spirituality (New York: Doubleday, 1982, 1994), p. 73. I am also indebted to Carol for her beautiful formulation of the Goddess as "intelligent, embodied love."

BIBLIOGRAPHY

Albert, Michael. *Thinking Forward: Learning to Conceptualize Economic Vision*. Winnipeg: Arbeiter Ring, 1997.

Ausubel, Kenny. *Restoring the Earth: Visionary Solutions From the Bioneers*. Tiburon: H. J. Kramer, 1997.

Ayers, Alex. *The Wisdom of Martin Luther King, Jr.* New York: Meridien, 1993.

Barlow, Maude and Tony Clarke. *Global Showdown*. Toronto: Stoddart, 2001.

Churchill, Ward. *Pacifism as Pathology: Reflections on the Role of Armed Struggle in North America*. Winnipeg: Arbeiter Ring, 1998.

Christ, Carol. *Rebirth of the Goddess*. Reading: Addison Wesley, 1997.

Clarke, Ben and Clifton Ross, eds. *Voice of Fire: Communiques and Interviews from the Zapatista National Liberation Army*. San Francisco, *Freedom Voices Publications*, 1994.

Cockburn, Alexander, Jeffrey St. Clair and Allan Sekula. *Five Days that Shook the World: Seattle and Beyond*. London: Verso, 2000.

Crimethink Collective. *Days of War, Nights of Love: Crimethink for Beginners*. Atlanta: CrimethInc Workers' Collective, 2001.

Danaher, Kevin, ed. *Fifty Years is Enough: The Case Against the World Bank and the International Monetary Fund*. Boston: South End Press, 1994.

Danaher, Kevin and Roger Burbach. *Globalize This!: The Battle against the World Trade Organization and Corporate Rule*. Monroe: Common Courage Press, 2000.

Davis, Angela. *Women, Race, and Class*. New York: Vintage, 1983.

De Villiers, Marq. *Water: The Fate of Our Most Precious Resource*. Boston: Mariner Books, 2000.

Dyson, Michael. *I May Not Get There With You: The True Martin Luther King, Jr.* New York: Simon & Schuster, 2000.

Erikson, Erik H. *Gandhi's Truth on the Origins of Militant Nonviolence*. New York: W.W. Norton, 1969, 1993.

Freire, Paolo. *Pedagogy of the Oppressed*. New York: Continuum, 2000.

Haley, Alex and Malcolm X. *The Autobiography of Malcolm X*. New York: Ballantine, 1999.

Hawken, Paul. *The Ecology of Commerce: A Declaration of Sustainability*. New York: HarperBusiness, 1993.

Hawken, Paul, Amory Lovins and L. Hunter Lovins. *Natural Capitalism: Creating the Next Industrial Revolution*. Boston: Little, Brown & Company, 1999.

Jack, Homer A., ed. *The Gandhi Reader: A Sourcebook of his Life and Writings*. New York: Grove Press, 1956.

hooks, bell. *Feminism Is for Everybody: Passionate Politics*. Cambridge: South End Press, 2000.

Jacobs, Jane. *The Nature of Economies*. New York: Modern Library, 2000.

King, Martin Luther, Jr. *I Have A Dream: Writings and Speeches that Changed the World*. San Francisco: HarperSanFrancisco, 1992.

—— *Why We Can't Wait*. New York: New American Library/Penguin, 2000.

Klein, Naomi. *No Logo*. New York: Picador, 1999.

Korten, David. *The Post-corporate World: Life after Capitalism*. West Hartford: Kumarian/San Francisco: Berrett-Kohler, 1999.

—— *When Corporations Rule the World*. West Hartford: Kumarian/San Francisco: Berrett-Kohler, 1995.

Laduke, Winona. *All Our Relations: Native Struggles for Land and Life*. Cambridge: South End Press, 1983.

Mander, Jerry and Edward Goldsmith. *The Case Against the Global Economy*. San Francisco: Sierra Club Books, 1996.

Miller, David. *I Didn't Know God Made Honky-Tonk Communists*. Oakland: Regent Press, 2002.

Mollison, Bill and Reny Mia Slay. *Introduction to Permaculture*. Tyalgum: Tagari Publications, 1994.

Monbiot, George. "Raising the Temperature," *London Guardian*, 24 July 2001.

Moyer, Bill. *Doing Democracy: The MAP Model of Organizing Social Movements*. Gabriola Island: New Society Publishers, 2001.

Outwater, Alice. *Water: A Natural History*. New York: Basic Books, 1996.

Robin, Vicki and Joe Dominguez. *Your Money or Your Life*. New York: Penguin, 1992.

Roszack, Theodore, Mary E. Gomes and Allen D. Kramer, eds. *Ecopsychology: Restoring the Earth, Healing the Mind*. San Francisco: Sierra Club Books, 1995.

South End Press Collective. *Talking About A Revolution*. Cambridge: South End Press, 1998.

Spretnak, Charlene, ed. *The Politics of Women's Spirituality*. New York: Doubleday, 1982, 1994.

Starhawk. *Dreaming the Dark: Magic, Sex, and Politics*. Boston: Beacon, 1982, 1997.

—— *The Fifth Sacred Thing*. New York: Bantam, 1992.

—— *Truth or Dare: Encounters with Power, Authority, and Mystery*. San Francisco: Harper & Row, 1988.

—— *Walking to Mercury*. New York: Bantam, 1997.

Teish, Luisah. *Carnaval of the Spirit*. San Francisco: HarperSanFrancisco, 1994.

Tobocman, Seth. *War in the Neighborhood*. Brooklyn: Autonomedia, 1999.

Vaughn, Genevieve. *For-Giving: A Feminist Criticism of Exchange*. Austin: Plain View Press, 1997.

Weisman, Alan. *Gaviotas: A Village to Reinvent the World*. White River Junction: Chelsea Green Publications, 1995.

Welton, Neva and Linda Wolf. *Global Uprising: Confronting the Tyrannies of the 21st Century*. Gabriola Island: New Society Publishers, 2001.

Zerzan, John. *Future Primitive*. Brooklyn: Autonomedia, 1994.

INDEX

271

ABOUT THE AUTHOR

STARHAWK is a committed global justice activist and organizer. She is a veteran of progressive movements for over thirty years, from anti-war to anti-nukes, is a highly influential voice in the revival of earth-based spirituality and Goddess religion, and has brought many innovative techniques of spirituality and magic to her political work.

She is the author or coauthor of ten books, including *The Spiral Dance* (now in its 20th anniversary edition), *Truth or Dare* — which won the Media Alliance Meritorious Achievement Award for nonfiction in 1988 — *The Fifth Sacred Thing*, winner of the Lambda award for best Gay and Lesbian Science Fiction in 1994, and *The Twelve Wild Swans*.

She lives part time San Francisco in a collective house with her partner and friends, and the rest of the time in a little hut in the woods of the Cazadero Hills where she practices the system of ecological design known as permaculture. Her website is: www.starhawk.org

Printed in the United States
124301LV00013B/223/P

9 781897 408131